Praise for ON MY OWN

"*On My Own* looks at the joy, pain, and necessity of living solo in a society that still views unattached women as spinsters and old maids . . . An engaging read, [it] empowers more than it prescribes . . . the ideas here are important and Falk presents them with a comforting combination of analysis and empathy."

—*Body & Soul*

"[Falk] argues that solitude can be an empowering force—one that doesn't supplant relationships; it enriches them. Autonomy unleashes creativity and purpose, and a woman discovers her true self."

—*The Mercury News*

"Fascinating . . . [Falk] demonstrates the riches and creativity that can emerge."

—*Today's Diet & Nutrition*

"Falk offers plenty of material to help [women] . . . appreciate the healing and nurturing benefits of solitude."

—*Publishers Weekly*

"Florence Falk's *On My Own* is a provocative, smart read for any woman who is alone, wants to be alone, or is figuring out how to be alone. An empowering, emotionally honest book that is long overdue."

—AMY SOHN, author of *Run Catch Kiss* and *My Old Man*

"In *On My Own* Florence Falk bravely and soulfully invites women to reimagine aloneness—to see it as a gift rather than a failure. Her book is a call to wholeness, independence, and empowerment."

—EVE ENSLER, author of *The Vagina Monologues*

"Finally, an insightful and powerful book that guides us towards inner freedom that is possible when we befriend aloneness. This is for all women, single or not: The stories and practical guidance offered in this book teach us about living and loving fully."

—TARA BRACH, Buddhist teacher and author of *Radical Acceptance: Embracing Your Life with the Heart of a Buddha*

ON MY OWN

THE ART OF BEING
A WOMAN ALONE

FLORENCE FALK

THREE RIVERS PRESS
NEW YORK

For my mother Pauline, my granddaughter Juliet, and

the wonderful women in my family

Copyright © 2007 by Florence Falk
Reading Group Guide copyright © 2008 by Three Rivers Press, an imprint
of the Crown Publishing Group, a division of Random House, Inc.

Published in the United States by Three Rivers Press, an imprint of the
Crown Publishing Group, a division of Random House, Inc., New York.
www.crownpublishing.com

THREE RIVERS PRESS and the Tugboat design are registered trademarks of
Random House, Inc.

Originally published in hardcover in the United States by Harmony Books, an imprint
of the Crown Publishing Group, a division of Random House, Inc., New York, in 2007.

Grateful acknowledgment is made to Houghton Mifflin Company for permission to
reprint an excerpt from "Saint Francis and the Son" from *Mortal Acts, Mortal Words* by
Galway Kinnell. Copyright © 1980 by Galway Kinnell. All rights reserved. Reprinted by
permission of Houghton Mifflin Company.

Library of Congress Cataloging-in-Publication Data

Falk, Florence Arlene.
On my own: the art of being a woman alone/Florence Falk.—1st ed.
If I am a woman alone, who am I?—What is aloneness?—Shame-in-hiding:
a woman's cultural heritage—The awakening: childhood—The hall of mirrors:
adolescence & young adulthood—Befriending aloneness—Stepping out—Reaping the
harvest: solitude, the sacred, & the rediscovery of the self—Aloneness and relationship.
Includes bibliographical references and index.
1. Single women—Psychology. 2. Single women—Attitudes. 3. Man-woman
relationships.
I. Title.
HQ800.2F35 2007
306.81'53—dc22   2006021213

ISBN 978-1-4000-9811-8

Printed in the United States of America

Design by Lauren Dong

10 9 8 7 6 5 4 3

First Paperback Edition

Woman must come of age by herself. This is the essence of "coming of age"—to learn how to stand alone.

—ANNE MORROW LINDBERGH, *Gift from the Sea*

No matter how much women prefer to lean, to be protected and supported, nor how much men desire to have them do so, they must make the voyage of life alone, and for safety in an emergency, they must know something of the laws of navigation. To guide our own craft, we must be captain, pilot, engineer; with chart and compass to stand at the wheel; to watch the wind and waves, and know when to take in the sail, and to read the signs in the firmament over all.

—From "The Solitude of Self,"
ELIZABETH CADY STANTON's last address to
Congress, 1892

Although she continued to knit, and sat upright, it was thus that she felt herself; and this self having shed its attachments was free for the strangest adventures. . . . There was freedom, there was peace, there was, most welcome of all, a summoning together, a resting on a platform of stability.

—VIRGINIA WOOLF, *To the Lighthouse*

Contents

WHAT DOES A WOMAN WANT?
Complete sovereignty over her body, mind, spirit, and soul, as well as the sanction and protection by the body politic of which she is a part of her life, liberty, and the pursuit of happiness, including the full measure of freedom and safety to pursue her life as she sees fit and the right to complete gender equality regarding access to, and movement in and through, public and domestic space and the redress of any and all grievances that interfere with or inhibit such freedom.

THE AUTHOR

Part I

THE MANY FACES OF
ALONENESS

Chapter One

IF I AM A WOMAN ALONE,
WHO AM I?

I t's January and breath-stopping cold, the kind of weather Lisa's Nordic blood thrives on. But today the tonic isn't working. Instead of her usual robust glow, Lisa looks wilted and solitary, as if she had rushed to get to a party only to find it was over. And in a way, this is true.

Four years after meeting at the hip downtown cabaret Joe's Pub and falling instantly in love, Lisa and Sam agreed to separate. The decision seemed to happen of its own accord, oozing out of their apathy like the insides of an egg from a cracked shell, and they were too battle-fatigued to bother cleaning up the mess.

Lisa used to say that in meeting Sam she had come as close as she could imagine to finding the right person for herself. Sam was a freelance journalist. Lisa thought he was the smartest, most exciting man she had ever met. "I fell in love not only with his mind but with his sexy bearishness—even his chipped tooth turned me on." She loved that he was left-handed and had a husky voice, the way he howled when they made love, how his body smelled. She marveled at his boundless energy, unfettered imagination, and a steady-handed discipline that allowed him to read an entire book or draft an article in one sitting. Above all, she loved that they were not only lovers but each other's "closest friend," often acting less like adults than five-year-olds, playing together in their own hermetic world, as if the one outside had ceased to exist.

A whole year had passed like that. Then slowly, subtly at first, things began to change. Was she imagining it, or was Sam becoming distant? He seemed less emotionally available. For the first time since they had been together, Lisa felt an empty space inside. She would have given anything to melt the distance between them. As time passed, the empty feeling came and went. When Sam was his lovable self, Lisa's world righted itself and she felt full again. But as soon as he seemed the least bit preoccupied or restless, she began to ache with disappointment and need.

Both Lisa and Sam had prided themselves on their independent spirits. They had even promised each other not to talk about their future. The problem was that despite herself, Lisa wanted more. She was surprised and disturbed by the feelings of longing Sam summoned up in her—feelings she didn't even know were there. But whenever she hinted at "longer-term possibilities," her cautious euphemism for marriage, Sam blocked her. "We're doing great," he'd say reassuringly. "Let's just see what happens." His resistance unsettled Lisa and made her doubt herself; in earlier relationships, she had always felt in control.

Lisa began to resent the very qualities that drew her to Sam. His writing seemed to take up more and more of their private time, and she convinced herself that Sam was using his deadlines as an excuse to "disappear." At first, Sam tried to smooth away Lisa's concerns, but as time went on, his anger flared. "Stop worrying about my work," he'd snap, "and worry about your own."

Before long, light kisses on the check replaced lingering kisses on the lips. Lisa complained that they hardly ever made love anymore. She and Sam began to argue all the time, hurling insults and accusations back and forth: his "need to be the center of attention"; her "crazy temper"; his insistence on always being "right"; her "godawful prying"; his "sadistic putdowns—especially in front of my friends"; her laziness. Fights that had once ended in renewed vows of love and bouts of passionate sex now drained all their energy.

But when Sam finally told Lisa he needed his own place, she was heartsick and filled with dread. For the first time since they'd been together, she let her mind stray to the one thought she had scrupulously avoided until now—being alone.

On the day Sam moved out, Lisa sat on the couch in stunned disbelief while he padded from bedroom to study to bathroom, sorting through clothes, books, CDs, even bottles of shampoo and vitamins, separating out *his* stuff from *hers*. When he was finished packing, Sam walked over to her. "Be good to yourself, darling Lisa," he said, planting a kiss on her brow. "No matter what, this has been a great adventure for both of us." The ease with which he had already seemed to slip back into his own life and away from theirs infuriated Lisa. She both marveled at and was enraged by his composure. "Just leave me the keys, you arrogant bastard," she shot back. With a sigh, Sam set them down beside her. Car service rang up a few minutes later, and he let himself out the door.

Feeling too drained to move, Lisa curled up on the couch and fell asleep. When she woke up, it was already dark. She had to pee badly, and her arm ached from lying on it, but she couldn't bring herself to move until a cramped foot forced her to sit up. Her body felt sluggish and weak, and she could barely lift her feet. The phone rang. Hearing her friend Katherine leave a message, she didn't bother to pick up. It was Sam's voice she was waiting for.

That night, Lisa couldn't bring herself to sleep in their bed, so she brought her pillow and comforter back to the couch and stayed there, zoning out on old movies. She slept on the couch the next night, too, and the next. With Sam gone, she found herself listening to the silence. It's odd, she thought. I've been by myself a thousand times when Sam was out. Only now it's different. Before, I was alone, but not really. I was *waiting* for him. Now I'm not waiting for anyone. She started to sob, and finally the pain and hurt came pouring out. She felt frightened and confused. This didn't seem real, but of course it was. He was gone and he wouldn't be coming back.

LISA IS A set designer who first came to see me when her "honeymoon" with Sam was over, and she was struggling to understand how a relationship so magical, so light and luminous, could have begun to collect the dust of ordinary existence. She wanted to be wanted again. She wanted Sam to feel her longing and respond to her longing with his own. In her heart of hearts, she wanted to hold on to the rosy candlelight glow of romance, rather than have to deal with the bright, sometimes glaring day-to-day life with another person. And who could blame her? To be spun off earth and float above it for a while is exhilarating. But real love must take root in the soil of reality; otherwise, it can't last or modulate into deeper form. Lisa and Sam's relationship didn't have such durability.

Still, for Lisa—and almost every woman I know—the problem is the hard landing that occurs when a relationship ends and she falls backward into the shaming belief that somehow she is to blame.

Today, the woman who sits across from me still feels too bruised to try to pick herself up. "It feels like there's something terribly wrong with me. I don't even understand why I feel so bad." Lisa speaks more slowly than usual, and in her eyes I see a threading of loss and bewilderment. "I think I knew for a long time that this day would come, but I didn't dare let myself think about it. I guess I swept it under the proverbial rug." She is silent while she struggles to make sense of her feelings. "It's not that I want to be with Sam. I mean, I *do*," she corrects, "but only if it could be the way it used to be, and I know it can't. It's just that . . ."

"Just that what?" I ask.

Lisa is staring at the floor. "That I'm *alone,* completely *alone,* and it's terrifying." She pauses for a moment, then looks at me helplessly. *"I don't know how to be a woman alone."*

I AM STRUCK by the intensity of Lisa's feeling—as if she had just described the greatest calamity that could befall a woman. What Lisa didn't know—at least not then—was that she was articulating the same fear, doubt, confusion, and sense of helplessness numbers of women feel at all stages of life when they must learn for themselves what aloneness is and what it is like to be a woman alone.

"I keep telling myself it won't be so awful after all, this living alone." Lisa sighs and straightens her shoulders. "All the same, I'm not sure I can do it. I'm really not." Yet, before she met Sam, Lisa *was* alone; she had a budding career, plenty of lovers and would-be lovers, good friends, and a lively curiosity about life. *Her* life. I remind her that she more than once described herself as "comfortable in my own shoes" before Sam came along. "Yes, but there were always other men around," she protests. "I never had to worry about what it would be like without one."

Like many of us, Lisa assumes that a woman alone must be miserable, and, worse, that she somehow deserves to be, as if she bears full responsibility for her manless state. Striking a vein of black humor, Lisa wonders if she is like Typhoid Mary, carrying some unmentionable flaw that sends men fleeing and might be contagious. Without Sam, Lisa's self-esteem has plummeted. She no longer knows who she is or what she wants. She struggles against two bullying emotions: *shame* for being a woman alone, and *fear* that she will remain one. She cannot, no matter what her rational mind tells her, shake the belief that a woman alone is statusless: an outcast.

Although this fantasy sounds exaggerated, some version of it hovers in the imagination of most women—whether partnered *or* alone. Indeed, the famous scarlet letter *A* that once stood for *Adultery* might now be said to stand for *Alone*. How is it that even the most seemingly self-assured woman falls prey to feelings of inadequacy if she is not with a partner? And where do her feelings of neediness and dependency arise from?

Lisa exemplifies a paradox that besets many women today who continue to live an "as if" story. A modern woman may be the very model of independence with respect to her worldly accomplishments—education, career status, and the ability to earn a decent living—but this is only half the story. The other half, which is often hidden, is her fear of aloneness. To be alone, after all, is a breeding ground for thought. And if we are confused or unsure of ourselves, the stubborn weed of inadequacy takes over the garden. Nowhere is this more apparent than when a woman enters a relationship. For no sooner does she feel an attraction to the other person than she begins to doubt herself. Suppose he thinks she is boring or a bad lover? That her legs are too short or her breasts too small? That she is not smart or witty enough? Spirited away by self-deprecation, she has already fallen out of relationship to herself. But her real fear—the hidden determinant that makes her needy and dependent—is her fear of being alone.

To say this burden is too heavy for a woman to bear is a gross understatement. And yet the fear of aloneness is enough to keep us in tow, often lagging behind our own desire for independence—despite the fact that we have been graced by the women's movement with a cornucopia of opportunities. Underneath, women are still terrified of standing on their own. Despite the tremendous gains of the last four decades in women's freedoms, too many of us still carry the baggage of women's long social and cultural history of being treated as second-class citizens and social rejects unless we are under the protection of a man.

I am often struck by the number of married women in my practice who are convinced that if they went out on their own, they would fail. That the thought of becoming a "bag lady"—or, in one woman's conjuring, "a Xerox lady feeding pages into a machine forever because that's all I'm good for"—can still provoke such dread indicates the pervasiveness of this fear in our age-and-status-phobic culture. Given the facts that more than a quarter of all single women over eighteen (13.5 percent) live below the poverty line, that 26.5 percent of single female-headed families live below the poverty line, that four times as many divorced women with children fall under the poverty line than married women with children, and that 19.6 percent of women alone over 65 live below the poverty line, the fear-based fantasies of these women unfortunately also have deep roots in reality. But the fear these women express is only partly about survival. They are also wrestling with deeply ingrained fantasies about what it means to be without the protection of a man.

From the beginning of recorded history, as Simone de Beauvoir reminded us in *The Second Sex,* woman has been defined exclusively in relation to man. As de Beauvoir explains it, man, caught between fear and desire, has deified and debased, adored and despised, woman, simply because she is "Other." In a primal, negative sense, woman, viewed by man as object, begins to see herself through his eyes. Fear of losing or never attaining social status leads her to gauge her desires according to *his* standards of measurement. Instead of asking Who am I? she asks, Who does he want me to be? Instead of pondering What do I want for myself? she asks, What does he want from me? No wonder, then, that aloneness is so terrifying to a woman. She regards it not as a state of potential liberty—what de Beauvoir called "sovereign solitude"—but of alienation, not realizing that the person she is most alienated from is *herself.*

For most women, being a woman alone is virtually a euphemism for being flawed—not with a modest flaw, mind you, some relatively superficial and fixable feature like a crooked tooth or poor eyesight, but *inherently* flawed, defective at the core. "To me being alone is— wow—what a loser!" says Martha, a writer in her mid-twenties who published a first novel based on her romantic relationships with men. "It means that, at bottom, you're not wanted. Because if you were wanted, you'd never have to be alone." Martha bounces from relationship to relationship, and, in real life, as in her novel, needs to be in control of everyone. Falling in love is how she escapes the aloneness she so fears. Her infatuations are short-lived, however, for as soon as she is sure the man adores her, her enthusiasm wanes and she starts planning her exit strategy. But just let the man signal that he has other things on his mind or isn't that interested, and Martha, like Lisa, scrambles to get his attention—and hold on to it. No matter what the cost.

When Martha can be on her own, when she is able to feel secure no matter how a man feels about her, when she doesn't feel the need to twist herself out of shape to gain his approval or judge herself critically if she fails, she will be on the path toward an authentic selfhood.

To be able to recognize—let alone understand and talk about—a woman's fear of aloneness has taken me almost a lifetime. At this point, I don't share Lisa's or Martha's terror of being alone; for me, aloneness is no longer fraught with confusion and fear. This doesn't mean I don't take those feelings seriously. My heart opens to the distress of all women who fear aloneness, all the more because their fears were once my own. My journey as a woman alone taught me that aloneness is a natural, dynamic state, and that when we run from aloneness, we are really running from ourselves. The market for self-help books is a thriving multimillion-dollar business, and the vast majority of these books are bought by women. We spend millions of dollars hoping to improve our self-esteem and boost our confidence—learning "simple solutions" to lose weight, rid ourselves of shyness or panic, or heal our anxiety and depression. Along the way, we might also discover (as certain popular self-help books promise) how to live successfully with screwed-up people, fight back and win, dance with our anger, and what the "rules" are to get a man and keep him. The baited promise is that we will discover what "happy people know," which usually has to do with rapturous sex and multiple orgasms 365 days a year. These books succeed because they speak to women's fundamental dissatisfaction with themselves. How much easier it is to divvy up this feeling into seemingly manageable, and "fixable," pieces than to acknowledge the deeper roots of that dissatisfaction in the shame and low self-esteem we carry.

My work with women has convinced me that aloneness has been and continues to be an overlooked and undervalued dimension of women's lives, one we will all experience and owe it to ourselves to learn about. Our fear of aloneness, which women rarely talk about, even among themselves, keeps us stuck in self-defeating behaviors. It is not uncommon for a woman who fears aloneness to stay in a bad relationship, rush impulsively into a new one, or use food, sex, alcohol, or drugs to dull the painful feelings it evokes.

Given the basic human need for connection, the acceptance of aloneness can be hard for both women and men. Still, one essential difference prevails: men who are alone are not marginalized. If anything, they are mythologized. Solitary males have a heroic patina; even their aloofness is deemed seductive. Bachelors are always eligible. Our culture perks up at the sight of an untethered man, whereas "spinsters," almost by definition, are ready for the pasture.

This doesn't mean that as a group men alone fare better than women alone. Socialized to conceal their emotions and their vulnerabilities, men are more susceptible to the stresses of isolation than women are. Depressed men, according to Terrence Real, author of *I Don't Want to Talk About It: Overcoming the Secret Legacy of Male Depression,* are far less likely than women to seek help. But women carry the baggage of our social history, a bred-in-the-bones belief that there is something wrong with us if we are not with a man. The social and economic progress we have made over the last four decades has not been enough to stave off the influence of a women-baiting culture whose media endlessly bombard us to be *more:* more beautiful, more sexual, and more compliant—in short, more of everything that will help us get, and keep, a man. Never mind that we are likely to become *less* ourselves in the process.

Aloneness is an opportunity, a state brimming with potentiality, with resources for renewed life—*not* a life sentence. Its cultivation should not be an apology but an art. In the space of aloneness—and perhaps only there—a woman is free to admit and act on her own desires. It is where we have the opportunity to discover that we are not a half but a sovereign whole. With that insight, we can then begin to discard the remnants of "thingness"—the spoiling belief that gives rise to our timidity, insecurity, and fear—so that we can realize true autonomy, with or without a partner.

ONE DAY—it was after my second divorce—I realized most acutely that no one ever prepared me to be a woman alone. Daughter, sister, lover, wife, mother, teacher, member of this committee or that organization—absolutely—but a full person unto myself, rather than merely a woman-in-relationship, never. I learned at my mother's knee that women nurtured others—men, children, family, and friends—but not themselves. My mother fulfilled her domestic roles to capacity, devoting herself to me and my two brothers, and catering to the needs of my autocratic, demanding father. But as a first-generation immigrant fresh from the farmlands of the Ukraine, she didn't finish high school, let alone go to college. At sixteen, she met my father; at twenty, she married him; and a year later, she was wheeling me to the park in a baby carriage. She had no sense of who she might have been on her own. I know that as the world changed around her, she hungered for more for herself, and I'm certain she passed along that sense of deprivation to me. It wasn't until after my father died that she began to grow into her fullness as a woman.

Fortunately for me, I had certain advantages my mother did not: I received a good education, and I was able to ride the beginning waves of the women's movement. But at the same time that I was taking advantage of women's increased opportunities, I was clueless as to who I was, what I wanted, or how to get it for myself.

Like Lisa, I cast my line for the prince and was hobbled by the distance between my dreams of romantic love and reality. Had I not felt the same fears, I would not have gotten married at eighteen. Nor would I have stayed married for several years after I knew for sure that I was not in love and never had been. My husband was a cellist. He was a wonderful person. But it didn't matter. I was not in love with him; I was "in love" with his music. For the length of time it took him to play a cello sonata, I was passionately and devotedly his. But between those times there was all that great space to fill—the maw of my own dissatisfaction. When another man appeared and offered new adventures, it was easy enough to step out of the marriage; after all, I had put only one foot in.

Soon, the magic of the new relationship wore off, and I was truly on my own. But roaming free as men do through a public world as wide as the plains felt too open, too windswept and real, for comfort. I worked for pennies in off-off-Broadway theaters, lived alone in grungy apartments, and found myself hoping that the arching branches of something or someone would give me shelter. Once again I married, this time to a man who was a human rights activist and writer and taught international law and politics at Princeton University, and once again I wasn't prepared for how alone and lonely I felt, still largely invisible to myself despite the triumphs of bearing two adored sons and earning a doctorate in English literature and a teaching post at a major university.

Have I felt Lisa's terror of being a woman alone since then? Many times. Aloneness is always hovering around the borders of our lives. Sometimes we seek and welcome it, as when we steal a few quiet hours away from our busy lives to read or knit or have lunch with a friend; sometimes it crashes in sideways, as when a beloved partner dies unexpectedly; and sometimes it enters so quietly that we are barely aware of its presence, as when we feel the first intimations of our mortality. One way or another, aloneness insistently refuses *not* to be acknowledged.

Between lovers, before and after my second marriage, and sometimes most acutely *during* these relationships—when it became clear to me that I relied on men to fill up the empty spaces in my life—I realized that I had been running away from aloneness, and that I could no longer avoid its challenge. For the first time in my life, I understood that simply because I was alive, aloneness would be intermittent in my life. Obliged by circumstances to learn how to be alone, I had to wean myself away from my long-held fantasy of rescue. Gradually, as my own fear lifted and aloneness no longer felt like a threat, I began to explore its many facets and discovered that rather than being a place of shame and loneliness, it was a place of healing. I could begin to feel the many parts of myself coming alive—even visibly—and I realized that, far from being the flatland I had believed it to be, aloneness was in fact an expanding realm of possibilities. In that spirit, I began to define myself as a *woman alone:* a woman who was ready to accept responsibility for my own fate. Carving my own way with renewed energy, sometimes lonely but mostly not, I reared my two sons, took steps to become financially independent, and discovered the pleasures, and riches, of solitude.

On My Own arrives from the confluence of two major streams in my life. The first is my personal experience of living alone and teaching myself a relatively new mode of existence. The second is my work as a psychotherapist, where the shadowy presence of aloneness in the lives of many of my female clients was first revealed to me. I had to reconsider long and deeply embedded cultural assumptions I had unwittingly accepted in my practice with other women undergoing the same struggle. Bearing witness to their aloneness and coaxing it into visibility then began to inform our work together and became a dimension of their lives worthy of serious exploration.

Since my second divorce, aloneness has achieved a solid-state steadiness; having befriended it, I can count on it as an assured companion, cherishing its gift of solitude as a space to center and renew myself and to live creatively. I have also discovered that as the richness of aloneness enters our lives, we are not likely to give it up lightly. Will I always be a woman alone? The answer begs another question: How could I possibly know what will come to pass in the next moment, let alone the rest of my life? Nor do these questions matter, for they only steal energy away from the things I care about here and now. What I can say, however, is that any future relationship I might have will be based on what I've learned about myself as a woman alone and the strength of who I am.

To be alone out of choice is one thing. Even women who fear the permanency of that state may long for the solitude it offers and welcome its repose. But to be alone out of necessity is another story—and a sad one, at that—limp with the draining energy of shame and fear. These issues are ones we need to come to terms with. But I didn't yet fully know these daunting facts when Lisa had her sad epiphany and called out for help.

Ironically, if one of Lisa's friends were to admit that she was in a bad relationship, Lisa would say, "Why stay, then? You're better off without him." She might even feel twinges of contempt. "Why would she want to be with someone like that? It's degrading." Lisa wouldn't realize that her disdain was a decoy distracting her from her own belief that aloneness is a humiliating punishment.

I don't know how to be a woman alone. Lisa's words touched me. Only now I had turned her words into questions: What does it mean to be a woman alone? *How* to be a woman alone? The answers became the subject of this book. In simplest terms: *Women need to befriend aloneness.* This is the only way we can develop the art of being a woman alone—each of us in our own way.

WHO IS A WOMAN ALONE?

Inasmuch as all of us inevitably find ourselves alone, not once but many times during our lives, I use the term "woman alone" to refer to all women. By default, choice, or necessity, we all experience our own particular life crossings that set us apart. Whether we prefer it or not, feel shame or pride in being there, this means that we may be separated, divorced, widowed, homeless, unmarried, never married, between partners, a woman artist with (or without) a "room of our own," a gay woman, a welfare mother, a single mother, an aborting or miscarrying woman, childless, sick, old or dying, a jilted woman, a depressed woman, or alone in a loveless or troubled relationship. A woman may feel alone when she finds herself a seat in a crowded movie theater, waits in a hospital corridor for a radiation treatment, or makes love with her partner in dull silence. For among the species of aloneness, one of the most painful to endure is to be in the presence of someone who arouses a need but does not satisfy it; another is the unblinking stare of indifference, which repels the exchange of concern, love, or compassion between people. A woman—any woman—is alone when she feels emotionally or spiritually separate and apart from others and herself.

Here are other "just causes" when being alone becomes an unacceptable state:

- if the culture disvalues her gender, objectifies her person, and encourages her to feel powerless;
- if she is obliged to live in conditions of social or economic deprivation or isolation;
- if she is physically and emotionally unprotected and subject to the violence of others, whether that violence assumes physical or emotional form;
- if she feels marginalized or abandoned;
- if *being* alone makes her feel stigmatized and ashamed;

- if she cannot assert her own voice or feel the full strength of her creative energy without the compulsion to apologize for it;
- if self-doubt and stealth make her mind opaque to itself—confused, defensive, and uncertain about its own originality;
- if she is invisible to others or to herself.

For most of us being alone means unmarried. When we are young and single, say, between eighteen and twenty-nine, we usually relish our freedom. At thirty, however, singledom can become worrisome. Many of us grow impatient with serial dating, stale relationships, or too many breakups, and wonder if we will ever find the "right" partner. Having been reared to expect marriage and, usually, children, we wonder if something is wrong with us when expectations fail to materialize. That's when we begin to feel the weight of aloneness and, with some measure of guilt, shame, and sadness, identify ourselves as women alone.

Past examples of women alone, for the most part, have not been cheerful. "I'm not sure I wish to marry anyone," says Isabel Archer about her wish to explore life as a single and "independent" woman in Henry James's *The Portrait of a Lady;* later, she falls haplessly backward into a tragic marriage. Lucy, the (self-declared) "horrid flirt" in Bram Stoker's *Dracula,* recklessly imagines herself marrying not one, not two, but "three men, or as many as want her," and is straightaway "staked" as a vampire (the nineteenth-century equivalent of being burned as a witch). Because the stakes are so high (and flammable), it's easy to see why so many women speak softly among themselves about the possibility of *not* marrying, or else stay mute altogether. Yet in *Writing a Woman's Life,* Carolyn Heilbrun notes how little "has been told of the life of the unmarried woman who, consciously or not, has avoided marriage with an assiduousness little remarked but no less powerful for being, often, unknown to the woman herself." Can it be that a woman would choose *not* to marry without being conscious of her decision? The writer Gail Caldwell "really did forget to get married," she said. In her twenties and thirties it just didn't seem necessary. By the time she was into her forties, Caldwell had "wandered" on alone—without, it seems, turning into either a witch or a bag lady.

In the world we live in there are endlessly varied reasons why some women stay married, others divorce, and still others never marry at all. Imagine what it would be like to know our real thoughts and desires. Imagine what it would be like to express them without having to hear loud whispers from the culture's prompt box, reminding us that the rewards we seek are exclusively marriage-bound—especially those who "forget" to think about marriage, or who choose to create their own forms of partnership.

In *On My Own,* I want to offer a new paradigm that embraces all women, both within marriage and without—including those who sculpt their own kind of "marriage." Women should be free to ask aloud the questions they once only dreamed about in the dark. They would probably still begin with the question Freud put to Marie Bonaparte (and which neither of them was prepared to address): *"What does a woman want?"* At the beginning of the twenty-first century there are, however, plenty of other questions we should be asking ourselves:

1. As a woman alone, who am I?
2. As a woman alone, what do I want?
3. Does our society respect my rights, encourage me to feel my own worth, and protect me?
4. If not, how can I ensure that my needs will be addressed?
5. Who can help me in this process, and how can I best help myself?

At this moment in history, the surge in the number of women alone is startling. Single women over the age of eighteen now represent a stunning 48 percent of the female population. More than thirty million American households—about three in ten—are maintained by women with no husband present. Ten million of these women are single mothers with children, up from three million in 1970. And yet the subject of aloneness that affects each and every one of them seems to have slipped through the cracks of the culture.

The subject matter of women alone is hardly new. But "woman alone" as *subject*—as *I, myself,* speaking as the central narrator and charting the inner territory of my aloneness on my own behalf—*is absolutely new.* So is the designation "woman alone." As a distinct category within women's culture, it formally elevates our presence and status, helps us to achieve visibility and expression, and allows us to redress our marginalized state.

For as aloneness becomes less a punishment and a condemnation, it becomes a resource and an opportunity for growth and transformation. The act of reimagining aloneness will make it possible for us to incorporate it into our lives in a new and integral way, because we will have finally realized that to be a single woman is a prerogative rather than a plight. We will also discover that aloneness doesn't negate our need for relationships any more than relationships negate our need for aloneness. We need both. Imposed aloneness can then become inspired aloneness. In that spirit we could also begin to embrace the special concerns of women who are not only alone but isolated and at risk, including (but not limited to) women of color, disabled women, battered women, homeless women, sick women, older women, or any other woman who has been deemed "invisible" and feels hopelessly "alone."

Many stories make up the quilting of this book. First and foremost are the stories of my patients, who in many ways have been my mentors. I've often wondered what it would be like if they could meet one another, and pass on the lessons they have learned about aloneness in their everyday lives. Perhaps this book will be their common meeting ground; if so, one of my fantasies will have been realized. For myself, I can only say that from each meeting a gem has been dropped into my lap.

I also include stories drawn from interviews with women whom I've sought out, hoping that their variety of experiences, good and bad, might offer useful information, and that they themselves might be helpful mentors and role models. Other stories are based on conversations with friends and colleagues who have generously shared their personal versions of being alone. Wherever appropriate, I have drawn on my own history. There are many other drawers to look in, and I have opened many of them: myths, novels, plays, essays, spiritual texts, paintings, films, songs, and newscasts. My perspectives are psychological, sociological, cultural, and spiritual. Finally, my sources are disguised as composite figures to keep their identities anonymous, except when people felt comfortable being named and granted me permission to do so.

If my offering is successful, it will pass from the hands of one woman to another—from mothers to their daughters, daughters to their grandmothers, aunts, and cousins, and, from all of them, to their female and male friends in open-ended dialogue.

Chapter Two

WHAT IS ALONENESS?

It is 5:30 A.M. I lie awake in my Vermont house listening to the silence. It has moved into the foreground—so complete, you can almost hear the birds turning in their nests. This is the slivered instant just before night turns to day, a hallowed breath of stillness when everything is bare potential. I watch the slow striking of metal against metal of the wind chime outside my bedroom window. Its thin silver tubes look as though they are treading air. Soon a solitary bird will shake its feathers and sing a morning raga; within moments, others will begin answering.

A little past six I get out of bed, take a quick shower, dress, and go outside. The late August air is tangy, the grass is frosty under my bare feet. I do some stretches, though truly I can't wait to go back inside and warm myself. Other than a few humming insects and a spider spinning its web across the front door, there is nothing but the familiar static inside my brain to pay attention to.

Afterward, I eat breakfast and read. The house creaks, a pickup truck climbing the hill switches into second gear, the electric water heater fires up, then turns off again. In a while I'll turn on the computer. But first I'll read one more chapter to stretch the time. I am steeped in aloneness, and it feels warm and bracing and good.

IT TOOK ME a long time to appreciate the special beauty of aloneness. Like many women, aloneness wasn't a subject I thought about—until it fell smack into the forefront of my life, as impossible to overlook as an inkblot on white paper. In the years leading up to my divorce, aloneness felt like a burden to me because I couldn't pretend it wasn't there: the widening gap between two people growing apart won't allow it. In the years following, the weight of the burden lifted, only to be replaced by a newfound sense of aloneness—the stark reality that I was going it alone in the world as I struggled to find and build a career that both satisfied me and would support the two sons I would be raising—alone. That my sons would receive support from their father was a comfort, but it scarcely obviated the greater challenge I faced: to discover who "I" was.

Twice I had entered into marriage in the throes of romantic love, and twice I had been disappointed. Like Lisa, I wondered, Who am I if I am a woman alone? Like her, I felt afraid. Having reached the place where I could no longer dream of being rescued by a man, I understood, fully and irrevocably, that I was the sole agent of my fate, no matter how many relationships I entered into and whether or not I found another great love.

What I eventually discovered changed my life: having let go of the fantasy of rescue, I had crossed some invisible boundary. For the first time, I was ready to accept being a woman alone, only now it was no longer a default position but a state I could inhabit in a prideful way. This shift of perspective was at once radical and ordinary: radical because, as I shed my shame and fear, it forever transformed the way I thought and felt about myself; ordinary because it allowed me to go about my daily life with a clarity and strength that had long been missing.

THE MANY FACES OF ALONENESS

There is a 1945 recording of Bessie Smith singing Cole Porter's "What Is This Thing Called Love?" that always makes me stop whatever I'm doing, sigh, and wonder along with her. Bessie sings with the wistfulness of someone who knows she will never get a satisfying answer. Still, it didn't stop her—or, for that matter, any of us—from trying to probe love's mystery, nor from rushing ahead to climb its slippery slopes.

Would anyone, I wonder, write such a song about aloneness, a condition that carries its own mystery, though hardly one we are eager to solve, let alone rush into? There are plenty of songs about loneliness, beautiful haunting ballads in which we nurse our pain, wait for our man to show up or come back. But the subject of what we would or could do on our own just doesn't excite our interest; we much prefer to wonder what we did wrong and whether there will be a next time. And yet, although aloneness is as basic to the human condition as our deep-rooted need for connection, and has the potential to fulfill our need for self-understanding and self-expression, it remains a woefully neglected subject.

ALONENESS IS SINGULAR in the breadth of connotations the word itself carries. The dictionary definition of aloneness—*"apart from others"*—is simple enough. But there are many ways to be alone. We may be far away from people we love and still feel connected to them. We may share our bed with someone and feel utterly alone. Angry words with a loved one can leave us feeling abandoned. A chance meeting with a stranger can ignite a spark that signals the potential for relationship. Hours we spend alone may pass in the blink of an eye; minutes alone can feel endless. Few of us are literally all alone in the world: we usually have parents, siblings, other relatives, friends. But we can feel alone if our relationships don't nurture us, that is, if they don't strike any chords of shared experiences or mutual recognition.

Aloneness is an interior state as well as an external condition. Deep in our hearts we probably understand that aloneness is a natural part of life, but existential aloneness, the awareness that within us is a core self that no other human being, no matter how intimate, can ever touch, can be unsettling. The great activist for women's rights, Elizabeth Cady Stanton, put it this way: "Our inner being which we call ourself, no eye nor touch of man or angel has ever pierced."

Just reading the dictionary's synonyms for aloneness—"solitary," "lonely," "lonesome," "lone," "forlorn," "desolate"—underscores our apprehension. We need to demystify aloneness, to rid it of the taint of isolation and despair, and to understand that it is an essentially "neutral" state. On its vast spectrum, our experience of aloneness can veer from the loss and emptiness of isolation on one end to the spaciousness and plenitude of solitude on the other. The direction women need to pursue is toward *solitude*. That is where we will find the nourishment to harvest our inner resources. The question is: What stops us?

ALONENESS AS PUNISHMENT

From an early age, we are conditioned to associate aloneness with punishment. "If you do that one more time," the mother says, "you are going straight to your room." "If you don't quiet down," the teacher threatens, "you will have to play by yourself." The child who yells or talks back to adults is labeled "naughty" or "difficult" and is isolated from the people she needs most—parents, siblings, and friends—until she learns to behave. The message is clear enough: to be alone is to be at fault and unworthy of the company of others.

A depressed, bored, or passive parent may stay in her room, watch TV, talk on the phone to friends, or hand the reins to the nanny, thus letting her daughter fend for herself. The child who cries too much, who expresses her raw feelings, or is too rambunctious— who, in short, does not conform to the established patterns of behavior in her home—may see her parent turn her back, tighten her lips, withdraw. To be ignored or exiled from the family circle is a punishment of a different sort. An unseen child begins to feel unworthy, and she begins to associate aloneness with loneliness, alienation, and disempowerment.

In the most severe cases of parental neglect or child abuse, a child's self-denigrating feelings get ratcheted up to disturbing proportions. Doors slammed shut, doors that don't open no matter how much a child pleads or sits on the floor outside crying her heart out, doors that muffle the sound of whispering voices and a life she is excluded from, doors that cannot shield her from the sharp barks of parents' shouting matches or the battle cries of physical violence—all of these closed corridors and shut-out places create isolation chambers. Many women tell me that as children they often felt powerless and terrified when they were alone—away from where the action was, left out in the cold, so to speak, like the miserable child in Hans Christian Andersen's classic fairy tale *The Little Match Girl*. One of childhood's most unsettling fairy tales, it tells the story of an orphan girl who lives in a village where no one pays any attention to her. To support herself, she sells matches on the street for pennies. One bitterly cold winter night, she wanders the streets begging strangers to buy her matches, but no one does. Her only solace is to watch the warm glow of a cozy, well-fed family through their living room window. Later that evening, the little match girl freezes to death in the cold. No more woeful childhood story of exclusion exists.

The absence of a loving connection during childhood will haunt our adult years: the dreaded feeling of not being wanted by a beloved parent later on becomes a fear of not being liked by a friend or wanted by a lover. Sometimes the fear of abandonment is enough to impel us to stay in unfulfilling or even damaging relationships; or, alternatively, to isolate ourselves as a preemptive strike against the anticipated pain of rejection.

ALONENESS VERSUS LONELINESS

Not long ago, *The New York Times Magazine* published a photograph of an attractive middle-aged woman named Meera Kim sitting alone at a kitchen table. On one wall behind her are a photograph of her son taken when he was a child and a drawing he made as an adult. The caption explains that she has just returned from visiting her husband in Korea. She is glad to be home, but is thinking about "how everybody's alone"—her husband, her mother, herself—and says that unless her children visit her, she is lonely. Mementos of her family fill the house and help to ease her loneliness. "But I am not always lonely," she continues. "And sometimes when I am all alone, I am so happy and quiet. I think what I like to think, do what I like to do." Kim has made a clear distinction between loneliness and aloneness. She is lonely when she feels the absence of her family, yet she has no trouble entering aloneness when she reflects on the privilege of having her own private space in which to think and do what she pleases.

We often mistake aloneness and loneliness for each another, but they are not the same. It is true that loneliness is embedded in the aloneness experience—if only because we carry an existential awareness of our mortality and the fragility of our existence—and in that sense, loneliness is a natural feeling that colors all our lives, even if only as a faint background tint. There are of course different intensities of loneliness, ranging from the benign, such as when we want to be with people and no one is available, to the aching loneliness when a loved one dies, to alienation from one's self and from others that can result from childhood experiences. At times, our loneliness is related to our natural desire for connection with someone who, for whatever reason, is unavailable. The issue for women alone is not that we will never feel lonely. The issue is how aloneness makes us feel about ourselves. What the dictionary definition of aloneness does not make clear is the essential distinction between loneliness and aloneness: that to be "apart from others" means to be in the presence of oneself.

But suppose we have a diminished sense of self? Or believe, as many women do, that we are less than we pretend to be? If so, being alone and free of our usual distractions can actually feel dangerous, calling up our unconscious doubts and fears that, in the words of women I've worked with, we are "inadequate," "fraudulent," "unworthy." We fear coming up empty, but of course this isn't so. We are never empty. What we are is love-starved and in need of the kind of recognition and support we likely missed while growing up. This is when we are most likely to seek someone or something outside ourselves to fill us up, to "complete" and make us whole.

Meanwhile, the marketplace flourishes, tempting us with endless distractions. When we feel the twinge of loneliness, we can always work ten-hour days, glue ourselves to the cell phone, party or shop till we drop, zone out in TV land, drink or get high, surf the Internet, or "makeover" our bodies, faces, and homes. Yet our feverish efforts to stay "connected" in this wireless age are symptoms of a deeper distress. Despite the proliferation of cell phones, Palm Pilots, iPods, BlackBerries, and the burgeoning repertoire of new gadgets at our disposal, we still feel lonely.

Even when the culture makes it very easy for us to journey away from ourselves, there comes a point when our deeper longings no longer allow such escape. Women alone are then bound to grapple with painful and uncomfortable feelings. But this is a good thing. As we sort out and come to terms with the fact that there will be no rescue, we have a choice—either give up and escape, which some women do, or turn inward to harvest our own resources. In this way, a lonely woman begins her journey back to self. For the lonely woman who resigns herself to her "fate" is a needs-based woman. She is still looking for answers outside herself, whereas the woman alone has given up her fantasy of rescue. No longer despairing of aloneness, she is ready to befriend it—transmuting the shame that has hobbled her into pride in her own sovereignty. Does she still feel lonely at times? How could she not? But she accepts loneliness as part of the human condition and gets on with the rest of her life.

ANNA CHRISTENSEN IS a psychotherapist and Buddhist teacher who lives and works in New York City. Slender, with shoulder-length blond hair and deep blue eyes, it is hard to believe she is a grand-mother. Divorced after several years of marriage, Anna went on to raise her daughter as a single mother and to start a successful busi-ness on her own. With many visitations of loneliness in her young life related to parental neglect, Anna might easily have grown fearful of aloneness. Instead, the acceptance of aloneness became a great chal-lenge as she grew into adulthood. She describes how as an adult she learned to transition from loneliness to aloneness. "I can remember feeling very lonely around the holidays, or on summer weekends when the streets seemed quiet, empty. I used to imagine that every-one but me had someplace to go, people to be with. Almost immedi-ately, the feelings gave way to the sense of failure."

At the time, the view from her window of empty Manhattan streets was a visual metaphor for her childhood experiences of lone-liness. "Sundays were particularly bad. My brothers would watch TV, which was 'boys' stuff,' while my parents were busy with other things. If I was ever to feel alone, it was Sunday." Growing up, Anna's mind began to tag certain weekends and holidays—"when there's *nothing happening*"—with the same kind of loneliness. "That's the mental state I was caught in," she says. As an adult, Anna sought clinical help for depression around the issue of such pervasive loneliness. One of the assignments her therapist gave her was to go to the Metropolitan Museum of Art and count the number of people sitting on the front steps with a companion, then count the number sitting alone. "I was stunned. I couldn't believe how many people were alone," Anna says. "That moment broke a spell. It taught me to question some of my assumptions."

Like Meera Kim in *The New York Times Magazine* photograph, Anna learned that there is a way to accept loneliness so that it *opens* into aloneness. "By now," she says, "I actually *covet* aloneness. I'll try to explain what it means to me. Let's say I get up, it's dreary outside and raining, and my mood darkens. I try to physically locate the depressed feelings—it is a kind of heavy weight in my chest. My mind begins its litany of complaints—'This is so awful'; 'I wanted to take a walk this morning'; 'I don't think I can stand one more day of rain'—and the words always drag me further down. But if I don't put any more energy into those thoughts and shift my focus to the feeling in my chest, the heavy weight begins to lift, and the words fall away; there's nothing for my depression to hold on to any longer because I'm no longer feeding it with words."

Anna chooses to stay with those feelings for one simple reason: *that's what's there.* By separating out her feelings from the emotional dead weight of words—words that over time have served to reinforce and intensify her depression—she can begin to think completely different thoughts. A "dismal day" might, for example, turn into a "gray day," only now she has the sense that this is perfectly okay. It may not be her favorite weather; then again, it doesn't have to be. For even though conditions remain exactly the same, once the old words are swept away, Anna has a clear field: she's no longer using her story to create the world that made her depressed.

Anna has learned from experience that we have everything to gain by acknowledging our feelings, and nothing to gain by wading into the marshland of old attitudes and behaviors. One of the critical lessons her example teaches us is to stay alert to old ways of thinking that hold us prisoners in dead-end stories about who we are if we are alone. As an old Buddhist scripture says, "A tenth of an inch's difference and heaven and earth are set apart." Anna was able to make that

180-degree turn; when she did, the aloneness that started out as a sense of despair shifted into an aloneness that, in her words, "is full and whole. It has a sense of completeness, and I don't need anything to make it better or different." Perhaps most important, Anna's inner movement from loneliness to aloneness is a reminder that we, too, have the power—and the skill—to transform our experience of aloneness so that it may begin to serve, rather than defeat, us.

Ironically, for those of us who fear aloneness, one of the most profound truths is that *we need to be alone in order to begin to think differently about being alone.* What gets in our way is our old reflexive tendency to equate aloneness with personal failure. Fear and shame strip us of our rightful inheritance: we pull back and, in so doing, turn away from what will ultimately serve us best—to learn how to befriend aloneness and establish a vital and working relationship with it. Only then will we be able to find the dynamic creative energy that can nurture, revitalize, and replenish our inner resources.

ALONENESS AND RELATIONSHIP

Women often fear that accepting aloneness means they will always be alone, that there is no room for aloneness in a meaningful relationship. To accept aloneness in one's life, or being a woman alone, by no means rules out having a relationship—either in the present or in the future. On the contrary, our willingness to embrace aloneness expands our potential for intimacy.

The more serious question is whether we stay in relationships that aren't working because we are afraid to be alone with our loneliness and use relationships to fill up our emptiness, or we get stuck in regret and remorse because a relationship has ended, or live in romantic "if only" fantasies about finding a new relationship. We are meant to be in relationships with other people, but, just as surely, we are meant to partake of aloneness. To deny this part of our existence is a little like trying to walk the earth on one foot instead of two.

Yet, all too often, fear and anticipation of having to endure the absence of a "significant other" causes a psychic backlash that sends us rushing into someone's waiting arms, whether or not the relationship is right, or even good. "It was marriage that taught me anxiety looks like devotion," says the writer Vivian Gornick about her own marriage in *Approaching Eye Level.* Gornick is not the only woman who feels this way. Loneliness tempts many women into believing that romantic love will save them. The real fear, however, is to be with one's self. And to avoid that confrontation, the desire to be with someone, sometimes anyone, can take on an urgency verging on obsession.

When we fall *in* love, we almost forget we are distinct individuals, as if we exist only in relationship with another person. When we are *out of* love, we divide once more into separate entities. But "one," so the old nursery rhyme taunts, is like the cheese that stands *alone*—not only "apart" from love, but seemingly out of relationship altogether— as if "one" had no standing on its own, no self-integrity, self-pleasure, or self-motivated pursuit—had, in fact, nothing to commend it at all, other than Three Dog Night's pop music distinction of one being "the loneliest number that you'll ever do."

To fall in love is one of life's greatest offerings. But it sometimes seems we are more in love with the idea of being in love than we are with the person. When Brad Pitt and Jennifer Aniston split up after a four-and-a-half-year marriage, *New York Times* journalist Gina Bellafante marveled at the vast number of people who were emotionally invested in their union. We peer into the lives of the rich and famous for vicarious pleasure—trying to get a glimpse of what makes life beautiful and meaningful and, in these difficult times, to find some fantasy version of ourselves we can live with. Similarly, in real life we search for that special someone, hoping to find in him or her the best of ourselves. We wait for the "chance meeting" that is bound to happen—or so we are taught to believe—at least once in our lives. "You had me at hello," Renée Zellweger says to Tom Cruise in the

Cameron Crowe comedy *Jerry Maguire* (1996). And while we may wonder at the weightlessness of her collapse, one thing is certain: our dream of finding the "other half" who will complete us is as alive and well as it's ever been.

But in all relationships, it eventually comes to pass that two people anxiously trying to merge into one discover they are really two. This realization is a transformational opportunity—an open space where the exhilaration of romance can begin to mature into a *whole*some relationship based on mutual love and respect between two autonomous people who actually like each other as they are, and who do not wish to change the other. Nothing in our lives can be more satisfying than this kind of partnership; in fact, underneath all our romantic fantasies, this is what we long for.

But when this essential sea change does not take place—when, becoming two, we decide that our "other half" is no longer what we think we want, or vice versa—our fear of abandonment may still keep us from going our separate ways. In fact, the terror of disconnection is often a stronger bond than love; it keeps many couples together in spent relationships. "I crave and fear being alone" was how one unhappily married young woman described her dilemma to me. By masking our true feelings and pretending things are fine when they are not, we can forestall the dreaded moment of separation when our partner walks out the door for the last time, leaving us feeling stranded and alone.

If we do decide to go it alone, or if circumstances demand it, loneliness is usually the droning accompaniment to this condition. It is natural and normal to grieve our loss, as if in mourning, even if we have left a bad relationship behind. Our sadness may even be masking a host of other emotions—among them shame, unworthiness, envy, jealousy, resentment, rage, and despair. Any of these responses brings us into the realm of what Nietzsche called "dangerous knowledge," which the heart ferociously resists, fearing to be disabled—fearing, in essence, its own salvation.

NO ONE BETTER understood the interplay between aloneness and connection than the English pediatrician and psychoanalyst D. W. Winnicott, whose writings on a human being's capacity to be alone remain seminal in the field. Winnicott knew that the feelings each of us carries forward from birth gather, if we are lucky, into an ever-evolving sense of self. His work with infants and children led him to the core paradox that governs *all* our relationships—not only to others but to ourselves: *"It is only when alone (that is to say, in the presence of someone) that the infant can discover his own personal life."* Quite simply: We learn how to be alone by first being in the *presence* of a nurturing caregiver who, in the deepest sense, respects and therefore validates our being. This requires a relaxed, abiding form of attention that includes listening with the heart as well as keeping a vigil of sustained watchfulness with body and mind. In this way, the child can grow secure enough to develop a personal self, for she will be able to rest comfortably in the kind of creative musing that solitude provides.

So vital yet understated is this revelation that we hardly realize it reaches to the heart of our self-shaping power. In describing the relationship between connection and aloneness, Winnicott paved the way for the understanding that, at the very least, the capacity to be alone is as important as the capacity for relationship as a measurement of emotional maturity, psychological health, and, equally important, a creative life. These alternating life currents of separation and connection instill in us a sense of agency that allows us to become our own mapmakers and move into the uncharted territory of our lives.

SOLITUDE AND THE SELF

In his groundbreaking book, *Solitude: A Return to the Self,* psychoanalyst Anthony Storr has tried to restore the balance between connection and aloneness. Storr questions the pervasive tendency among psychotherapists to emphasize the ability to form successful relationships as evidence of a healthy self. What they overlook is the equally vital truth that the creative self is often best nurtured and realized in aloneness—more specifically, in the animating form of aloneness we call solitude. Love and friendship, while critical to making life meaningful, are not our only sources of happiness: "Our expectation that satisfying intimate relationships should, ideally, provide happiness and that, if they do not, there must be something wrong with those relationships, seems to be exaggerated." In other words, personal relationships are no more and no less worthwhile than the solitude that can return us to the self.

Why is solitude necessary? The self requires solitude so that it may have time to sleep and to rest; to sort and integrate new information and experience; to solve problems; to live creatively; and, should the longing arise, to find fulfillment in some form of religious experience. Operating throughout our lives, Storr reminds us, are two opposing drives: one impels us toward close connection with our fellow human beings; the other toward our equally important need for the sovereignty of selfhood that only solitude can shape. We must heed both drives to bring our lives into balance. As yet, the psychological community has not made a sufficient effort to restore the balance between them— partly because it has directed its focus toward relationship, and partly because the message that aloneness is a state to be cultivated has not yet seeped deeply enough into its collective consciousness. Until this happens, the development of our capacity to be alone will continue to get short shrift—a hardship for women alone, who need, perhaps most of all, to cultivate a deep and compassionate attitude toward aloneness.

THE AVERAGE LIFE expectancy for women is about seventy-nine years. Given the grand arc of our lives, this means we really don't have scads of time to bring ourselves into being. To help us, what we need—in fact, *depend* upon—is solitude. Nothing else allows the green sap of selfhood to flow more easily or readily, nor provides a more fertile space in which we can establish our vital self-governing center. And no other form of aloneness offers so reposeful a sanctuary for the self to mature.

But what exactly is this "self" that occupies so much of our attention? Only a few decades ago, the psychological community spoke instead about the ego, id, and superego; nowadays, that vocabulary is largely obsolete. Next to the impersonal ego, rambunctious id, or tyrannical superego, self seems closer to the essence—or, rather, *our* essence—as the knowing center of our being, our felt awareness of continuity and initiative that we assume to be localized somewhere inside us.

The self is like a river coursing through the center of our existence. What we feel periodically when we stop to take the pulse of the self is its ongoing unity. Whenever we feel lost or estranged from our selves, what we really mean is that we have lost our sense of self; when the self feels absent, so do we. Conversely, when we feel alive and fulfilled, we are speaking out of our sense of self. The self is our subjective reality—that which breathes life into being, doing, making, feeling, communicating—and its evolving form begins at birth, if not before. Each threshold crossing of experience in our infant life is eon's wide. Yet the through line of the self persists from our first breath until our last.

Most women learn early in life to keep the self—*our* self—in hiding. We discover that there are penalties to pay if we express who we are and what we desire. The good-girl syndrome that afflicts women makes us prone to putting the needs of others before our own. Naturally, we would like more for ourselves, but we often feel too guilty or undeserving to put our own needs first; our ability to act on our choices usually comes only after great amounts of struggle and suffering to reclaim the better part of who we are. And because our bodies never lie, we know by how unfree, how constricted, we feel that parts of us are in hiding, just as we know by the free flow of released energy when those parts have come alive again.

It is notable, looking back at our childhoods, how often the moments we felt most alive were in solitude. Christianne Zehl Romero is a Tübingen professor of German at Tufts University. A thoughtful and vigorous woman now in her mid-fifties, she grew up outside Vienna, where she spent her summers enjoying the company of her two older brothers and three cousins. "But from the time I was ten or eleven, I always needed to go off by myself—to the Danube, or the vineyards, where I could sit and just be." In her twenties, Christianne married Laurence, who was, she says, "in many ways my soul mate." Even so, she still wanted to reserve time for herself. "At first, Laurence used to say, 'Why do you think you're so special that you need that?' Then he grew to accept it. I needed solitude for my work but also to have time to contemplate. Now that Laurence has died, I think I need it even more."

Jan Roy, whose penetrating blue eyes sparkle with life and wisdom, says she has many busy women friends who manage to find private time for themselves in the early-morning hours or at the end of the day. Jan, who lives in rural Vermont and is Coordinator of Academic Services at the University of Vermont, likes to make a distinction between her need for private space and solitude. "My work usually involves other people, so when I come home, I often find I need private time to close the day." When the house is quiet, Jan sits down and knits or reads for about an hour. I ask her to explain the difference she finds between private space and solitude. "Private space," she says, "is for quieting my mind and stilling myself; whereas solitude has a more transcendent and creative function. The other morning, I was enjoying myself picking flowers, letting my mind go off in different directions. That was solitude. It has a more formal, grander aspect—the larger nature connection. All these flowers are like gifts from God, and I think it's important to see what's around me and to receive. That's what came to me in that moment—that solitude was about taking in—not just about giving, which is much easier for me to do. For me it reflected the reciprocity and the hope in everything. It's the complete circle."

Zeborah Schachtel, a psychoanalyst and sculptor who lives and works in New York City, came to value solitude later in her life—and only after she had spent many years learning to deal with her loneliness. "I think I always felt lonely," this lively and curious eighty-year-old woman tells me. "I was an only child, and only felt alone. Only means one. And alone and only seem to me to have the same root because I felt alone all the time. I think I ran away from aloneness because there was so much sadness in it from early experiences of deprivation and not being taken in by my mother." For many years, Dr. Schachtel's answer was to stay "very busy and very social. This was my personal role solution to being lonely."

Dr. Schachtel was fifty the first time she remembers taking in the experience of solitude. It happened late one afternoon when she was walking alone on the beach in Cape Cod. "I recognized I hadn't felt that way before . . . that I'd never had a positive experience. Now I was in nature and also being a companion to myself, and it was remarkable. I could take pleasure in myself—I could receive myself. An internal change had made that possible." She experiences a different kind of solitude when she sculpts. "Before I began to do sculpture," she says, "I had no way to form and express my inner experience. But the interesting thing is I always experience solitude as being quiet and listening to the still quiet voice from within. To hear it, I had to stop the jittery mental activity—the many other voices inside clamoring for attention. For me solitude is a state of communion with myself."

For each of us in different ways, aloneness is the portal we enter to find our way into solitude and to the harvesting of the self. Stable and enduring relationships—whether between partners, parents and children, or friends—are based on the solid foundation of a secure self, rather than a shadow-self swollen with need, and the capacity to be alone is essential to their formation. To accept aloneness offers a welcome paradox, inasmuch as it enhances our potential for relation-ships that are neither fear-based nor, in a literal sense, *self*-depriving or, worse, *self*-defeating. Eventually, we learn through aloneness as much as through relationship to nurture ourselves, and this makes nurturing relationships with others possible. We discover *for ourselves* that aloneness is natural, just as we learn that the forced togetherness of any relationship we cling to, or that feels coerced, is unnatural.

In all things, it is a matter of wholeness. Aloneness and connected-ness (or separateness and unity) are complementary aspects of our existence; together, they shape our connection to the world. Our capac-ity to be alone, then, is crucial. We must first learn to tolerate, then to accept, aloneness, so that a true connection to the self can be made. How ironic it is that this relationship to oneself is the one we are least familiar with, and yet it is the building block for all others. Our strength, our stability, and the integrity of *all* our relationships depend on forging this vital connection.

To RETURN BRIEFLY to my Vermont morning: at some indetermi-nate point—it would be impossible to say when exactly—the alone-ness I experienced there moved into solitude; no longer neutral, it felt spacious, fluid, and open, alive to possibility. What I might once have interpreted negatively as "time to fill" or, worse, "time to kill" turned into "my time alone," with generous proportions of time to be silent, to think, and, above all, to just *be,* come what may. I had to *accept* the state of aloneness and agree to be in it *before* I could enter the alive-ness and creativity of solitude. I also had to accept that right at that moment, and for whatever indeterminate length of time, I was a woman alone.

It was still early when I closed my book. Without deciding to, I let myself putter: water the plants, stack magazines, move things from here to there, open a window. But even as I plumped the pillows and made myself a second cup of tea, my mind was already limbering up.

I had caught up with myself and set the rhythm for what came after—which was to turn on the computer a half hour later and start writing.

Having tilled the field of aloneness for a long time, I have discovered that solitude is a gift. This same life-altering experience is available to all women. But to develop the right relationship to aloneness, we need to discover for ourselves that aloneness does not mean loneliness, or emptiness, or isolation, or alienation, or failure. Sorting out these differences became one of my primary tasks as a woman alone, and a major preoccupation of mine as I worked with the women in my practice. I am convinced that no group can profit more from a true understanding of aloneness than women who are, in any sense of the word, alone.

Chapter Three

SHAME-IN-HIDING: A WOMAN'S CULTURAL HERITAGE

THE SPINSTER REVISITED

The first spinster I ever knew was in summer camp. To a seven-year-old, which I was at the time, she seemed ancient, as old as one could possibly be and still *be;* indeed, she teetered at the Very Edge. She was hard of hearing, to put it politely, though "stone deaf" would have been more accurate, since she couldn't hear a word without holding a curved horn to her ear. "Speak loudly," she would say, "I have a horn in my ear," which was a strange request, since she presumably used the horn to magnify sound. After a moment, she would repeat, "Speak louder." And then, "LOUDER STILL," each time inclining a bit more toward the person she was addressing, so that by her third command, she nearly toppled over.

She wasn't particularly kind, nor was she cruel. She didn't smile, and she never seemed to get angry. Ancient as she was, she went about her business with gusto. Flapping the folds of her long black skirt as if to move faster, she resembled some obsessed black bird pecking for seeds in a field. Her conversations with other people were like traffic run-ins she couldn't avoid. When their words bumped into her, she would cock her horned ear like a turn signal, as if to acknowledge she knew they were there and would try to move out of their way faster the next time. The protruding horn extended like a winged antler that had grown out of her naturally and steadily as she aged.

What was this spinster doing in a children's summer camp? She was there because, after writing her story, I played her in a one-woman show that made my audience howl with laughter. But what I could never figure out was where she actually came from. How was it that the first spinster I knew was the one I created myself?

Now I understand that it was the culture I inhabited—or rather, that had begun to inhabit me—and in seemingly benign and innocuous ways was already systematically instructing me about marriage, aging, being alone. In a society that still portrayed marriage and family as every woman's goal, being a spinster was the ultimate booby prize, like finding a thimble in your slice of birthday cake instead of the gold ring. It meant that your fate was to be sad and lonely, that you had somehow fallen short of the mark, and that no one wanted to marry you.

The card game Old Maid ritualized these instructions. Young girls played Old Maid usually during those transitional hours after school ended and before homework began. As soon as the cards were dealt, they would grab hold of their hands to see whether the one "old maid" in the deck was among them; if so, the object was to pass her quickly to the next person so as not to get stuck holding her. Whoever couldn't get rid of her was the old maid—the loser. The medium was the message.

Once upon a time the spinster was, quite simply, a spinner of thread. And since spinning was most commonly done by young unmarried women, the term came to represent unmarried women in English legal documents dating from as early as the 1600s. By the following century, it was used to describe any "woman still unmarried and beyond the usual age for it." Over time, this spinster morphed into *The Spinster:* female archetype of the once luscious woman gone to seed, also known by such various synonyms as "thornback," "stale maid," "old maid," and "antique virgin."

There were plenty of spinsters in the novels we read, but we certainly didn't spend much time thinking about *them*. Instead, we identified our longings and our fears with the heroine's, whose chances for marriage were often in jeopardy. Usually, this heroine had the good fortune—the only acceptable fortune—to be sought after by, won over by, and eventually marry Mr. Right. That's where the story ended, and we closed the book. That was the future we all placed our bets on.

LOOKING THROUGH A book of paintings by the American artist Thomas Eakins, I came upon a nearly perfect description of the spinster stereotype by its editor, John Wilmerding. Describing Eakins's portrait of a young woman name Addie, he writes: "Everything about this portrait represents 'spinsterhood,' as it was conventionally constructed at the turn of the century. [She] is, to use the familiar modifiers, prim, terse, tight, overdressed, schoolmarmish, and puritanical. The chin high collar, fastidious hairdo, drawn lips, and perpendicularity of posture were all stereotypical signifiers used for characterizing an unmarried woman of middle age or older."

What unmarried woman past thirty could have withstood the scrutiny of this harsh male gaze? Lurking in the spinster's background was the suggestion of some grand, unconsummated passion—the love that might have been, whose plaintive "if only" helps explain why she became associated with two singular attributes: shame and sacrifice. She understood that her presence in society was largely tolerated in exchange for services—sewing, mending, cooking, tutoring, or, in maiden-aunt fashion, taking care of her nieces and nephews. Unless independently wealthy, she was obliged to accept a subordinate status to her married sisters in the social hierarchy. No matter that in real life, beneath the surface pallor of their seemingly lackluster lives, their numbers included hundreds, perhaps thousands, of strong, brilliant women, such as Jane Austen, whose novels registered the merciless attitude of society toward women who couldn't, or didn't want to, secure husbands; the poet Emily Dickinson, who spent the last sixteen years of her life cloistered in her father's Amherst, Massachusetts, home writing some of the boldest poetry in American literature; or the eminent writer and scientist Rachel Carson, whose classics *The Sea Around Us* (1951) and *Silent Spring* (1962) presaged the formidable environmental hazards now upon us.

Today, the designation "spinster" seems to have passed from the mainstream; that is, we don't automatically call unmarried women spinsters anymore; it is not politically correct to do so. But the archetype of the spinster is still alive in our unconscious: she has simply morphed into her present incarnation as the *woman alone*—that is to say, into the stoic, sometimes quietly mournful woman who has missed out on the possibility of finding a partner and carries some shame and guilt about it.

This is not to suggest that all women alone feel bereft, or that the awareness of being alone is our constant preoccupation. On the contrary, more women than ever before have the financial independence to pursue life choices that don't involve marriage. But many of those same women still wrestle with personal shame and guilt, brace themselves at parties for the inevitable question about whether they are married, avoid going out to dinner or the movies alone, worry that new people they meet are really thinking they are "losers."

With 27 percent of the more than 114 million adult women in the United States unmarried, personal choice certainly must account for a good number of them. Some statistics are noteworthy. Between 1970 and 2000, the median age at first marriage for women increased by 4.3 years to 25.1 years. In 2000, 81.8 percent of women aged 15 to 24 had never married, versus 56.4 percent in 1950; while 29.7 percent of women aged 25 to 34 had never married, versus 11.3 percent in 1950. This means that when the survey was taken in 2000, roughly 25 percent of all adult women would have said, "I have never married." This statistic was mostly drawn from women who were under 24; nonetheless, it is a snapshot of all American women, a quarter of whom had never married. Still, the prevailing cultural attitude holds that unmarried or unpartnered women are deprived, sad, even desperate. Turning the mirror the other way, many women alone see themselves in the same light.

No wonder, then, that in our culture of abundance, women alone tend to feel scarcity—as if they are deprived of life's full bounty. As Lily, a thirty-something single woman, put it, "The only real passion driving me all my life is that I want to be loved by someone, and love feels utterly remote." Filled with shame and a crumbling sense of self-worth, Lily has ensconced herself in the cul-de-sac of victim-hood, where she bemoans her "C-minus existence as a woman alone" and fantasizes about the fairy-tale prince who might save her. How ironic that on an emotional level, Lily is not so far removed from her once-compliant kin, the spinster, who also believed that the "proper" life was a married one.

SHAME-IN-HIDING

Women in our culture breathe in shame like oxygen and don't even know it. That's how particlized this negative energy has become—and how infectious. We all know the biblical account of shame's origins: in the King James version of *Genesis,* curious Eve, pleased at the sight of the apple hanging on the Tree of Knowledge and liking the idea that "the tree was good for food, and that it was pleasant to the eyes, and a tree to be desired to make one wise," bit right in (3:6). We also know what happened next: how this First Woman dared to wander off the garden path *alone* and was branded, stigmatized, and exiled—not only for her curiosity, but because she asserted herself. For her stunning act of independence, both she and Adam were shamed.

In the story of Eve and Adam—which of course is also ours—shame generates consciousness: "And the eyes of them both were opened, and they knew that they were naked." (3:7). Translated in terms of our human development, consciousness always precedes self-consciousness—but just barely: self-consciousness blooms immediately thereafter. Once we become conscious, we are primed to feel shame. Thereafter, events small and large will contribute to the burden of shame we carry.

"My father tried to kill my mother one Sunday in June, in the early afternoon" begins Annie Ernaux's *Shame,* a memoir about her shame after witnessing that excruciating event at age twelve. The family is sitting down to Sunday lunch. Her mother is in a bad mood and starts an argument with her husband that continues through the meal. After the table is cleared, she keeps criticizing him, while her father says nothing. Suddenly, he stands up and grabs her. Ernaux runs upstairs to her room and throws herself on the bed. Moments later, her mother screams out her name and she runs down the stairs shouting for help as loudly as she can. At that point, says Ernaux, all she can remember are "sobs and screams. Then the three of us are back in the kitchen again. My father is sitting by the window, my mother is standing near the cooker and I am crouching at the foot of the stairs. I can't stop crying." She recalls her mother saying, "'Come on, it's over.'" Afterward, the three of them go for a bicycle ride in the nearby countryside. The incident is never again mentioned, but in that terrible moment, Ernaux's childhood ends; shame seeps into her, and she becomes a sliver of her former self, a transparency, feeling not merely exposed but devoid of a self, empty.

Later that summer, she and her father are eating dinner at a restaurant. At a nearby table, Ernaux sees a girl a few years older than herself, laughing and talking with a man who could be her father. Suntanned, wearing a low-cut dress, she seems completely at ease, unphased by her surroundings. Then Ernaux catches sight of her own reflection in a mirror, "pale and sad-looking with my spectacles, silently sitting beside my father, who was staring into the far distance." Suddenly, she understands the dividing nature of shame: it puts us at war with ourselves and separates us from other people. This impermeable barrier is perhaps shame's most distinctive and enduring feature. The shame-filled person feels defective at the core, unworthy, capable of criticizing, judging, condemning, punishing—but never simply observing herself without attaching blame.

WHAT DID I DO WRONG?

About three-thirty on the morning of Ash Wednesday, Stephanie Gonzalez was jolted awake when a strange man grabbed hold of her arm. Pulling her out of bed, he proceeded to rape her at knifepoint. Afterward, he grabbed hold of Stephanie's neck and forced her into the bathroom, pressing her face into a corner of the shower stall and threatening to kill her if she moved. For interminable seconds the world ceased to exist, as Stephanie surrendered to the fact that she was going to die. The next thing she heard was the sound of tennis shoes squeaking across the tile floor and away from her. When she was sure the man was gone, she turned on every light in the house. Then she called the police.

An accomplished career woman, at the time of the rape Stephanie had just started her second term as secretary of state of New Mexico. Stephanie's first reaction was to congratulate herself for staying calm and composed as she told the story to the police and, later, to the doctors and nurses at the hospital. Of course it was terrible to be raped, but she wanted to put it behind her and get on with her life. A few days later, she went back to work telling herself that she was over it.

Then came the backlash. Within a few weeks, Stephanie began to feel anxious when she was around people. Instead of socializing with colleagues as she usually did, she started going straight home after work, citing fatigue as the reason. "I could feel myself shutting down," she said. Soon, she distanced herself from a promising relationship with a man she'd started dating about three months before the rape and began staying in on weekends, too. It got to the point where she didn't want to leave home even to go to the grocery store or post office.

Despite the fact that she'd kept it secret, Stephanie became convinced that everyone in town knew about the rape and blamed her for it. She began to take frequent showers. "It seemed like I could never get as clean as I wanted to, as I needed to be. I felt dirty, inside and out."

Spurred by guilt, Stephanie kept circling around the same questions. Why had the attacker singled her out? Had she crossed paths with him and inadvertently been rude? "It was like, what did I do to make this happen?" She reviewed her past compulsively, scanning it for evidence of misdeeds. The fact that the rape happened on Ash Wednesday fed her growing belief that it was punishment for being "bad." "It felt like it was my fault. I should have tried to stop him. I should have been more careful about locking doors." She even convinced herself, unrealistically, that had she fought back harder, she could have overpowered her larger, stronger assailant.

Only after Stephanie sought help from a therapist did she begin to understand that the "dirt" she was trying to get rid of by showering obsessively was her own shame. She was also able to identify her feelings of hopelessness, restlessness, and inertia as symptoms of depression, driven by her unacknowledged shame. Eventually, the therapist helped Stephanie understand that what had happened wasn't her fault, that she could neither have prevented nor stopped the rape once it started without risking her life. "Once I could accept that, it was no longer a question of what I had done but of what the perpetrator had done. I am almost abashed now at how ready I was to deny the impact of the rape and then turn around and blame myself for it."

Stephanie's experience is but an extreme example of women's tendency to always blame themselves, although it is not uncommon, given the fact that one out of every six American women has been the victim of rape or attempted rape in her lifetime, and that 17.7 million women have been victims. Surely, Stephanie's experience speaks to the insidious nature of guilt and shame. These two emotions are often intertwined, though they are not the same. Guilt's energy is invested in "shoulds" and "oughts," and it plays these notes unremittingly. We feel guilty for something we've done or didn't do or for having forbidden thoughts. Preoccupied with guilt, we spare ourselves the more disturbing feelings of unworthiness underneath—where shame has burrowed in.

Shame and guilt may be the dominant emotions that afflict women in our culture. They grow out of what I believe is a woman's fundamental social fear: not being liked or accepted *as she is.* Nothing undermines a woman's self-esteem more quickly than to feel judged, and when "as she is" includes being a woman alone, she expects disapproval. How can she help it when the social climate she inhales is replete with messages reminding her that she should aspire to the status of marriage and motherhood, and that the satisfactions of work and success are meaningless otherwise? To accomplish this goal, women must prove their desirability to a man—if single, by vamping it up; if over thirty-five, by finding ways to remain forever young. "Give me everything I want and nothing I need," croons a Victoria's Secret ad featuring a sultry blonde in a black lace push-up brassiere. Clearly, her seductive charms have earned her the right to ask Mr. Right to fulfill her every desire. As for the rest of us unfortunates, we know what we must do to capture a man: buy some sexy see-through, that's what. This is Victoria's real secret.

Meanwhile, the 30-plus million of us past thirty-five, which seems to be the cultural dividing line for acceptable singledom, are made to feel anxious and ashamed of our single status, especially if we haven't already proven our sexual mettle—or don't believe we have enough of it—to snare a man. Still, it's not too late—provided we emulate TV's come-hither sex goddesses, as they toss their Panteened tresses, flash "supersmiles" through whitened teeth, and scent themselves with CK's perfumed promise of Euphoria. If that isn't effective, virtually every women's magazine on the market hawks self-improvement with a vengeance so we can "Take 10 Years Off Today"

(*Eve*), "Get Dewy Skin, Sex-Kitten Hair and Lips That Stay Up All Night" (*Jane*), renew "Sexual Energy: Get It Tonight!" (*Redbook*), and "bliss out" on the "The Beauty Makeover That Really Works"(*Elle*). For if we can no longer be young goddesses, at least we can plasticize, Botox, liposuct, and otherwise cosmeticize ourselves to "look like" them—or, as one cosmetics ad assures us, "stay perfect" and improve our chances of catching or keeping a mate. The women's movement that fought for equal rights in the 1960s and 1970s has been superceded by the women's antiaging movement in this first decade of the twenty-first century.

"In a world where many women either get divorced or never get married, it is now a status symbol to snag a married name," writes Maureen Dowd, Pulitzer Prize–winning columnist for the *New York Times* and author of *Are Men Necessary?* Better to be a "desperate housewife"—as the same-named prime-time hit TV series reminds us—than to stay single and forlorn. In subtle and gross ways, the bias against unmarried and unpartnered women is stronger than ever. The Spinster, updated and retrofitted, is alive and well.

"WHAT DID I do to deserve this? I wonder what's so wrong with me that someone cannot love me for who I am?" asks Heather, one of the contestants on ABC's prime-time hit *The Bachelor,* a reality series in which twenty-five women compete to be an eligible hunk's made-it-to-first-place soul mate. Heather became a leading contender before bachelor Aaron rejected her. Her sobbing when she didn't win was the raw footage of shame. Not once did Heather question Aaron's desirability as a potential husband. He was the prize in a game she desperately wanted to win. Like too many women, when she didn't win, she believed herself defective.

The difference between Heather and the rest of us is that she went public with her doubt and shame and broke down in front of millions of people. Still, her story is a dramatic example of how low self-esteem reinforces women's tendency to blame ourselves when we aren't validated by a man. Words like *stupid, lazy, fraudulent, boring,* and *ordinary* creep into our vocabulary all too easily, along with phrases like "I'm not good enough," "I'm a failure," and, above all, "It's no use trying." Aligned with this toxic form of self-blame is the fear of being thought of—and, worse, seeing ourselves—as "too greedy," "demanding," "selfish," "indulgent," or just plain "too much" that scores of women have guiltily expressed to me when they dare to do things for themselves instead of other people.

Eventually, these inner voices become like white noise, droning monotonously in the background with such compulsive insistence that they fill in all the vacant spaces where our real voice might break through, the one that allows us to accept ourselves as we are. Strange as it may sound, Heather's one authentic moment—when she was not performing but actually being herself on *The Bachelor*—was when she lost control and started to sob. That was when her real self slipped through.

Yet when we hear other women put themselves down, we almost reflexively think, "No, that's not me, I don't feel like that." Shame is called the hidden emotion precisely because it is so difficult to feel, let alone acknowledge. But there's an infallible way to test shame's power: all we need to do is pay attention to the occasions when we feel self-conscious, overly self-critical, or when we turn away from choices we would like to make. Our shame as women alone reveals itself in the most ordinary decisions, like deciding to order the same old boring take-out rather than eating a nice meal alone in a restaurant, or staying home rather than going to the movies, the theater, a party, or on a vacation. Shame creeps in around the holidays, or after a divorce when old friends stop inviting us to dinner parties, or when we find ourselves bingeing at three in the morning, or when someone calls us "Mrs." once this form of address no longer applies, or when it begins to seem that everyone but us is coupled, or when a friend finds a partner or marries while we watch from the sidelines.

The feeling of shame women alone carry always revolves around the theme of not being good enough as we are, and invariably our response is to try to be "better." But "good enough" is not quantifiable; it is a goal that, like the receding horizon, can never be reached, no matter what we do or how hard we try.

NO ARM TO CLING TO

In *A Room of One's Own* Virginia Woolf wrote: "if we face the fact, for it is a fact, that *there is no arm to cling to* [my italics], but that we go alone and that our relation is to the world of reality and not only to the world of men and women, then the opportunity will come . . ." By "world of reality" Woolf means our own inner world where, alone, we are free to mine the sources of our creativity. And yet, more than seventy years after these words were published, many of us still cringe at the fact that there is no arm to cling to, caught as we are between our genuine desire for autonomy and our deeply held dependency fears about what it means to be "unpartnered" and alone.

Our conditioning for such behavior runs deep. At the end of the nineteenth century, suffragists did their best to dismantle the Cult of Domesticity that kept women tethered to home and family. The "new woman" who emerged between the 1890s and the 1920s, when the term was coined, had, as a result, far greater freedom to pursue public roles and express her individuality than ever before. But progress is nonlinear. We don't just climb steadily uphill, but, like Jill, often tumble down again. Recounting the feminist movement of the 1960s and 1970s, Maureen Dowd writes, "Maybe we should have known that the story of women's progress would be more of a zigzag than a superhighway, that the triumph of feminism would last a nanosecond while the backlash lasted forty years."

It is little wonder that women continue to be confused about their roles and their identity. The media's subliminal message to us is that everything we do must be calculated to make us desirable to a man, which, by logical extension, means readying ourselves for marriage. In other words, we are expected to be irresistible sirens before transforming ourselves into wives and mothers. The thrust toward becoming strong, independently minded women has folded back on itself. Whether unpartnered or in relationship, we are still not prepared, in Woolf's words, to accept the fact that we "go alone"; nor are we ready to accept that, for each of us, the "world of reality" refers to the fulfillment of our own personal life. As yet, most women don't have a clear understanding of what such a personal life entails or why the "art" of being a woman alone is worth protecting and fighting for—whether we are literally alone or not.

Freud asked, "What does a woman want?" The real question is, what does each one of us, as a woman, want? To be taken care of by a man? To stand on our own? In truth, women today seem desperately to want *both;* hence, our role and identity confusion. But if this is so, then we must be willing to admit our dependency needs and to recognize that for as long as we "cling," we barter away our freedom for the sake of being rescued. The double standard still prevails. We still want the man to "prove" his love by paying for our dinner or the mortgage. We still wait for a man to tell us how to think and feel. We still look up to the opposite sex, waiting for his approval—and his marriage proposal—largely unaware of how deeply we have internalized the prevailing biases of the culture and its ambiguous response toward being a woman alone. In this brand-saturated environment, we still accept simplistic "rules" to achieve coupledom, turning ourselves into "products" a man will want to . . . buy. Ellen Fein and Sherrie Schneider's *The Rules* and Rachel Greenwald's *Find a Husband After 35 Using What I Learned at Harvard Business School* are just such working manuals. Greenwald's premise is that by the time we reach thirty-five, meeting Mr. Right is much harder than when we were younger. For, while older men, especially well-heeled ones, are considered desirable and can have their pick among nubile twenty-year-olds, women face steep competition and go downhill fast. Still, not to worry, says Greenwald. Love, after all, is for sale. We are the "product," the "personal brand," the "commodity," as long as we are willing to learn from her how to market ourselves—in fifteen easy steps. Learn, in other words, how to distinguish ourselves from all other "brands" so that (god willing), we still have the opportunity to divest ourselves of singledom, a low-yield investment, and follow the high-return trajectory of marriage and children. As if our salvation depended on escaping singledom.

WOMAN AS NURTURER

Recently, I got a desperate call from Nell, a woman I worked with years ago when she was single, dating, and a budding writer; she is now the mother of an energetic two-year-old boy. The problem, Nell explained, was that her live-in partner was away for a few weeks on a business trip, and her nanny was sick with the flu; she was, for the time being, a full-time mother and not loving it. "What's wrong with me?" she anguished. "I love my two guys, and I love my home. But work is my home, too, and I don't know how to do the mother thing full-time." Nell felt ashamed for not behaving the way she thought mothers were supposed to. "I'm handicapped, I have two left hands," she told me, "and child care is relentless."

Hearing her distress, I decided to tell Nell how, as a young mother, I almost lost my sanity wheeling my two young sons in a stroller around Princeton until I realized that, instead, I could bundle them in the car and take them to wonderful places. One of our favorites was the American Museum of Natural History, where, up close and together, we could marvel at the forty-nine-foot-long Tyrannosaurus rex and stare at the diorama of a killer whale. Nell breathed a sigh of relief. I could almost hear her exhaling shame, along with some of her guilty thoughts that mothers are supposed to be cheerfully self-sacrificing. "It's amazing that, even today, we still don't even know the expectations we carry," she said.

As a mother who is well aware of how much her life has been enriched by nurturing her two sons, I know that one of the great rewards of being female is to create and bring forth life and to care for that life until it can take care of itself. But I also remember the agonies of conflict I felt each time I went against accepted conventions of mothering by desiring something for myself. When I tried to be available to my children and also follow my own personal and political interests, I felt torn apart by guilt. My sons were grown before I understood the price women pay for doing what comes naturally. For as we nurture other people's lives, we often neglect to nurture our own.

I don't mean the kind of nurturing that a bubble bath or pedicure might fix—delightful as they may be. Rather, I am talking about deep and regenerating forms of nurturing that have to do with living our personal lives. To nurture others is an essential part of our femininity, but when the role of nurturer becomes the way we justify our existence and define ourselves—"I am a nurturer" rudely upending "I am a woman who, among the many other choices I make, also nurtures"—it is almost always at the expense of self.

MEDIA LESSONS WE SHOULDN'T BE LEARNING

The debilitating effect of media exposure on women's self-esteem is nothing short of astonishing. It should come as no surprise that the direct route to reach us is through our bodies—whose size, shape, beauty, and adornment are constantly being mirrored back to us as defective. We are easy marks, not only because advertisers capitalize on our shame and low self-esteem but because so few of us fight back. According to the media's house-of-mirrors philosophy, appearance—how we look rather than who we are—is what matters. And, to an alarming degree, we buy it.

From the time they get their first Barbie, as 90 percent of girls from three to eleven do, young girls are confronted by a role model of the unattainable body. Plenty of research has documented the link between the increased incidence of eating disorders and the rise of the ultra-thin fashion image as the ultimate standard of beauty. One study recorded young women's reactions to pictures of models in magazines and found that exposure to the thinness ideal produced depression, body displeasure, stress, and, of course, guilt and shame. A Stanford University study sampling of female undergraduate and graduate students found that 68 percent felt worse about their own looks after reading women's magazines. Other studies have found a direct relationship between media exposure and eating-disorder symptoms. The tendency among girls to compare themselves to models only increases with age. How can any merely mortal female feel good about herself when bombarded with images of stars and models whose physical imperfections have been airbrushed out of existence? As women alone, we apparently lose on both counts: we have failed to excite a man's interest, and so the prize—marriage, home, and family—eludes us.

By saturating us with words and images of thinness as the body ideal, the intention is to make us desire *more* by aspiring to be, quite literally, *less*. In plain language, we are being inducted into a life of addiction, the hungry-ghost realm where envy, the feeling of being "less than," causes endless craving and where dissatisfaction is the norm. On the one hand, feeling hopeless, we console ourselves by consuming whatever we think might fill our emptiness; on the other, we pursue the false hope of transformation and renewed possibilities through "makeovers"—forgetting that the change we seek comes from making *internal* choices rather than external ones. In our effort to reach some unattainable image of beauty, we seem to forget that we are people, not marketable commodities.

What are we searching for with such addictive fervor? The answer, I am convinced, is love. But love rarely grows true and strong in the desolate fields of shame and envy. Limp with shame, we are needy lovers, not forthright ones, seeking in our partners what we cannot find in ourselves. When that effort fails, as it must, we begin to look for it in *things*. In her thoughtful exposé of the advertising world, *Can't Buy My Love,* Jean Kilbourne shows that advertisers have moved beyond the false promise "Buy this and you will be loved" to the yet more hopeless one: *"Buy this and it will love you."* Forget about having relationships with real people. When all else fails, we can fall in love—even have autoerotic sex—with inanimate objects. All we have to do is run our new "hot" Dyson vacuum cleaner, "pump" ourselves up with a Lexus car engine, or "Bacardi by night."

In this worldview, there is no need to change the world or ourselves: products will do that for us. So will words, hollowed out to mean whatever the advertisers want them to mean, turning "live words" that can light up the heart with their wisdom and energy into "dead words," with all the truth squeezed out of them. In this world of weightless words meant to convince us that we are free and independent, "revolt" means buying the right brand name of designer jeans or identifying with models wearing black nail polish; "think for yourself" means having enough style sense to buy the latest "hot" fashion; "spirited" is the newest celebrity scent. We don't have to glow from within: gold-flecked foundation takes care of that. Promotional campaigns costing millions of dollars try to tame and subdue us, so that we will keep buying our image of freedom instead of forging it from within.

And it starts early. From childhood on, everything a young girl dreams about, thinks about, wants for herself, is turned into the pap of product—trivialized so as to become meaningless. Jane, a young mother, was dismayed when her five-year-old daughter, Elise, was teased by her classmates for wearing the wrong kind of snow pants. "This is kindergarten, no less! Sometimes she's teased for not having the latest cool snack food in her lunch box." Jean Kilbourne puts the emphasis squarely where it belongs: "Just as she is entering womanhood, eager to spread her wings, to become truly sexually *active,* empowered, independent—the culture moves in to *cut her down to size.*" We grow alienated from who we are and what we truly want for ourselves, extinguishing the spark that ignites the self. For any woman, this kind of disconnection from self breeds loneliness and need, for there is nothing nourishing about the deliberate subversion of one's selfhood. One of the more painful moments I remember in my therapeutic practice was when a young, dark-haired woman confessed to me that "no matter how smart I am or how well I put myself together, I always feel small unless a man tells me how terrific I am. I should have been tall and blond. I was *born wrong*."

FEAR AND VULNERABILITY

In the collection of clippings I've saved over the past years, outstanding in its offensiveness is a double-spread Dior ad featuring a young girl sitting in a white car, dressed to become roadkill. A long red zipper strung like a lasso across her black see-through blouse stretches down between her spread-eagled legs. Eyes closed, lips parted, her body soiled with grease, it looks like she, rather than the car she's in, is about to get a lube job she'll never forget. In the second image, the girl, now clad in a black bikini, leans against the car's hood, legs still parted. Sullen and abject, she looks like one of the lost souls in advertising's netherworld, utterly, and almost winsomely, defeated. In what amounts to a celebration of statutory rape, a single word completes this image: the "Dior" insignia of approval.

From images to excruciatingly real events, women commute daily along the highway where sex and violence intersect. Given the media's insistence on exploiting female sexuality, we learn—some of us the hard way—that when we venture alone into unknown places, a certain amount of fear is appropriate, that caution is prudent.

Melanie, a pretty redhead with soulful eyes, remembers walking with a boyfriend in England at age sixteen. "There was an underpass in the road, and he just headed for it instinctively. I hesitated, but he said, 'No, no, let's go this way, it's quicker'. I would never have gone that way by myself, and it made me realize how different the world must look to him: he wasn't afraid of going into a dark, deserted tunnel."

Sometimes, we take risks anyway because it feels like there is no other choice. Marla Ruzicka, a twenty-eight-year-old American aid worker who founded the one-woman aid group in Iraq, Campaign for Innocent Victims in Conflict, to help civilians caught in the cross fires of war, became a casualty herself when a suicide bomber's attack on a convoy of security contractors also hit her car on the airport road in Baghdad. Ruzicka surely understood the danger inherent in the work she chose, and her death transcends gender distinctions. In many parts of the world, women don't have the luxury of making personal life choices: they are attacked simply *because* they are women. In this country, good fortune allows us to believe we are relatively risk-free until some life event shocks us into awareness, and so we tend to "forget" the many ways this culture devalues women. Violence comes in numerous guises, not all of them as raw as rape, battering, or incest. So deeply have we internalized shame and guilt, women scarcely notice that the culture's fingerprints have stained our sense of self-worth, or realize that we have the power to remove them. Yet, to the degree that we refuse to take notice, we are psychologically, and often morally, compromised.

Many unpredictable shamings are reserved for our gender alone, as these few among countless examples illustrate:

Crossing the threshold into lesbianism, as Joyce did at age twenty, "feeling really vulnerable and visible, like the moment I stepped out in the street, I had 'Lesbian' written all over me." And although Joyce said the relief was "actually fabulous," she also had to go through a "very intense phase of feeling isolated from some of the friends I had before. People were shocked, homophobic, really nasty. At Barnard College! Who knows what that is, except that there's a lot more homophobia in this society than we acknowledge." Having fallen in love with a woman who "looks butch, not girlishly feminine like me," Joyce is painfully aware of how differently they are treated in unfamiliar public settings. "If I'm alone, guys whistle at me, but if Clara and I go to a restaurant, they seat us right next to the restrooms."

Calling an abortion clinic to schedule an appointment and being berated by a pro-lifer who had somehow managed to intercept the line. "Here I was, twenty years old," Jamie, now thirty-three and happily married, tells me, "and she's saying, 'Are you sure this is what you want to do? Because it's a sin, you know, and you have other options.'" Days later, Jamie was at the public clinic, sitting alone in a blue paper robe almost frozen with fear waiting to go into the operating room. And though she was not able to see behind the thin partitions, she heard the sounds of other women crying. In the grim atmosphere of a public clinic, the gray institutional pallor registered an unconcern as profound as it was punishing. "It's hard to believe this could have happened to me, but sometimes I still think about it. The pain doesn't really leave."

Being treated like an object, as Gena was before giving birth to her second child at the age of thirty-two. A vibrant, hardworking woman alone, Gena still remembers the horror of "knowing something was wrong and no one telling me." On welfare at the time, Gena went to a local clinic. "You're just a number, you see a different doctor every time, mostly men, and it's not like you have a personal relationship with anybody." When Gena was two weeks overdue, doctors examined her; not sensing much activity, they decided to induce contractions to see how the baby reacted. "They didn't say there was a problem; I thought it was probably just that I was overdue."

The next morning, the nurses prepped Gena and wheeled her into the delivery room and hooked her up to monitors. "No one was saying anything. Then a female resident came and looked at the monitor. And I knew it, I could feel something inside me, and she goes, 'Something's not right here.' And that's all she had to say. My whole life changed that minute." A group of doctors came into the room. One of them scanned Gena's stomach with a stethoscope. All he said was, "Well, that's where the heartbeat should be." The doctors never looked at Gena or talked to her directly. It wasn't until that evening that she was told her baby had died in the womb.

First reactions to menopause, which Louise, a novelist in her early fifties, called "a major geological shift," took hold of her unawares and made her feel she had to reevaluate her "sexy woman" self-image. "I felt attractive only to the extent I believed men found me attractive. Now I just feel old." Eventually, Louise understood that she needed "to find my own sense of myself, not the one *they* had conferred on me." She says she has a ways to go.

Divorce, menopause, the shape of her nose or the size of her body, delivering a stillborn child, becoming a teenage mother, a single mother, a battered wife—the list of cultural phenomena that can elicit women's shame is legion. But because shame usually occupies the invisible center seat in our lives, it is hardest to recognize, let alone disown. Often it takes years before we become aware of how profoundly shame erodes our life force or feel ready to acquit ourselves of the emotional pain that has knotted our lives.

OUTING THE SECRET OF THE INJURED SELF

The impact of cultural blockage on women's lives cannot be underestimated. For to the degree that we accept—and abide by—the rules of socially invasive, and false, doctrine about who we are and who we ought to be, we will continue to suffer from low self-esteem. The formation of self will be drastically, perhaps irrevocably, compromised.

There is, however, a power-laden alternative: *to disabuse ourselves of shame and fear by outing its secret lair inside us.* How? By first growing conscious of the emotional and spiritual hold these host energies have on us. This is exactly what Stephanie Gonzalez did after she was raped, as, little by little, her attitude, then her actions, began to change. For two and a half years Stephanie kept her rape a secret. Meanwhile, she was reading about case after case of rape in the newspapers—and gaining strength and resolve. "Finally," Stephanie said, "I made a decision that turned my life around: I would no longer live with the crime—or the secret. Instead, I would tell the public about my rape."

Stephanie called Barbara Goldman, the executive director of the Santa Fe Rape Crisis Center, and volunteered to tell her story on TV. After the program aired, Stephanie was inundated with calls from women and men who wanted to offer support and share their own stories. "They would say, 'This happened to me several years ago, and I'm going to get help.' Or, 'This happened to my mother, and my father hasn't been able to deal with it, and we all need to get help.' A woman who is now a district judge told me it had happened to her. The outpouring was incredible."

The experience of outing her secret transformed Stephanie. "I'm not the same person," she says. "I don't feel ashamed anymore." By admitting to and uncovering her own invisible wounds, Stephanie went through a profound educational process. She was no longer content to accept a dysfunctional mode of social "behavior"—that of the nice, obedient, and voiceless woman—by silencing herself, or turning suppressed anger into self-disavowal, or allowing feelings of shame, guilt, and anger to translate into depression. Such acquiescence would have only created more inner emptiness. Instead, Stephanie's therapeutic work allowed her to confront her own secret shame *in solitude*. Indeed, that act was itself a form of self-assertion, and it permitted her to give a name to hitherto unknowable and inchoate feelings that had been choking off her sense of personal freedom. Most of us do not have to endure such terrible misfortune before embarking on the journey to selfhood; yet whatever circumstances bring us there, this is the same path every woman alone must travel. Indeed, once we step foot on it, we will savor the solitude that transforms our lives.

A WOMAN'S SELF

A woman's self is a strong, yet delicate, thing. I know this firsthand from the privileged space of my office, where I have a panoramic view of women's selves. Their appearances vary: outside, some are broken, tough, wispy, empty, hungry, ravaged, or ravenous; inside, all shine with the same hallowed light. Appearance isn't important. What is important is that no matter how faint the silhouette, these selves stubbornly persist. For the self insistently shows up, shape changing according to its need for camouflage and the degree to which it feels brutalized or neglected: in a word, *unseen*. To be unseen is, frankly, an intolerable form of aloneness. It means that we are invisible to others, or, if even vaguely visible, that we simply do not matter. Nothing is more devastating to a woman's self than that: for to be unseen by others means that we are truly unable to see ourselves. This is surely how Stephanie felt after the rape and before she was ready to come to terms with what had been inadmissible knowledge. But it is also a looming reminder to the rest of us who are quick to cast the first stone—at ourselves.

THE DIMINISHED SELF-ESTEEM that leads us to fear, and then turn away from, the solitude we need for personal and spiritual nourishment, is a river fed by two tributaries. The first is the social and cultural tributary I explore in the first three chapters and that creates the climate whose air woman alone must breathe in every day. The second, equally important tributary concerns the development of our personal identity, which I will turn to next. It is important for a woman alone—indeed, *all* women—to understand how some of the fundamental experiences of growing up female—from childhood through young adulthood—affect the way a woman's sense of self evolves—*specifically in relation to our early experiences of being alone.*

When we take into consideration the many cultural messages that encourage a woman to think of herself as less than—to not accept herself as she is—together with the many assaults to the self that are personal and individual, we can begin to understand why the uncomfortable feelings we carry make us veer away from aloneness. The challenge to women alone is to confront these feelings so that we can enjoy the creative rewards of solitude.

Part II

ON SHIFTING
GROUND

Chapter Four

THE AWAKENING: CHILDHOOD

WHEN YOU FIRST KNOW YOU'RE YOU

The moment arrives for all of us. On an ordinary day, something extraordinary happens. An insight stirs us to wakefulness as insistently as an alarm clock, and we know consciously what had been only an intimation before: *I am myself and can only be myself.* Following behind is its corollary: *I am absolutely different from every other creature in the world.* "I remember at a very young age looking at my hands and being struck that I existed," says psychologist Alexandra Bloom, describing her moment of awakening.

For most of us, such an insight usually occurs by the time we are nine or ten, though the timing is different for different girls. On a continuum of development that begins at birth, this revelatory moment marks the start of what Jung called individuation, the ongoing process by which each of us becomes distinctly ourselves. The drive toward selfhood progresses through childhood and adolescence until it reaches that elusive state known as adulthood. But if childhood experience is characterized by immediacy, "in-the-momentness," when we are still relatively free of the self-consciousness that begins to plague us by the time we reach adolescence and continues to plague us in one way or another into adulthood, then this moment is remarkable because it marks the *beginning* of active self-awareness. It is as if the blurred outline of self suddenly grows sharp and clear, illuminating with unerring accuracy the knowledge that we are unique. Natalie described her moment of recognition at age ten or eleven this way:

"It was a hot summer afternoon and I was lying on the floor of my room, legs propped up on the side of the bed. I may have been reading; more likely, I was daydreaming. I was wearing shorts, and I remember so clearly looking at my legs as if seeing them for the first time. I studied the shape of my calves, feeling cautiously pleased. They aren't so bad, I thought, already aware that to have thin, shapely legs was considered 'good' and made one attractive to boys and that fat, chunky legs were 'bad.' Then I undid that perception by reminding myself that they looked wider when I stood up. Still, I remember my fascination, as if getting to know the shape of my calves was a way of getting to know me. My calves didn't look like the calves of any of my friends; they were mine."

It is in such moments that we first intuit the meaning of privacy. "I thought of my mother," says Natalie, "and knew somehow that these thoughts weren't something to share with her, even though we were close. I think I understood then that there would always be things about me that were mine and mine alone, utterly private." Nor does the realization last. "Looking back, it seems clear that it was then that I began to develop an inner life," she continues. "But I underwent no obvious transformation. I'm quite sure that just minutes later, I ran outside to join my brothers' softball game and didn't give it a second thought. Still, some ineffable presence called 'me' took up residence inside my being. It was as if my Self, planted in infancy and taking root in childhood, had sent up its first tender, young shoots."

Not surprisingly, such awakenings usually happen when we are alone. Mine took place one early spring afternoon as I was walking home from school. There was a maple tree on my block. I passed it every day, but on this day, it caught my attention more than usual, and I reached up to grab one of its leaves. Turning it in my hands, I suddenly noticed the contrast between its shape, texture, and vivid green color and every other thing around it—the spindly brown branch from which it emerged, the pale, smooth concrete sidewalk below my hand, and, most of all, the soft, pink flesh of myself. I remember feeling the leaf's aliveness, and suddenly feeling alive to myself as I never had before, part of some great, mysterious energy that also animated whoever "I" was. Of course, I could not have articulated any of these ideas at the time. Still, the impact of that moment endured as a memory, one that retained the sweet trace of promise—of the self I would become.

From my countless discussions and interviews with women, I have come to believe that in this moment of awareness—our intuition that the kernel of our potentiality lies within—is one of childhood's greatest offerings. It is a moment of pure communion with our private, true self that may not come again for a long time. The world closes around us again all too quickly for this experience to last.

THIS REVELATION DOES not arrive without some anxiety. For all the joyousness in Alexandra Bloom's newfound awareness, she also remembers "feeling different from the other kids." It was as if graced by specialness one moment, Alexandra feels herself fall from grace the next. The collaboration between sameness and difference—first with our parents and then with other people—continues throughout our lives. Our perception of difference is inevitably followed by a stern reminder of our inherent separation from all other beings: Yes, I am me. And yet, the moment I celebrate my uniqueness, I feel my separation from others: I am reminded that not only am I in relationship with others, I am also alone.

TO BE A "THING-FINDER"

*She had no mother and no father, and that was of course
very nice because there was no one to tell her to go to bed
just when she was having the most fun, and no one who
could make her take cod liver oil when she much preferred
caramel candy.*

ASTRID LINGREN, *Pippi Longstocking*

Hard as it is to believe, one of our first models of a woman alone is
now "a woman of a certain age." Pippi Longstocking's coming-out
party was in 1950, the year Astrid Lindgren's book was published in
Sweden, when Pippi was just nine. Nine years old and all alone,
except for a horse who lived on her front porch, a monkey named
Mr. Nilsson, and a suitcase full of gold pieces she could dip into as
needed, Pippi still reigns as the quintessential representative of the
spirit of childhood—its unfettered imagination free to roam where it
wishes, unencumbered by adult rules and laws and conventions.

Pippi was an orphan, a literary conceit for all that is unknowable
and undecipherable about childhood. Physically stronger than anyone around her, "so very strong that in the whole wide world there
was not a single police officer as strong as she," no one could get the
best of her. Pippi made all her own decisions. She didn't go to school,
not simply because the teachers couldn't stand having her there—
and they couldn't!—but because she didn't want to and said so loud
and clear. She went to bed when she liked, never did the "Friday
cleaning," and walked backward when it suited her—mowing down
social conventions like so many cluttering weeds. What flowered in
their place was a cosmically comic slant on the world and her boundless generosity toward others that informed her vision of how life
ought to be lived, which was to do exactly as she wished. Aloneness
gave her imagination its vast playing field.

"What are we going to do now?" asked Tommy.

"I don't know what you are going to do," said Pippi, "but I know I can't lie around and be lazy. I am a Thing-Finder, and when you're a Thing-Finder you don't have a minute to spare." . . .

"What's that?" asked Tommy.

"Somebody who hunts for things, naturally. . . . The whole world is full of things, and somebody has to look for them."

As adults, we have to work hard to recall our own childhood capacity to be thing-finders—the sense of wonder we brought to each experience simply because it was new. At age eight, Vicki's mother taught her the "art" of washing dishes—how to fill the sink with hot, sudsy water, sliding in the silverware to soak while she washed the glasses first, then the plates, silverware, and finally the pots and pans. "I did it so mindfully," she says. "I know it sounds silly, but the experience felt sacrosanct." Now, as a grown woman and mother of two adolescent children, Vicki's dishwashing is a routine, mostly pleasureless, chore that "I can do in my sleep." The freshness and wonder of these first childhood experiences fades, and no matter how passionate we remain, the bubbling vitality of childhood that Pippi represents never again repeats itself in quite the same way.

Surely this is why adults were appalled by Pippi, while children adored her. She embodied the rogue energy, the wild-card side of young girls—gangly, coltish, awkward, pre- (and) sexual, precocious, adventurous, iconoclastic, nonsensical, nonconformist, poetic, and piercingly aware. To be a "Thing-Finder," as Pippi declared herself, also aptly describes the imagination of young girls, which, under ideal conditions, is so liberated, so free-flowing and animated, that everything feels magically alive, including stones, shells, and stuffed animals—and ourselves. We marveled at Pippi's adventures, wanted to breathe in the pure air of her unconfined freedom, no doubt sensing that she was there to give us courage as we started taking on the world. Pippi is a robust metaphor for being *out there on one's own*—in other words, having a self, declaring it, and surviving.

But even the frankest and most fearless among us, unlike Pippi, grow up feeling a sense of restraint. Most young girls have to go to school and are bound by adult rules there as well as at home. We did our homework, helped with dinner, fought with our siblings, watched movies and TV, did or didn't do well at school, were rewarded or punished, praised or ridiculed—all the while sucking in images and messages of how young girls ought to behave.

We also experienced childhood woundings—divorce, a death in the family, illness, a parent's shaming, a sibling's bullying, a friend's betrayal—that obliged us to come to terms with disappointment and loss when we were far too young to absorb their intensities. The events of childhood test and shape us, even if all the action takes place beneath the surface. As the developmental psychologist Carol Gilligan described it in *In a Different Voice,* her compelling study of girls' loss of confidence, we often don't realize that something has begun to change in us until we reach puberty, when self-doubt creeps in and the lilt in our voices starts to lose its spring.

PROTECTING OUR PRIVATE SELF

If childhood marks the awakening of our potential, and the budding awareness of our individuality, it is, just as important, about our intuitive knowledge that we need to protect the core of our newly discovered self. For the story of growing up female in this culture is too often one of loss of exuberance and spontaneity: fear and self-consciousness make us want to hide behind some form of protective coloration. Each of us probably has our own childhood story to tell about the joy of discovering a self and how it was "lost" to us. But whatever the reasons, we can be sure that the confluence of both tributaries—our socialization as young girls and the personal traumas we experience—eventually drive our self into hiding. Thus we rein ourselves in, learn not to say what we think or feel or desire, and instead become some version of the "good" girl—desperately striving for an A-plus life to please our parents—or the "bad" girl—falling into a C-minus life as if indifferent to anyone's love. In more extreme cases, we develop a false self to conceal our loss, hurt, and fear. This is rarely a conscious act. We simply want to be loved, accepted, or, sometimes, just tolerated by the parents we so desperately need. Still, its effect is devastating. For when the kernel of self is lost to us, we are lost to ourselves.

In childhood, this loss usually goes undetected, partly because childhood is an unbridled time of life, exploding with new experiences, yet, from the outside looking in, giving the appearance of seamless growth and change. In "The Effect of Loss on the Young," Winnicott, who as a pediatrician and analyst studied the lives of young children, writes about the "liveliness" of children "that deceives everyone except the child. The child knows that the liveliness has to be paid for." In part, this can't be helped. Children *are* distractible; life does "come bubbling up whether they like it or not." But unless we recognize that there is life flowing beneath the visible surface of a young girl's demeanor, it is easy to misinterpret her needs—especially if they center around rejection and loss.

For all the psychotherapeutic focus on childhood and the glorious literature that has been written about it, childhood still remains a vast, uncharted country. No wonder people write memoirs, trying to puzzle out and fit together the missing or forgotten pieces. Childhood perplexes and confuses us; many of us are not sure *how* to think, or feel, about it. All too often, what we shy away from is the spell—and sometimes the pall—that this period casts over the rest of our lives; more particularly, we retreat from the "child" still trapped inside our adult bodies and the feelings she conjures up. Yet to the degree that we refuse to recognize how beholden we are to this child we left behind, our longing to rescue her wars with our equally ardent wish to ignore her suffering and distress.

On the deepest level, the genuine aliveness that belonged to us in childhood, the life force that Pippi represents and not the false liveliness Winnicott speaks about, is exactly what women need to reclaim. Sometimes our efforts to forget childhood, to leave it behind as soon as possible, hide our urge to scramble back inside its boundaries and stay there. In fact, it is precisely because we leave such a big chunk of our self adrift in the past that we lose the art of seeing the child part of ourselves—and of *seeing into* childhood—that is, being able to sort, decipher, and integrate the world of our true, personal childhood selves into our adult lives.

Childhood is where many of us parked our sense of freedom. Women trying to retrieve lost parts of themselves inevitably will say, "I remember being so happy—*then*," "I had extraordinary energy," "I was fearless," "I was fiercely independent," as if these buoyant selves have sunk to fathomless depths. Yet our growth, our freedom, and our joy require that we retrieve the lost, and secreted, child part of ourselves.

In Margaret Atwood's novel *Cat's Eye*, Elaine Risley, a successful painter, returns to Toronto, the city of her childhood, for a retrospective of her work, and is flooded with memories. In flashbacks, the novel describes the initiation rituals nine-year-old Elaine endures when she tries to befriend Cordelia and her friends Carol and Grace. Cordelia is the leader who holds the other girls in her sway. Sometimes she attacks Carol or Grace. But Elaine is her special target. What makes Cordelia so powerful is that she acts as if she likes and wants to help Elaine. She tells her that she is not "normal . . . like other girls"; on the school bus she whispers into her ear to "stand up straight!" and not to "move your arms like that"; she assigns Carol to report on what Elaine does and says all day and metes out her punishment accordingly. Under the guise of friendship and in utmost secret, Cordelia is relentlessly and mercilessly cruel.

> *In the endless time when Cordelia had such power over me,*
> *I peeled the skin off my feet. I did it at night when I was sup-*

posed to be sleeping. . . . I would go down as far as the blood.
Nobody ever looked at my feet, so nobody knew I was doing
it. In the mornings, I would pull my socks on, over my
peeled feet. It was painful to walk, but not impossible.
The pain gave me something definite to think about,
something immediate. It was something to hold on to.

By the time they enter high school, the roles have been reversed;
Elaine is the strong one. But the damage is done and imprinted in
her unconscious. Eventually, Elaine learns that Cordelia ended up in
a mental institution after having tried to commit suicide. Still,
remembering how well she managed to hide her pain from her
parents, Elaine anxiously watches her daughters for signs of similar,
hidden distress: "I scrutinized their fingers for bites, their feet, the
ends of their hair. I asked them leading questions: 'Is everything all
right, are your friends all right?' And they looked at me as if they had
no idea what I was talking about, why I was so anxious. I thought
they'd give themselves away somehow: nightmares, moping. But
there was nothing I could see, which may only have meant they were
good at deception, as good as I was."

This is not to suggest that our secret lives are inherently painful,
for they indeed carry great beauty as well as pain. Even so, the surface calm of childhood often hides haunting memories that begin to
surface only later in life. The very unruliness of change often makes
us long both to remain a child—for what child actually wants the
responsibilities of being an adult?—and to "grow up"—which our
far-flung fantasies equate with freedom.

DISORDER AND EARLY SORROW: JUSTINE

For Justine, the wounding started when she was six, the year her
glamorous socialite mother, remote and distant to begin with, took

sick and virtually disappeared from Justine's life behind a closed bed-room door. Almost overnight, the atmosphere in the house changed. The voices of adults dropped into whispers, there were long phone calls between her father and her aunt, and for weeks at a time she wasn't allowed to see her mother. Alone, and much of the time forgotten, she remembers circling aimlessly through the living room, waiting for someone to pay attention to her.

Justine's mother had breast cancer, and, despite chemotherapy and radiation, it eventually metastasized. "They didn't tell me my mother was sick, and only later did I find out she wanted it that way. She kept saying, 'Don't tell her, because when I get better, I want it to be as if nothing ever happened.' My whole family was like that. They don't want anything unpleasant to disturb their beautiful life." But it did happen. Justine's mother died two years later, at the age of forty-six. Justine was eight.

At twenty-nine, Justine, a strikingly beautiful single woman, spends most of her time working as a volunteer fund-raiser for a small arts foundation or traveling to Paris to be with her boyfriend or visit friends. She has a restless energy, as if she were still circling the living room of her childhood waiting for someone to notice her. This is one side of her. The social side—poised, gracious, seemingly confident—a reflection of her privileged upbringing—usually masks it, which is why I was surprised by her ardor, and the quiet despera-tion behind it, when she first came to see me because of panic attacks and a growing inability to make decisions. "Do I want to buy an apartment? Get married? Have a baby? Do I want to be alone? It's horrible. No choice seems better than the other." Justine is depressed, the legacy of having no real mothering as a child, no one saying, "Yes, you can do it," when she tried to make decisions for herself.

Since then, we have been searching out her feelings about the mother she barely remembers and what it was like to grow up in a family where children were mostly seen and not heard, and whose emotional lives were deemed virtually nonexistent—unless, of course, their feelings grew too powerful to stay submerged. After her mother's death, Justine began to have chronic stomach spasms that made her double up in pain, and by the time she was ten, she had developed a phobia about eating solid food for fear that she would vomit. Even then, neither her father nor the pediatrician who treated her regarded her symptoms as evidence of emotional distress; it was "Justine's nervous stomach acting up."

Justine doesn't remember crying or feeling sad when her mother died. She does remember lying in bed at night, picking at the wallpaper and making scratches on her night table, feeling completely alone and abandoned. Justine's father was devastated by his wife's death and too preoccupied with his own grief to give Justine the love and attention she so desperately needed. Instead, Justine became her father's caretaker, comforting him as well as she could within the limits of her child's capacity to do so. It was her way of keeping her place in his heart intact and reassuring herself that her world had not completely slipped away—that he, and they, would be able to stay afloat. Eventually, Justine's father started dating again. "Most of his girlfriends were short-term, but there were two I grew really attached to: Michelle, who lasted about two years, and Sandra, who my father almost married but didn't." Not wanting to be a burden and wanting desperately for them to like her, Justine became the perfect good girl. "I knew how uncomfortable it was for them if I acted sad around them. So when they'd ask, 'How are you?' I'd say, 'Just fine.' But what I really wanted to do was sit in their lap for hours and cry." When Justine talks about how close she grew to these two women, and how abandoned she felt after they left, there is still sadness in her voice.

For her father and the other adults in her life, Justine pretended that she was okay. Yet she withdrew into herself, as if the shadow of her mother had fallen upon her. Not only was she transformed by the loss, but she unconsciously assumed responsibility for it, and, by adolescence, directed the abandonment anger she felt toward her mother against herself. In high school, she was taking drugs and drinking herself into blackouts. It wasn't until the police called Justine's father one night from the hospital to let him know that she had overdosed on heroin that he finally stopped pretending to himself that things were all right.

The child who suffers a loss writes her own text as she goes along, and does so alone. Justine suffered, as children generally do, in silence. As much as she needed the love and protection of the adults in her family as a child, she could not ask for it because at that time she had no way to understand what she *was* feeling. Instead, she let her stomach spasms and food phobia "speak" for her, and in adolescence used drugs as a way to numb and soothe herself. Helplessness in the face of urgent need is a hallmark of childhood loss, when cries for help are often soundless. Adults can't help because they have lost the compass that could lead them back into their child's world. At best, they can be gatekeepers and guardians, waiting with outstretched arms to soothe their child's distress. The adults around Justine did not perform even this role. Justine was thus obliged to enter spaces and accept the burden of this new experience without any markers—or reliable models—to guide her. In the context of loss, this degree of self-initiation is not paralleled at any other phase of our development.

WHEN WE ARE mourning, we often lose interest in worldly matters; all of our feelings revolve around the loss of the loved one; there is no room left over for other interests, no doors open to admit pleasures of any kind. As early as 5 B.C., the Greek word *melancholia* has been used to describe symptoms we nowadays associate with depression—loss of appetite, sleeplessness, irritability, restlessness, despondency—due to a lingering form of grief and fear. Melancholia's overtone of sadness seems particularly suited to a grieving child's loss of innocence. In the heaviness of her heart, she *knows* that something is responsible for her loss. Sometimes she is given a reason to hold on to: "Your mother is ill"; "Your father is depressed"; "Your mother and I won't be living together anymore." Other losses—say, when a parent withdraws love from her daughter, or keeps finding fault with her, or favors a brother or sister—are harder to give a name to, though they inflict as deep a wound to the developing self.

Yet no matter the cause, a young child feels that she is to blame. Were she more "lovable" this would not have happened, and the fact that it did deals a crushing blow to her self-esteem. Terrible feelings of self-doubt and self-blame often accrue. In *Mourning and Melancholia* (1917), Freud writes that "for the most part," the occasions of loss extend beyond a literal death to include "all those situations of being wounded, hurt, neglected, out of favor, or disappointed, which import opposite feelings of love and hate into the relationship or reinforce an already existing ambivalence."

The problem for the child is that the more empty and impoverished she feels, the more prone she is to idealize what or whom she has lost. Justine had to reconcile the beautiful mother in the photographs whom everyone admired with the real one who "withered away, hairless or with a big wig, and coughed all the time" and was lost to her, even before she died. Justine used to write her mother letters, composing special ones for each anniversary of her death:

> I had been through so many stages with her, and one of the things that is so amazing is that when a mother dies when you're that young, you don't end the relationship . . . the relationship keeps going . . . and she's gone, so I had to invent the relationship. Every stage I went through with my father, I went through with my mother. But she wasn't there, so with her I had to figure out if I was like her. I had to figure out if I did or didn't look like her. I had to figure out if I could succeed past her limits. I still haven't figured out if I can live past her age—that's a big one.

To make up for the emptiness inside her—the lack of something real to hold on to—Justine, in effect, improvised their relationship as she went along. Idealizing the lost mother became a way of life, and for a long time she tended to project her mother's best attributes—real or imagined—onto both the women and the men she met and was inevitably disappointed when they couldn't live up to them.

THE CHILDHOOD LOSS of mothers, fathers, siblings, friends, fans out to include faith, hope, and beliefs. But the greatest loss of all is that of the child's sense of self, which is often greatly diminished by the lack of nurturing, mirroring, and support that the presence of the absent person may have provided. Annette, a gifted potter now in her sixties, grew up unable to escape her mother's depression, which seemed to fill all the corners of the house. Stretched out on the carpet near the sofa like a cat, or by the bed, where her mother would lie folded up for hours at a time, Annette kept vigil, trying to lift her mother's dark moods. She would comb her mother's hair, or they would look at fashion magazines together and gossip about her mother's friends. Annette's mother died when she was a teenager; as a grown woman, she is given to forming dependent relationships with men in which she acts as caretaker, re-creating her past experience.

Anya's father walked out of their Budapest apartment late one afternoon after the authorities ordered all the young Jewish men to assemble in the local square. At the first landing, he turned and waved good-bye, as Anya stood in the doorway watching him leave. That was the last time she ever saw him. She was nine. Part of her remains trapped in that moment, for ever since, she anticipates that any man she gets involved with will, like her father, walk down the winding staircase and out of her life. More than once, she has fallen in love with an unhappily married man, waiting in vain for the day he will divorce his wife and marry her. Now in her late fifties, she has virtually given up on finding the "right" man and resigned herself to being alone.

Bertha was the youngest of five children whose mother, worn out from work, never paid attention when her older siblings picked on her and called her names and made a point of excluding her from their activities. Bertha's reaction, which was to yell back at them longer and harder, angered her mother. Sent to her room without dinner, she waited to be called downstairs, but it never happened. Each day, the fighting would begin anew and end with her banishment from family life.

Each loss shakes the soul to its foundations. Some prove so disruptive that they may compromise a woman's ability to confront aloneness later in life. The challenge for women alone is to learn how to sit with those disquieting feelings of loss and pain and the anxiety they are likely to engender, rather than find ways to escape. Fear and anxiety can grow particularly acute when we dare to enter the feeling of emptiness that is inside us. As one woman describes it, "That's when I feel like a bottomless pit of need." By sitting with these feelings, they start to lose their stranglehold over our lives. Solitude allows us to discover that we are more than the sum of our pain; it helps to shift our longings, so heavily invested in our own sense of neediness and dependency, toward meaningful and life-affirming pursuits. Gradually, we gain back our voice, and the self breathes free. Thus begins the "art" of being a woman alone.

BETRAYAL

As a child, Pauline spent every August with her family on an island off the coast of Maine. On the ferry ride across, Pauline always watched excitedly for the moment their hillside cottage came into view. At first, the cottage always had a damp, musty smell, but her parents threw open all the windows, and by evening the salt winds had cleansed the air, lulling Pauline into a happy, contented sleep. Every year, Pauline went with her parents to visit their close friends, the Averys, who lived on a nearby farm. The two families always gathered in the Averys' large kitchen, and, while the adults caught up on the island news over coffee and freshly baked muffins, Pauline would sit on the porch and play with the Averys' two cocker spaniels. But the summer she is six is different. Mr. Avery invites Pauline to see the new barn. On the way, he holds her hand and asks her about school and whether she's made new friends. He tells her what a pretty girl she is and that she shouldn't grow up too quickly. Behind the barn is a haystack. Mr. Avery sits down, leaning his back against it and puts Pauline on his lap. Patting her knees, he sighs deeply, squints at the sun, and keeps on talking. Pauline feels restless and wants to move away, but she has been taught to be polite, so she merely watches Mr. Avery's hand begin moving in small circles up her thigh. The touch of his fingers feels soothing on her skin, though she can see that his hand is trembling slightly. Engrossed in the story he is telling her, she barely notices as Mr. Avery slowly unzips his pants with his other hand. Then he cups Pauline's hand inside his own and places it gently on his penis. As yet, Pauline doesn't know what a penis is, so when the soft thing she is touching suddenly grows hard, it frightens her. She wants to pull away but is afraid to say this to Mr. Avery, and her hand, helplessly lost in his, continues stroking his penis until it swells as long as Pinocchio's nose. Continuing to whisper smiling words, Mr. Avery reaches between Pauline's legs and reaches into her pants. "Where is Tinker Bell?" he asks, while a searching finger strokes her vagina before it finds its way inside her, twisting and turning—until a great shudder overcomes him and he suddenly lets go of her.

Afterward, Mr. Avery and Pauline stroll back to the house. It is a hot day and the sky is blue and cloudless, but for Pauline a darkness has settled in. "We just had a wonderful tour of the barn," Mr. Avery exclaims a bit too loudly when they enter the house. Mrs. Avery hands each of them a glass of lemonade, and Pauline's mother gives her daughter a hug. Like most abused children, Pauline doesn't say a word to her parents about Mr. Avery, though she knows something terribly wrong just happened—something she feels she is to blame for that will make them very angry. As psychologist Judith Herman writes in *Trauma and Recovery*, "The conflict between the will to deny horrible events and the will to proclaim them aloud is the central dialectic of psychological trauma." Pauline is just past fifty when she tells me this story, and though her mind knows otherwise, part of her still believes she did something wrong.

The enormous magnitude of violations such as rape, beatings, and incest cannot be underestimated: they are devastations to the self, shattering a child's trust and innocence, sometimes forever. Pauline trusted Mr. Avery because he was one of her parents' closest friends, and because in her young and protected life no one had ever broken her trust. She was never the same after the betrayal. Yet because there were no visible signs of damage, no one noticed any change, not even Pauline herself, whose memory of the event disappeared into her unconscious. Just one thing bothered her, not in an interfering way, and not all the time, she told me, almost as an aside, some forty-five years after the event took place. Rather, it was a thought that started to nag at her only recently. "I have no idea who I am," Pauline told me. "I know now that I never have. I don't even know what it would be like." Pauline said this a few weeks after that terrible moment suddenly and unexpectedly exploded into consciousness. It was the first time her elegant, ladylike persona yielded to the inexpressible sadness that she had been carrying for so many years. She cried that day for her lost self, which had been almost entirely covered over by the press of social commitments—but she also felt a new fear: suppose she had no interior life, or if she tried to reach it, she would come up "empty." The fear—that there is "nothing inside"—keeps many women from venturing into aloneness.

In a relative sense, *every* child suffers some form of betrayal at the hands of the people who are supposed to protect her. It may come in the subtler shape of a lie or broken promise—a father who fails to keep his word that he will be home to help with homework, a mother who "forgets" to pick her child up after school or arrives after all the other children have left—or the grosser form of physical violence or sexual abuse. If the lie or the broken promise is small and happens seldom, its bitterness grows dilute. But if the betrayal is large and repeated, the child's capacity to trust grows as barren as winter. Situated in a place of innocence and absolute powerlessness, she has, as yet, no way to understand the terrible thing that has happened—is happening—to her; even worse, she is bound to the act, whatever it may be, by her own unremitting confusion. She is, after all, in the family nest; there is food on the table, a bed to sleep in, a brother or sister to curl up near, schoolwork to do, a TV show to watch. So she pivots back and forth, from love to dread, from warmth to feverish chill. The power of a child's love astonishes. No matter how she might suffer, her love persists; she will rally behind her parents—or at least one of them—with indiscriminate loyalty. Searching for understanding and wanting desperately to forget the incomprehensible, she forgives the lie, the broken promise, the violence done to her. She even forgives her abuser. The one person she does not forgive is herself.

MAGIC CIRCLES

Am I inside or outside the magic circle? This is one of the fundamental questions every young girl wonders about. She can't help herself. The desire to be part of a group is one of our basic human urges. In childhood our need to belong feels urgent, and the question of whether we do or don't can sometimes take on an almost obsessional significance, perhaps because belonging is so intimately connected with a developing sense of self.

As a young girl first begins to notice that circles exist, she is bound to feel that she belongs or does not, that others accept or reject her, that she is "part of" or "left out." In a sense, circles—family, school, community—govern her existence. Circles teach the young girl new and deepening lessons about intimacy, bonding, and community; depending on whether she feels included or excluded, they can also provoke anxiety, fear, anger, envy—emotional energies that are bound to affect the young self-in-formation.

I WAS EXCLUDED from a "magic circle" just before my eighth birthday. It happened in summer camp one Friday night in late July. After dinner, the counselors told all the kids to put on clean white shirts and shorts and assemble at the campfire site for a secret cere- mony. Rumors had been spreading through the camp all week about the elite society made up of the counselors and a select group of campers—those who had already proven their mettle as model camp citizens. The purpose of the evening ritual was to induct a handful of new members into its ranks. The whole camp was in a state of fer- ment, everyone wondering if she would be chosen.

At eight, everyone went down to the campsite. Two counselors told us to form a single line. As we filed into the circle, they handed each of us a silver cardboard star, with a white, unlit candle in its center. Then, for what seemed like an eternity, we waited for the ceremony to begin. Finally, someone blew a couple of long, solemn notes on a bugle, and a procession of "elders" made up of counselors and older campers entered the campsite, their candles lit and glowing, and began to make their way around the circle. In front of each chosen girl, the leader would pause, light the child's candle with her own, and motion to her to join the procession. How I hoped the leader would stop in front of me. I even held out my star, just in case she failed to notice me. As the procession grew nearer, I held my breath and waited for the footsteps to stop. Instead, it continued right past me, the leader looking straight ahead as she moved on to the next chosen one.

The next day, one of the counselors explained that I wasn't ready to be a member of this special "society"; I was too much of a mischief-maker, she said. But if I could learn to be a better camper—"You know, not giggle after lights-out, make up your bed without creases, be the first one up the morning instead of the last, that sort of thing"—there would be another opportunity in August.

At first, I bristled. Then I gloated. By the time August rolled around, I'd built a wall around myself, glued together with as much real mischief as I could dream up. Was I willing to be responsible? Helpful? A team player? Sure, I was. Just watch me catch flies and put them on whiney Miranda's pillow, sneak out of the bunk at night, refuse to sing the camp anthem. The last thing I wanted was to belong to a magic circle full of "goody-goodies"—as I defensively labeled members of the group from which I'd been barred. I even formed a circle of my own, made up of other swaggering, mischief-prone "misfits" like myself. Still, I never forgot what it was like to be kept from that star-lit magic circle.

SOME OF THE most potent circles are those forged by the link of friendship. *"Best friends, best friends, never never break friends; if you do you'll catch the flu and that will be the end of you."* Growing up, Lithe Sebesta, coauthor with Maura Spiegel of *The Breast Book,* remembers saying these words, almost as an incantation against danger. The lines of this childhood rhyme are a reminder of the rules and penalties governing young girls' friendships. Nowadays, the words may differ, but the rituals of childhood friendship are the same: arms or crooked pinkie fingers entwined, oaths of fidelity are exchanged, as if one's very life depended on it. The anxiety of *not* belonging to a magic circle is simply too much to endure, which is why young girls promise to stay friends forever, why allegiances are recklessly abandoned or renewed. What we cannot bear is to be excluded from the security of the circle's shelter. These wounds are variations of Hans Christian Andersen's *The Little Match Girl,* the child watching from an unbridgeable distance the warm embrace of a family circle, a life from which she is forever barred.

THIRTEEN-YEAR-OLD Abby describes herself at age eight as a "dork," in her lexicon, "someone who doesn't dress well, who's kind of annoying, who's not into things that most other kids are." The daughter of ex-hippies-turned-academics who taught at the local community college in their small New England town, Abby had always been a bright, outgoing child who made friends easily. But in third grade, she became the object of cruel teasing. The other girls made fun of the way she dressed, the wheat-bread-and-sprouts sandwiches in her lunch box, and her "mop" of red hair that frizzed up when it rained. They couldn't believe she didn't watch TV and had never heard of Britney Spears or *NSYNC. Abby, who had never paid attention to popular culture, began to realize that her classmates thought she was weird. "All of a sudden it wasn't about little kids all running around together having fun. There were different social groups—and I didn't fit into any of them." She began spending a lot of time at home, which didn't suit her outgoing personality.

For the first time, Abby started to worry about not having friends. Her parents tried to explain that turnabouts like this were often temporary and, while not fun, were a normal part of growing up. They told her to try to ignore the teasing. But Abby couldn't. "It made me feel really bad. Everybody kept telling secrets about me." To cope, Abby built a wall around herself; an avid reader, she became even more bookwormish than before.

Fourth and fifth grades provided a welcome reprieve. Abby had two good friends who shared her interests. Having a place to belong, she began to let down her guard socially. But with her sixth-grade entrance to junior high, her problems started again. Her two friends had gone off to private schools, and once again Abby found herself the object of ridicule. This time, she tried to make the other girls like her: in class, she let them see her test answers; she offered to give them her clothes; she loaned them money; and she began clowning around a lot to make them laugh. Nothing worked. "They just mocked me for trying too hard and called me a dork to my face. I got so depressed. I would just lie around all the time. I didn't want to do anything except read."

Abby blamed herself. "They seemed so cool, and if they didn't like me," she said, "I figured it was because there was something wrong with me, that I really was a dork." When her mom said that the other girls were probably jealous because she was smart and pretty, Abby got angry and countered that "being smart and pretty only made things worse." The seventh grade was no better for Abby, and she tried even harder to ingratiate herself. "I was pretty annoying. I kept telling them how mean they were being. I'd say, 'I want you guys to be nice to me.' They'd say, 'Okay, fine,' but then they'd be mean again. Finally, they wouldn't even talk to me. That's really when I felt alone."

When aloneness feels more like an expulsion than a choice, a child will seek acceptance by muting the self. For the goal is to be included at almost any cost. No wonder that the fear of being left out, of not belonging, can, over time, interfere with a young girl's appreciation of solitude. In fact, the danger is that she may retreat into a defensive aloneness rather than willingly enter a creative solitude.

Victimization like Abby's is not uncommon. Social cruelty in girls, overt or hidden, is an old story, except that until recently it was kept under wraps—the ghost in our attic, so to speak. In our culture, girls aren't supposed to be aggressive, much less cruel. On the contrary, we are reared to be the gatekeepers of harmonious relationships. In *Odd Girl Out: The Hidden Culture of Aggression in Girls,* Rachel Simmons interviewed schoolgirls in three different parts of the country, letting them speak about their experiences as either the perpetrator or the victim of bullying behavior by their peers to expose the meanness and manipulation that often lurks behind the "nice girl" façade. Such aggression is never direct but, as these girls describe, takes the form of backbiting, excluding others, spreading rumors, and name-calling. And because it is kept silent, it is all the more anguishing.

When Kate, aged sixteen, noticed *Cat's Eye* on my library shelf, she said, "I hated that book. I don't even like looking at it." Kate considers second grade the worst year of her life. That's when the other girls, taking the lead of the ringleader, made merciless fun of her because she had to wear a patch over one eye to correct a condition known euphemistically as lazy eye.

Kate didn't peel the skin off her toes like Cordelia, but just seeing Atwood's novel brought back the raw blisters of her own suffering. Like many girls, she kept her pain from her parents. "It wasn't that they wouldn't have tried to help, they definitely would have been concerned, but somehow I just didn't think they would understand." Parents often can't detect their child's longing to be inside a magic circle, the price she might sometimes pay to get or remain inside, or the terrible pain she feels if she is excluded. Many times they have forgotten, or blocked out, the intensity of their own childhood experiences. Or they aren't even aware of circles in their child's world, being caught in circles of their own.

We live inside some circles, we live outside others. And sometimes we can feel like we're going around in circles, depending on whether we feel good about those we're in and those we're not. "With respect to circles," as my colleague Sidney Mackenzie says, exaggerating only slightly, "we're all five years old."

OUR SECRET GARDENS

No one knows the need for a secret garden better than young girls, whose lives are largely cultivated in gardens of their own making. Perhaps that is why, among all the ages and stages of womanhood, they are most adept at finding them. Secret gardens are our sanctuaries, refuges where we can be ourselves without artifice. The attic, a special corner of the room, the niche behind the staircase, a window seat—almost any space can function as a secret garden, as long as it allows us entry into our own private world, giving us the opportunity to stretch and make limber our mind and body, to till our own soil, so to speak.

As metaphor, the secret garden is where we go to find a world all our own—a world that belongs to us and no one else. It is "secret" because we alone have the key, because no one else knows how to get there, and because it holds our deepest longings of our private self.

IN THE SPRING and early summer, Katherine spends hours tending the real garden behind her house. For her, weeding is less a chore than a quest; it mimics her daily struggle to regulate the tension between chaos and order in her life. In the rest of her life, Katherine spends enormous amounts of energy obstructing her own desires— as if they are weeds that she must uproot before they grow unruly. In fact, what has grown "wild" inside her are the internalized messages of her Hungarian refugee parents. And because she has begun to challenge those voices by daring to express what she wants for herself—sleep till nine on weekends, leave the office on time, buy sexy clothes—and forfeit her "good girl" role, they clamor more loudly than ever.

The child Katherine bore the burden of her parents' immigrant pain at having been uprooted. Not wanting to add to their suffering, she readily acquiesced to all their efforts to further their gifted daughter's accomplishments. They expected her to get straight A's in school, to excel at ballet and violin, and so she did, often sacrificing her social life to study and practice. A home movie of a recital she gave when she was ten reveals a pretty girl in a pink dress playing the violin before a rapt audience of relatives and friends, but the look on her face shows duty rather than pleasure. Her parents felt no happiness in life except their pride in Katherine's accomplishments, and their unspoken message to her was that self-delight is an indulgence, to be swallowed only a few spoonfuls at a time. Desperate to break free from the "dutiful life" she felt morally bound to live, Katherine feels guilty heeding her own desires.

That's why it wasn't surprising when she brought me her dream about a garden. "I looked out my bedroom window and saw it down below," she began, "except that it wasn't like my real garden at all. This one was extraordinary . . . filled with ravishing flowers of every sort. I wanted to rush downstairs and go into it, but something stopped me. Then I saw a woman. She was on her knees planting flowers, quiet and completely absorbed, and I wondered who she was and why she was there instead of me. . . ." Katherine's voice trails off. "Why do you think?" I asked. "I'm not sure," she said, "but it felt like I could only look at the garden from the outside, I couldn't go in." Katherine suddenly seemed immensely sad, and she was quiet for a long time. Finally, she spoke: "It felt dangerous for me to be there. Besides, I wouldn't have known what to do once I was inside. I couldn't take care of it."

Since then, we've talked a lot about Katherine's garden, real and metaphorical. Part of her would love her garden to "grow a bit wild, like some English gardens I've seen," but she is terrified to give into that yearning, lest she "lose control" of the garden—and her self. She knows that it could be her place of refuge, the "room of one's own" she so longs for. Yet she is painfully aware of the irony that to be in its solitude fills her with anxiety. "I can't just relax and let the sun warm my back because I immediately start worrying about everything else that I'm not doing and should be. It's like I can't allow myself to enjoy it."

EMMA'S MOTHER GAVE up a promising career as an art historian soon after she married Emma's father, a successful film editor. The couple had four children, of whom Emma was the third, and seemed to lead a charmed life. They traveled widely, attended openings, and lived lavishly. Emma remembers her father as a gentle, mild-mannered man who enjoyed being with his children. When she was seven, her father took her to the movies, and at dinner afterward a male friend of her father's joined them at the table. As they were leaving, her father asked Emma if this could be their "secret."

Two years later, her mother found out that her husband had been living a double life; that he and his "friend" had been having a homosexual relationship for years. Perhaps resenting Emma's closeness to her father, her mother became aloof, her reproaches expressed in long silences punctuated by fault-finding. "Her eyes bore into me," Emma said softly. "I would do anything to get away." To escape, Emma would spend hours in her room poring over her mother's old copies of *Vogue* and *Harper's Bazaar,* dreaming herself into other lives.

"There was one picture I loved more than all the rest," Emma continued. "When I found it, it was as though I had found my own version of perfection." It was a picture of a beautiful young girl in a turquoise bathing suit standing alone on a white-sand beach, palm trees behind her. Looking at it, Emma entered a virtual reality; safe from her mother's contempt, the island became her secret garden and she was the girl in the bathing suit who lived there. "Mostly, I was there alone," Emma said, "but sometimes I imagined my youngest sister, Monica, and my brother, David, coming, and we'd roam around the island and swim in the sea. But then I'd make them leave again." Emma laughed. "I guess I wanted to be in control of my paradise."

BOOKS WERE MY salvation, dependable escorts into more adventurous worlds than my own, mirroring versions of ideal families I wanted to belong to—while I kept my own parents at arm's length so they could not intrude on my dreaming time. Books offer respite through the stories of others; diaries—and, later, journals—offer a similar conversation with oneself. Books can lead a girl to seek solitude, a nice, quiet place free of distractions. Diary or journal writing requires active solitude: we take up a pen or go to the keyboard and write our secret garden into existence. This is how we connect to the private self that is forming.

In Erick Zonca's film *The Dreamlife of Angels* (1998), waiflike Isa begins to salvage the remnants of her life, but only after she finds her own story written into another girl's diary and realizes that resurrection is indeed possible: "I am starting this diary on a sunny day," she begins, "like a mirror to tell me who I am." The role of diaries and journals as friend, counselor, even therapist, often passes unnoticed by members of the adult world, which is just as it should be, so that young girls can hear the sound of their own voice speaking back to them without the noisy traffic of parents and siblings. Having this medium of exchange with other parts of ourselves may well be how many of us have learned to survive and endure.

Angela, now in her late twenties, began keeping a diary at age eight. When we started working together, she asked me to read her diaries and hold them for her. What struck me most was not what Angela said but what she left *unsaid*—declarations like "I hate Phoebe Marks more than ever," no explanation why; or "DD, I'm doing great in violin," followed a mere twelve days later by "I quit violin," again, no reason given. Angela's life was hard: a father who abruptly left the family, an ill and depressed mother, and being poor in an affluent community. Angela carried the residue of shame and boredom that settles in when time feels endless and nothing good seems to happen. The best that she could do was record her life in the form of lists and upcoming events; what she could *not* do was examine it. That would have to wait until she had grown into womanhood and dared to enter solitude; then her self—precious, pure, and intact—could come out of hiding.

"ONE OF THE best-kept secret gardens I know is the stable," Sidney assures me when I ask what other sorts of gardens she can think of. Sidney is speaking for both herself and her eleven-year-old daughter, Emily, who spends most of her free time inside them. And of course she is right. Step across the stable's threshold and you're standing right on the damp earth of a protected archetypal realm. On weekday afternoons and weekends, clusters of young girls are busily grooming their horses, sometimes speaking to the powerful animals they are learning to handle, ride, win over, control—gaining mastery of them while experiencing their own power as they do so.

In the stable the horses snort and neigh; their sensuality charges the atmosphere. "Well known it is that young girls love horses, love the wild underside of themselves, loving the long neck and hot ears of seduction," Jeanette Winterson writes in *The World and Other Places.* Heather combs Windswept's mane. Jesse brings her horse, Salvation, water after a brisk ride. Sarah grins toothily and tells me why she wouldn't miss a day, if she could, to be there. "I love it, I love my horse more than anything; there's no place I'd rather be," she says enthusiastically, patting Jezebel's flank and sniffing in the pungent aroma of the place as if she were inhaling the scent of rosewater or chicken soup.

Secret gardens are meant to be places of solitude, not isolation, and between these polarities our worldview can easily come apart. For isolation is a dead garden where nothing grows, while solitude is a vessel of potential that can hold all sorts of experiences, even quantities of loneliness. Freya Stark, one of the most audacious solo travelers of all time, whose taste for adventure in the early part of this century led her to disguise herself as a man so that, at age thirty-five, she might enter the forbidden territory of the Syrian Druze, attributed her sense of freedom to the "emptiness" of her early years when she first learned to cultivate "the habit of solitude." Her later journeys were clearly a manifestation of the great breadth Stark felt inside herself. Studying other versions of solitude can help us claim space inside ourselves—reap our own legacy of freedom as we develop the capacity to tolerate a spacious interior life.

What all these hideaway garden spaces have in common is a sense of privacy, stillness, and sometimes mystery; above all, they are always about potential: the unrealized coming into being. But the young gardener must make sure to keep the key that allows her to step *inside,* even if others are invited in. When Mary Lennox, the lonely and surly child in Frances Hodgson Burnett's childhood classic *The Secret Garden,* finds her garden, she knows at once that it is different from any other place she has ever known:

> *What was this under her hands which was square and made of iron and which her fingers found a hole in?*
>
> *It was the lock of the door which had been closed ten years and she put her hand in her pocket, drew out the key and found it fitted the keyhole. She put the key in and turned it. It took two hands to do it, but it did turn.*
>
> *And then she took a long breath and looked behind her up the long walk to see if any one was coming. No one was coming. No one ever did come, it seemed, and she took another long breath, because she could not help it, and she held back the swinging curtain of ivy and pushed back the door which opened slowly—slowly.*
>
> *Then she slipped through it, and shut it behind her, and stood with her back against it, looking about her and breathing quite fast with excitement, and wonder, and delight.*
>
> *She was standing* inside *the secret garden.*

Orphaned at the age of nine, Mary has been sent to Misselthwaite Manor on the Yorkshire moors to live with her uncle. There, for the first time, her shriveled world begins to open up. She befriends the old gardener, Ben Weatherstaff, and his robin; best of all, she stumbles as if by magic upon the secret garden. At first she fears the garden may have died but soon discovers "tiny growing things" in the damp earth. Though she doesn't know a thing about gardening, the fact that something is "alive" is all the inspiration she needs to start weeding and give whatever is growing the chance to breathe. Mary not only finds her own salvation while tending the garden, she also restores the health of her invalid cousin, Colin Craven, and discovers the joy of friendship with the children and grown-ups in the world around her.

THE LUCKY ONES among us are able to hold open the gates to these hideaway places where our private self begins its slow unfurling. Most of us, however, are not as fortunate. As time passes and fear and shame seep inside, we begin to doubt ourselves and lose direction. "How did I lose my inner world?" asks Sonya at forty. "I can tell you how," she continues. "Ridicule. Ridicule and dismissal." Sonya tells me some of her worst childhood memories: about the friend of her mother's who heard her singing and pronounced, "Well, now we know what you're *not* going to be"; about the dance teacher who said her steps were "too wild," and pushed her feet—and imagination— into cramped rectilinear spaces; about the piano lessons that were deemed "out of the question" because having a piano posed decorating problems her mother didn't want to deal with; about another family friend who told her some years later that her writing was "not commercial." The derision of those around us can take the form of sudden storms or subtle peltings; either way, it holds the power to bruise the petals of a young girl's desire for self-expression well before it has a chance to flower.

We need to understand why we left our gardens in the first place. Not that we intended to. We had to. As children, the peace and sanctity of our private space may have been threatened and disturbed, sometimes in terrible ways—physical abuse, molestation, rape, or incest among them—and often by the astonishing neglect of parents, unaware of or indifferent to their child's own sacred life. Later, as adults, though we may long for a secret garden, we usually feel unjustified in setting time apart for ourselves, either because of external pressures or because we lack the inner conviction to claim it. Today's world has little understanding, let alone patience or respect, for the need to be alone. Sadly, we succumb all too often to its invisible pressures.

As a therapist, my role is to accompany women back to these abandoned garden spaces and wait within hearing distance just outside their walls. It is very important, I've discovered, to let them enter their private, inner world *alone* until they come upon whatever they were searching for. When they're ready, and not before, I'll hear what happened to make them leave. Assuredly, whatever story they tell, it will always include someone who trespassed on, usurped, or exiled them from their private world. That's why I wait outside these secret gardens—until I'm invited in.

Young girls know how to find and make gardens. The pity is how often they are obliged to leave, and—like Katherine, Sonya, and the other women in these stories—move step by step away from themselves, until they can no longer consciously remember where their garden stood or are able to believe it is still alive. If we have lost the path to our garden, we need to remind ourselves of what young girls intuitively know: the garden does exist, and its bounty will replenish us throughout our lives. For whenever we try to retrieve lost parts of ourselves, we are bound to return to those early childhood years. The garden introduces us to solitude so that we may discover the private self; happily, it is also the precursor to the solitude a woman needs later in life to reclaim her self. Inevitably, this is where we started to bloom and where the soft growing petals dropped off our lives far too soon. But remember this: they are waiting in the dark soil of our garden— these "tiny growing things" that are the best parts of our selves.

Chapter Five

THE HALL OF MIRRORS: ADOLESCENCE AND YOUNG ADULTHOOD

On a weekday afternoon, I head downtown on a crowded New York City subway train. Sitting across from me on her mother's lap, a child no more than three years of age gently, even lovingly, combs her hair, spellbound by her reflection in the tiny hand mirror her mother holds up. It is just after three, school has let out, and the car is full of loud, exuberant teenagers. But the child is oblivious to everything but that small piece of herself she has caught sight of, which gazes back at her with remarkable insouciance.

On a nearby seat, three teenage girls sit talking together with manic intensity. They, too, are completely absorbed in their own world: the world of adolescence. Dressed to code—jeans, short leather jackets, multiple gold studs in their ears—they hunch together to share a morsel of gossip. As they talk, one of them reaches into her backpack, retrieves a tube of lip gloss, and deftly applies it, her attention shifting only slightly. She checks with her friends for approval. "Okay?" she asks. But they are busy crucifying a schoolmate for making a fool of herself with some guy named Lenny. "You should have seen her tripping over herself to get close to him," one of them says. "You should have seen *him* trying to get away," says the other. All three howl with laughter. But the lip gloss girl persists. "Is the color okay?" she asks again. "Yeah, it looks good," the others answer, "but why are you bothering to put lipstick on *now*?" It's not so much a question as a comment on her vanity, and it seems to throw the girl into self-doubt. She rummages through her backpack to find her mirror, then studies her reflection, her expression both smug and anxious.

Watching these two scenes side by side, I am struck by the vast distance separating childhood and adolescence and how it asserts itself in the way each of these girls uses the mirror. For the child, the mirror is an object of wonder. She is able to look at herself guilelessly, free from the snare of self-consciousness and self-criticism. Watching herself comb her hair, she seems to come alive to herself, stroke by stroke.

By contrast, the adolescent girl's relation to the mirror tells a story of ambivalence. When she looks at her reflection, she is measuring it against some idealized picture of how she should look that's in her head. But this is only part of the story. Ultimately, she is searching for something far more elusive: an affirmation that she is "okay."

MIRROR MEMORIES

Most of us are rich in mirror memories. Gazing into our reflection, it was as if we had found the map of an undiscovered country. We'd stare into our eyes, wondering if they really were the mirrors of the soul, and what people would see in ours. We'd scrutinize our body parts like diamonds under a jeweler's loop. We'd check for pimples and inspect the size of our pores, and obsess about the shape of our nose. Are those lines at the corners of my eyes crow's-feet? Is the faint shadow above my lip the beginning of a mustache? Why was I born with curly hair instead of straight? Adolescent girls zigzag from passionate attachment to a coolly clinical disgust. One minute we like what we see—it isn't unusual, for example, for a young girl to fall in love with her long eyelashes, or the shape of her breasts or upper arms. The next minute we feel disgusted, demoralized, and hopeless. Who are we kidding anyhow?

Yet vanity's glass is not all a mirror can be. It is also company on a lackluster afternoon or a weekend night at home. In its most positive aspect, the mirror is the adolescent girl's favorite transitional object—her growing-up version of the toddler's security blanket. It befriends us in some absolutely private space, usually the bedroom or bathroom, allowing us to act out different personas—from Cleopatra to Joan of Arc, from Marlene Dietrich to Reese Witherspoon.

At age fifty, Elizabeth still recalls her teenage mirror memories. Locking the bathroom door, she would stand in front of the full-length mirror and choreograph herself in one-woman performances. Leaning in close, drawing back, she vamped it up: caressed her breasts, lifted her chin to marvel at the arc of her neck, tried on different outfits, danced, grimaced, laughed, examined her body from every angle, spread her legs, studied her vagina, touched herself. "I didn't need the mirror to tell me I had defects. They were apparent to me— pug nose, full lips before it was stylish, a squint from being terribly nearsighted—I had plenty of self-doubt. What I needed was to feel special and comfortable in my body. That's what the mirror gave me. It reconstituted me, made me feel alive."

Moderate amounts of doubt can be a great boost to self-discovery. It makes us question ourselves and search for answers. But in adolescence, when our identity is in flux, too much doubt can be crippling. How does the young girl begin to trust her body when it is in a state of perpetual change? And how does she find strength in her private self at the very time she feels least integrated in her body *and* the world? Preoccupied with how her friends and peers see her, and negotiating new relationships with her parents, she is awash in uncertainty. Most likely, she has forgotten her childhood experience of having once felt the centering presence of a private self.

Adolescents don't spend much real time *in* their bodies at all; they are too busy being hypercritical observers. Fifteen-year-old Miranda tells me that she always feels "onstage" when she's with other people, even her friends. "Let's say we're just hanging out at a neighborhood deli. I'm talking and laughing and it looks like I'm having a good time, right? Wrong. Because I'm always wondering what they're thinking about me and how I seem." Like almost every teenage girl, Miranda is obsessed with how she appears to the world. But trapped in uncertainty, she can't tell. So she depends on others' real or imagined views of her.

There are, of course, golden moments when the adolescent girl genuinely feels herself. An A on a calculus exam, an aerobic workout that steams up her body, a standing ovation for her role in a school play—any such form of mastery can make her feel alive to herself. But when, say, her boyfriend teases her, or she has a fight with her parents, or gets a bad grade, she may fold up like a leaf in autumn, her confidence plummeting off its unsteady perch. Anxiety makes her prey to a steady stream of questions, most of them ending in the word *enough:* Am I beautiful enough? Smart enough? Good enough? Thin enough? Popular enough?

These sudden shifts from high to low self-esteem and back again are entirely natural at this tumultuous stage of development. By adolescence, a girl's sense of self has already been shaped by three powerful forces: her parents, who have provided her with a sense of identity; social pressures that may have already begun to undermine her feelings of self-worth; and the biological revolution taking place inside her that is changing the landscape of her body, awakening new and unpredictable feelings, including sexual desire. In *Reviving Ophelia: Saving the Selves of Adolescent Girls,* Mary Pipher refers to adolescent girls as "saplings in the storm" in recognition of their extreme vulnerability amid the gale forces of change and growth during puberty and adolescence. Just when we need it most, the steadying hand of reassurance loses its grip. Nowhere is this more evident than in our parental relationships, for no matter how supportive our parents are, they cannot stave off our burgeoning self-consciousness, nor quell the doubts that have begun to push their way to the forefront of our experience. The three-year-old child can still climb onto her mother's lap and be physically and psychologically soothed and supported. Over time, the reliability of this "containing environment," as Winnicott calls it, allows the child to achieve a stronger sense of self. Not so for the adolescent girl, who has moved into a far less secure world of shifting moods and wants. She wants to be "mothered"— and hates it. She wants to remain a child—and can't.

As she struggles to gain a better sense of herself, the adolescent girl relies on mirrors of every sort—her own reflection, a parent's frown, a teacher's encouragement, a girlfriend's snub, her boyfriend's caress. Whatever mirror we use, it is bound to inform, *mis*inform, and *re*form our vision of ourselves. The question is whether we find enough good mirrors to reassure us; for those that don't, that instead offer up harsh perspectives, can seriously threaten our fragile, newly forming self. When that happens, the likelihood is great that we will carry an impoverished self-concept, often way past adolescence.

Many adult women I've spoken to unfortunately suffer from this one-way mirror syndrome—looking outside of themselves for validation and measuring their self-worth solely through the eyes of others. A single woman is particularly vulnerable. Let the new man she's dating not text-message her the next morning, or not get back to her at all, and she instantly blames herself for some deficiency— allowing him to be the final arbiter of her worth. She is not merely disappointed, she is uncertain of her allure or of her self-perception.

It is one thing to be guided by good mirroring—something we all need throughout our lifetime—quite another to *depend* upon the way others view us, our sense of self rising and falling according to another person's opinion. Yet until we learn to value ourselves, we will not be able to gauge the world for ourselves, or act out of a sense of personal agency. For the many adolescents and women whose selves have been shaken or teased into submission by misguided parental or peer influences, the ongoing challenge of learning how to trust our own selfhood is bound to become the most rewarding practice of our lives.

A ROOM BETWEEN WISHES

When I think back to my adolescence, the first thing I see is my room at the top of the landing, on the second floor of my parents' house in Queens, New York. Twelve was my lucky year, the one time I can remember that my gambling-addicted father made more money than he lost, and there was enough to furnish my very bare bedroom. To replace the old chest with its missing bottom drawer and the child's desk I'd outgrown, I chose a set of sleek black-veneered chests connected by a vanity that doubled as my desk. It had a matching swivel chair whose black leather seat got broken in like a baseball glove from the hours I sat on it doing homework. My bed was next to a window that overlooked the garden. I remember staring out of it a lot—and dreaming.

My room was my repository, the place I stored my experiences and reflected on my feelings, mostly undeciphered. I longed to grow up, to be a child again, to fall in love, to stop being shy, to be acknowledged for who I was—even if I didn't know myself.

I experienced emotions I'd never felt before and each one made me feel like "me." The more wistful, sad, giddy, excited, angry, horny, silly, romantic, they were, the more "special" I felt. Later, I recognized these feelings as the early-forming self yearning for its own wholeness, at a time when the face we show the world tends to rely more on bravado than substance. They help to jump-start the self's motor into finding its own direction, as when a girl decides to forsake her anorexic behavior, chooses *not* to worry about her haircut, decides to stay home and practice the violin, joins the track team, or, with growing moral vision, works for an idea or a cause that is larger than the life she has been leading.

In her bedroom—if she is lucky—the teenage girl has an iPod or stereo system to block out family sounds while it revs up her hormones, poster-covered walls to enshrine her heroines and heroes, and a bed to support her fantasy life. The bed provides a rendezvous with the self. It is a nest, a forgiving place that can absorb some of her aloneness. Lying on it, dreaming, is the way she braces herself against the world and, if only in her imagination, turns it into a place she can control. By mid-adolescence, the bed will be the site of her sleep-fests—those long weekend cocoonings that often don't end until early afternoon—and quite possibly her sexual awakening, including masturbation and her first sexual experiences with a partner.

But when she leaves her house, her dreams collide with the real world—high school—where she comes face-to-face with the nuts and bolts of learning how to cope and stay afloat, let alone find herself, amid the endless swirl of her private expectations. And it isn't easy. High school is where she makes friends—or does not—falls in love—or does not—has her feelings reciprocated—or does not—feels good about herself—or does not. No matter what her achievements are during those years, when she shakes up the looking-glass of adolescent memories, she can see how deeply the "did not" memories settled inside of her.

In the 1999 movie *Never Been Kissed,* Josie Geller, a twenty-five-year-old rookie reporter for the *Chicago-Sun Times,* played by Drew Barrymore, is sent undercover to a local high school to write a story about teenagers. She needs to infiltrate the "in crowd," but Josie, who was a loner and major nerd in her high school days, can't do it. Instead, she finds herself reliving the horrors of outsider humiliation a second time around. Josie is befriended by the leader of the geeks. But when her popular, athletic brother convinces the popular kids that Josie is cooler than she seems, they claim her as one of their own. Immediately, her status changes—from outsider to center of the magic circle—and she begins to live a charmed life. Everyone wants to be like Josie. Only after she is chosen prom queen does Josie realize that she belongs with the nerds. Having been accepted by the cool kids, she finally gains the self-esteem she needs to accept—and be true to—herself. The movie is the ultimate return fantasy.

In real life we can't go back to high school to do it "right." And in truth, few of us would want to. Still, these four years are one of the more influential periods of our lives, a time, for many of us, when the negative feelings we carried made it much harder to feel the presence of a self, when our insecurities hardened and took root.

THE FAMILY KNOT: MOTHERS AND FATHERS

Parents of a teenager will tell you that they often feel like adjuncts, peripheral to her life instead of at its center, as they were when she was a child. Judging by the way her behavior toward them changes, their daughter's love is often hard to fathom. They get spun around by her moods, and it can be hard to remember what they intuitively know—that their daughter still needs them. Even the most well-intentioned parents sometimes lose sight of the fact that their daughter is engaged in a developmental struggle between opposing desires: the backward pull to be taken care of and remain a child forever, and the forward thrust to be an independent and autonomous adult. Needing our parents and hating that we need them, as teenagers we are still vulnerable to their opinions, deeply swayed by their behavior, and desperately in need of their approval.

MOTHERS

Every evening after dinner some version of this scene repeated itself during Sabrina's early adolescence: her mother washed the dishes, she dried and put them away, and during kitchen detail they talked and laughed and bonded together. Sabrina used to joke that she was like Rory and her mother was like Lorelai on the hit TV show *Gilmore Girls,* because of their teasing, playful relationship—though with far less snappy dialogue. True, Sabrina sometimes felt that her mother was too strict, but most of the time she thought her mom was "really cool . . . my friends really liked talking to her."

But by age fifteen, Sabrina was complaining that her mother "doesn't have a clue who I am. She doesn't let me do *anything* for myself. She only wants to buy me clothes *she* likes, but I hate the colors she picks. She's a nag. I have to be home earlier than any of my friends. And just because one time my boyfriend didn't get up to say hello when she came in the room, he's on her shit list. She's such a snob. But when I tell her that, she gets mad at me. Like *I'm* wrong and *she's* not."

Sabrina's mother is confused by the change. "I don't really get it. I try not to set myself up as an authority figure *per se*. I mean, I pull rank when I think it's necessary, which isn't to say I always get it right, but at least I'm *trying*." When I ask Sabrina about it, she is unequivocal. "It's her fault," she says. "She makes too many rules and wants to know everything, and when I don't tell her, she gets all uppity and silent. If I ask if she's angry, she always says she's not, but I know she is. She just won't admit it."

Like many teenagers, Sabrina has a tendency to make global, all-or-nothing accusations against her mother. Yet anger doesn't stop her genuine sadness over the distance between them. Feeling so misunderstood, it's hard for her to imagine that her mother may be just as confused and miserable as she is—that she may miss the close mother-daughter bond they used to have or even be lonely now that Sabrina has a boyfriend. On good days, Sabrina and her mother can still have a great time together. But the moment she thinks her mother is being overbearing, Sabrina bristles—like the time her mom sent her an e-mail to remind her to call the dentist. In a testy response, Sabrina wrote back: "Mom, I *made* the appointment. But in the future please don't keep reminding me. It's annoying. And they are MY teeth so if they rot and fall out, I have to live with that."

Yet with all the frustration and irritation, the pushing and pulling that goes on between them, the relationship between Sabrina and her mother is truly "good enough." This is Winnicott's tidy phrase to acknowledge the reality that all human beings, mothers included, are imperfect, and that good-enough mothering is as good as it gets. In Sabrina's case, while there is always room for improvement, the fundamentals of a healthy mother-daughter relationship are in place. For the most part, Sabrina can talk to her mother, and she knows she's loved. She is also fortunate in having a mother who listens to her criticism and tries to be more flexible.

What every teenage girl needs most is to be respected for who she is, even when she doesn't know herself. Nothing less will do, and, indeed, nothing less should do. For in adolescence, two competing urges tap-dance side by side: one is our potent drive toward autonomy; the other is our continuing need for our mother's love and approval. The push/pull of these two forces can make for a combustible mother-daughter relationship. In *Altered Loves: Mothers and Daughters During Adolescence,* Terri Apter describes the inevitable conflict that results when a mother fails to see or correctly interpret the enormous changes that her daughter is experiencing, while her daughter is demanding recognition and respect.

However clumsy, even maddening, a daughter's way of communicating her needs may be—crying jags, slamming doors, yelling, lying—she does *not* want to break the connection with her mother. Yet, all too often, this is exactly what happens. When her mother doesn't give her the love and support she needs, the daughter's emerging self is in danger of being compromised even before it has a chance to bloom.

Given their biological similitude, the disentangling process between daughter and mother is nothing short of miraculous. But the task of separation belongs to both parties. The daughter's challenge is to separate enough from her mother to become a person in her own right, yet still identify selectively with qualities she appreciates in her mother. The mother must allow her daughter to grow and mature, while not taking the apparent rejection personally. Knowing when to move forward and when to hold back is one of the most difficult and artful tasks a mother will ever have to achieve.

Finding the new footing is never easy, for the shift in their relationship can be hard on both of them. A long dance has been going on between mother and daughter, with intricate repeating patterns, endless variations, and lots of fancy footwork. Mothering always involves a double identification, for a woman is both mother and child simultaneously. As "child," we are likely to have some unfinished business of our own. To the degree that a woman remains in conflict with her internalized mother, and possibly her real mother as well, her own mothering will reflect some of those unconscious dynamics. No matter how determined a woman is to do it differently, her own unfinished story is bound to influence the way she sees her daughter and the way her daughter feels about herself.

For her part, a daughter must deal with the fact that her mother is not "other"; she is "like." She must be able to identify with her mother to confirm her own identity as a girl while still continuing the process of becoming a separate individual. The task of differentiating herself from her mother grows increasingly more complex as she matures sexually. Some daughters will feel good about themselves and happily be like their mothers; others will wish to be as unlike them as possible, especially if the daughter experiences her mother as intrusive, demanding, neglectful, or indifferent. All will depend on the daughter's ability to separate from her mother sufficiently to become a person—and woman—in her own right, and the mother's ability to tolerate her daughter's separation. For if either mother or daughter loses her footing—and who doesn't at times?—conflicts between them will inevitably occur.

Though it can take many forms, a daughter's anger toward the mother sometimes gets expressed in invidious physical comparisons. Diana, aged seventeen, imagines herself zipped into her mother's overweight body. "I hate her for being fat, for not even trying to lose weight. Her weakness repulses me." Arlene, who is the same age, bemoans the "fat thighs" that are her maternal inheritance. In a magical-thinking way, her "defective body," as she calls it, confirms the link between her mother and herself; that, try as she might, she will never escape the fate of being just "like" her. By the same token, the daughter of an exceptionally beautiful mother may feel so over-shadowed that she can never see her own attractiveness. Such comparisons are floating islands on which a daughter can maroon herself.

Here, too, the conflict goes both ways. A little girl has a vagina, but the rest of her body is a flat plain. Lacking her mother's womanly features of breast, waist, hips, and pubic hair, a daughter, then, is like her mother and not like her at the same time. But as her body shifts into woman's gear and becomes a closer version of her mother's, her coming-of-age inevitably throws the mother back on herself. Mirror, mirror, on the wall—a mother asks—tell me about myself, now and then. What was I like at my daughter's age? Was I as pretty? As smart? As talented? And what am I like now?

Suddenly her daughter is buying makeup and wearing dresses and earrings and shoes she might have chosen for herself—were she but young again. A mother cannot help but feel wistful watching her daughter blossoming, but, ideally, she will be able to keep her feelings in perspective. She will know that her youth isn't lost so much as ended, and understand that this is the natural order of things. She will also find beauty in this cyclic unfolding. If she has what she needs in her own life—love, work, purpose—she won't begrudge her daughter's wish to become her own person. Instead, she will cheer her on, giving her guidance and support when she needs it. But when a mother does not have a life of her own, when too many of her own needs remain unfilled or unresolved, watching her daughter come into her own can be a bitter pill to swallow, and she is primed to act out her resentment.

Unlived Lives and Unloving Mothers

A mother's unlived life can cause great suffering to her daughter: one way or another, she will expect her daughter to make up for her sense of lack. A "child mother," still in need of nurturing herself, may attempt to exchange nurturing roles with her daughter. A "friend mother" may try to be her daughter's equal, rather than a mother who is also a friend. A "victim mother," who complains bitterly of the sacrifices she makes or what she doesn't have, may induce guilt in her daughter for whatever brings pleasure to her life. An "envious mother" may try to cut her daughter down to size, or live vicariously through her daughter's achievements—or both. A "jealous mother" may attack her daughter's sexuality. A "passive mother" may disregard her daughter's emotional needs, perhaps turning a blind eye to physical or sexual abuse. Whether by ignoring her daughter completely or swamping her with her own emotional needs, an undernourished mother will divert attention toward herself to fill her own void. In every instance, a boundary is transgressed, a trust broken. Whatever form the *unl*oving relationship takes, part of the mother's intention, conscious or otherwise, is to diminish her daughter.

"If only you could see my mother not noticing me," Johanna says, sighing. "Good morning, I say, and wait, as I have these eighteen years, for her head to turn in my direction. It almost never does. And when I do happen to catch her eye, I swear she looks right through me. She's on the phone to her broker, or thinking about the captivating new man in her life and what she should wear when they have dinner tonight. She rarely eats dinner with me," Johanna adds ruefully. Yet Johanna's mother has no qualms about intruding on her daughter's life, offering unsolicited advice about the way she dresses, which of her friends she should "get rid of," which boyfriend is "someone you ought to hold on to." Johanna repeatedly tells her, "Mind your own damn business," until the tension between them erupts into screaming matches.

Even so, Johanna loves her mother and hopes, despite years of accumulating evidence to the contrary, that her mother will one day acknowledge her. It won't happen, of course; Johanna's mother is far too self-absorbed. Johanna was raised by nannies and spent a great deal of time alone. Her mother would schedule her in—a half hour here, an hour there—among her whirl of social engagements. When Johanna became a teenager, her mother, relieved that her daughter was busy with her own life, distanced herself even more. Eventually, Johanna's constant aloneness felt more and more like exile and brought her too close to her undernourished self. By sixteen, she was sleeping with lots of boys at school, using sex as a way to feel connected, and sometimes fooling herself into believing that the boys she slept with were truly interested in her. At the same time, she was also filled with self-loathing for "always being so nice to them. It was exhausting. But I didn't know how else to get what I needed." As a young woman, the vacancy in her, created by neglect, draws her to men who, like her mother, are ambitious, cold, and judgmental, yet, like Johanna, desperately needy—their clashing needs ending in fierce arguments about how the other is not there for them, until, emotionally spent and resentful, both retreat in sullen silence to nurse their wounds. The pattern continues with Johanna's present boyfriend. "Intellectually, I know I'm repeating history," she says, "but when Michael screams at me and takes one of his three-hour walks, it always feels like I'm being abandoned. I know I shouldn't put up with it, but it feels so lonely without him."

One of Carol's fondest childhood memories is of the baths her mother gave her, how playful they were, and how soothing it felt afterward when she would sit on her mother's lap wrapped in a towel, feeling her mother's body heat melting into her. For Carol, the bathing ritual was one of the few pure expressions of love she remembers between her mother and herself, the only moments she could relax into being the child. The rest of the time, Carol took on the mothering role, trying to rescue her mother from the pain of a failed marriage. "I saw it in her eyes—her need," Carol said. Yet Carol's mother seemed devoted to her daughter. She chauffeured her to high school without complaint, made sure she had nice clothes, helped her with her homework. But what looked from the outside like devotion often camouflaged neediness; and Carol became her mother's emotional caretaker. "I was always supposed to take her side. *She* was always the hurt one, the one who needed attention. And if I didn't give it to her, she'd freeze me out or act like a martyr. I'd feel so guilty, I'd never show my feelings; there wasn't room."

In high school, Rosa's artistic talent attracted the attention of two of her teachers, who encouraged Rosa's parents to send their gifted daughter to art school. Rosa never forgot that meeting. "My mother just sat there. She had this funny kind of half-smile on her face like she did when she was angry with me—sort of mocking. She told my teachers she'd think about it, but not to get their hopes up because it probably wouldn't happen; there wasn't enough money to send me to art school, and anyway, as far as she was concerned, art was a waste of time. I should take education courses in college, study to be a teacher. I felt like dying right then and there."

Not long after this meeting, some of Rosa's paintings were exhibited at the local Y. Rosa's mother didn't come to the opening night, but when she did pay a brief visit several days later, she barely looked at Rosa's work and instead praised Rosa's girlfriend Alegra, who was also exhibiting. "How very pretty," she exclaimed. "You're so talented, Alegra. You can do so many things." Rosa remembers looking at the walls as if to make sure her own paintings were still hanging there. Seeing them through her mother's eyes, she marveled at how awkward and ugly they seemed. Rosa's mother never did say anything about her paintings; nor did Rosa ever ask what she thought of them. To be able to separate out the strands of her mother's envy was the work of a far stronger person than Rosa was at that time. Instead, Rosa internalized her mother's disapproval. By her late twenties, she stopped painting altogether, convinced that she wasn't good enough to make it as an artist. It was years before she understood that her mother's mean-spirited lack of support grew from the depleted soil of envy.

There are bad mothers, okay mothers, and, fortunately, plenty of good-enough mothers. Even the best among them will sometimes feel conflicted about the role of mothering. Some will long for—but not receive—unconditional love from their daughters. Adolescent daughters will want the same. They need to have the mirror turned in *their* direction—but with sufficient support and recognition of who they are so that they may benefit from the warmth of its reflection. Less than that dispossesses us of our self-worth and encourages us to stray from ourselves—often without our realizing it until later in life. What we hear instead of our own voices is the cacophony of judging, criticizing, frightened, or condemning voices we have internalized. If we were neglected, chances are we learned to neglect our own best interests; if our desires were repeatedly thwarted, the likelihood is that we began to hide them, even from ourselves. Being in the presence of our wounded self can mean experiencing anxious, angry, depressed, or frightened feelings that we are usually at pains to deny. Lacking good nurturing, we do not know how to nurture ourselves. Least of all are we able to take advantage of solitude, for we are too hungry for love, or what may pass for it, to enter its healing space.

FATHERS

In her memoir, *The Shadow Man: A Daughter's Search for Her Father,* writer Mary Gordon asks, "Who is my father?" Her answer reveals how inextricably her identity was bound to his. He was "The origin and my source. My shame and my delight. The figure behind every story. The stranger on the road. The double, feared and prized, approaching from the distance." Gordon, who was seven when her father died, realized only much later that the image of the man she idealized was shot through with lies. Still, I'd wager that a great many women who grew up with their fathers would give a similar answer: instead of the father they long for, they see a stranger—a person whom they cannot talk to, reason with, or feel seen by. Many of the women I see in my practice describe their fathers as either emotionally inaccessible or overbearing. They, too, feel that they are missing something—a vital kinship with a father who is a supportive and ongoing presence in their lives.

In *Fatherneed,* Kyle Pruett, clinical professor of psychiatry at Yale University and the Yale Child Study Center, writes: "Fathers are still the single greatest untapped resource." Relative to mothers, fathers in this culture are a far more "shadowy" entity—even to themselves. This is, in part, because of the many barriers our culture erects to discourage competent fathers: corporate resistance to paternity leave, daytime scheduling of school conferences, media depictions of fathers as foolish or inept. Stereotyped as breadwinners and oriented toward the world outside the home, men tend to be less adept than women at reading the emotional text of their children. This does not mean men love their children any less than women do. It does mean, however, that their expressive powers are often limited, and, with their daughters especially, they can be emotionally awkward, rigid, or just plain unavailable.

It isn't unusual for a teenage girl to complain that her father still treats her like a child, or that he is the last person in the world she would confide in. She also tends to feel more affinity with her mother and is more inclined to understand her mother's point of view even if she does not go along with it. In contrast, she views her father as the arbiter of the law—the one who in the final analysis exercises control over her. Yet fathers are every bit as important to their daughters' development as mothers are. In fact, it is a thrilling source of pleasure and excitement for them to know that, though different from them, fathers are still part of them.

Father and Daughter: A Different Kind of Identification

Even when he is a nurturing, caretaking presence, feeding us, changing our diapers, singing us to sleep with lullabies, the father is not simply a mother surrogate; he is "other." Yet precisely because he is male, he represents many different and often exciting qualities a daughter wishes, and needs, to claim for herself. Research has shown that fathers are more likely than mothers to engage in the kind of play that encourages exploration and frustration tolerance. They are also likely to discipline with less shame and guilt. In *Fatherneed,* Pruett identifies five characteristics of "involved fathering" that actively promote the well-being of a child: feeling and behaving responsibly, being emotionally engaged, being physically accessible, providing material support to sustain the child's needs, and exerting influence in child-rearing decisions. On a more practical level, this can translate into anything from changing diapers to taking his daughter to school or to the pediatrician to learning about his daughter's likes and dislikes, fears, and desires. In short, the father needs to see his daughter wholly—that is, with a lens cleansed of perceptual bias and an awareness that includes sensitivity to her gender difference among all the facets of who she is now and might become. "Making allowances" because she is female simply won't do; not only does it deprecate his daughter but it devalues all women.

Peter never saw his daughter Rachel as limited because she was female. He taught her how to change lightbulbs and electric switches, how to paint houses and mow grass, and, as an adolescent, how to read maps and plan her own trips. When Rachel was four and wanted the training wheels removed from her two-wheeler—much to the horror of her mother—he did it. Thereafter, Rachel would pedal away alongside Peter when he did his three-mile run. Peter not only affirmed Rachel's competence but allowed her to identify with him as the powerful and beloved figure she could depend upon.

It is well-known that Freud saw little girls as "little men" without penises who try in vain to compensate for their "lack"—a view of woman's innate gender deficiency that held until the 1970s, when Freud's ideas on female development were first seriously challenged. What young girls want and need is something far more empowering than any part of the male anatomy: they want a strong father-daughter bond that allows them to identify freely with "male" qualities, like worldly assertiveness, and an orientation toward action that he embodies. As with mothers, an adolescent girl wants her father to recognize her for who she is, with an appreciative love that will help her separate into her own person. Good fathering requires the father's willingness to forge a close bond with his daughter.

When Father-Love Fails

But what happens when a father is unwilling or unable to form a close bond with his daughter? Or when their too-fragile bond constricts, instead of expands, her sense of self? Faced with rejection, the adolescent girl is bound to feel humiliated, her worth depreciated, and her sense of self degraded. She is also likely to choose men who represent an idealized version of him, or else live *through* a man's assumed power, while surrendering her own. Eventually, her sense of deprivation will breed envy, resentment, and anger, interfering with her ability to love and hampering her self-development.

At thirty-three, Kate loved to have intellectual sparring matches with her cerebral lovers, the only kind who appealed to her—until something they said, or didn't say, earned her contempt. She was a particularly good debater, having learned the art of mental jousting from her father, a lawyer whose worldly ambitions exceeded his success, and who compensated for his sense of failure by holding court at home.

By adolescence, Kate had become a pyrotechnician with words, always edging out her mother and brother in family debates, and feeling pleased with herself whenever her father smiled approvingly at something she said. But she quickly learned that the object of the game was to rush to the finish line but never quite make it over. If she bested her needy and narcissistic father, he would sulk and withdraw into himself. Kate relished her role as the "chosen one," but she lived in fear that her throne could topple over at any moment. By catering to her father's inflated emotional needs, she unconsciously absorbed the message that living up to her true potential left her vulnerable to rejection. She became a lawyer, as much to please him as herself, and, with high aspirations, chose international law as her area of legal expertise. For a while, things went well. Kate was hired by one of Manhattan's most prestigious law firms and threw herself into her work. True, her boss was a workaholic and had a reputation for being one of the most competitive men in the field, but he seemed pleased by her progress and Kate was flattered to have him as her mentor. However, when a client praised her handling of his case, Kate knew from her boss's sudden chill that she would fall out of favor unless she hung back and allowed him to be the star.

Fifteen-year-old Chloe has lived with her father since her parents divorced when she was eight. At ten o'clock, Chloe hears her father, just back from a dinner engagement, turning the key in the front-door lock and waits for him to come into her room, as he always does, even though she has asked him to knock first dozens of times. Ignoring the hour and the fact that Chloe is finishing up some home-work, her father proceeds to tell her about his evening. "I'm supposed to listen to his stories every night, but he never asks me a single question about myself." Chloe feels she has no choice but to put up with these intrusions. "If I say I'm busy or tired, he'll either act hurt or accuse me of being selfish. It's a no-win situation. And anyhow, I can't bear the guilt. I mean, I guess he's lonely." She tells me a story about sitting down with her father to watch a TV program. Before it started, Chloe asked her father to turn off the light. He did but then left the room immediately after and didn't come back until the show was over. Chloe anxiously asked whether he was angry with her. "No," he said, but she could tell by his clipped tone and the tension in his shoulders that he was. She asked what she did wrong, but her father wouldn't tell her, so there was no way to correct whatever "it" was. His narcissistic and emotionally manipulative behavior leaves Chloe terminally at fault, thus permanently guilty. She realized long ago that the only way to satisfy her father's consuming needs was to surrender her own. As a child, she remembers moments of feeling powerful, but they seem to have disappeared. Chloe sighs. "Sometimes I imagine putting a cardboard figure in my place—and watching to see if my father would notice. I bet he'd just keep on talking."

"Endlessly elsewhere" is the way Jennifer describes her emotionally absent father. She recalls how, as a child, she would try to get his attention by telling him stories and jokes. It never worked. Not yet emotionally mature enough to understand that her father's emotional terrain was completely separate from her own, she read his inattentiveness as disapproval, a sign of her inadequacy. In time, Jennifer's roots of shame and loneliness grew deeper, for the message she received was that her desires were not important enough to be met.

There may be many reasons for a father's inattentiveness; he may be worried about money or his career, overworked, or simply depressed. But if he is lost to himself, he will be a lost presence to his daughter as well. She will yearn for him nonetheless. For all that this kind of father is not, his daughter is ready to supply endless fantasies of who he might be.

Women often act out father longing with the men in their lives, so I pay close attention when they describe their emotionally absent fathers. A woman who has not felt the light of her father's eyes shining on her may find it hard to feel alive to herself, nor can she see clearly enough to understand that she has chosen a partner who is an idealized version of the father who disappointed her. When, inevitably, that person cannot live up to her projections, she begins to blame him, and what felt like love spirals down into contempt. The pattern usually repeats itself in subsequent relationships.

When women fall out of such relationships, usually, after a period of grieving, they are surprised at the relief they feel. The aloneness they feared suddenly seems welcoming; instead of living in the fraught, tense atmosphere of an exhausted relationship, they find themselves able to relax in its spaciousness. If, instead of rushing off into a new relationship, a woman alone uses the time after a breakup to look into herself and reflect on her own needs, rather than project them onto a partner, she is amply rewarded.

A father's passions, longings, desires—indeed, his pain—are inevitably transmitted to his child. Daughters of disappearing, demanding, depressed, intrusive, indifferent, judging, passive, bullying, incestuous, or remote fathers know this, consciously or not. Almost every night Claire used to watch her storytelling, gambling father change into his tuxedo, slick down his wavy hair, and tie the laces of his polished black shoes as he prepared to go out. He was six feet of charm, and she was enthralled by him. He was her hero—the man she adored even as she found him terrifying. His mystery, his smoldering, sometimes violent, temper, even the hints he dropped of other women in his life, created an almost unbearable tension in her. So did the hush that followed after he gambled away a fortune and left the family impoverished. Occasionally, there was a lull in his nightly disappearances, and for a few days Claire basked in her father's attention, feeling like the luckiest girl in the world. Then, just as it looked like he might be around for a while, out came his tuxedo and he sauntered off again, leaving her bereft and empty.

Claire sensed how well I understood her adoration, even though I didn't tell her until much later how close her story was to my own. She didn't know that I, too, had a gambling father who would suddenly erupt into violent storms of anger. My own father was a dandy and gambler Russian-style—meaning darkly handsome and brooding—with secrets studding his past and a compulsion to deliver his trust into the hands of swindlers. Money—making it, winning it, or, more often, losing it—kept him running in circles, hounded like a runaway slave. When his pockets were full, life was a horn of plenty; he would buy a house, a cabin cruiser, a few more handmade suits, and enough caviar and sturgeon to fill the stomachs of a small army. But when his pockets were empty, our world went dark; he would sit and brood, mentally revising his list of "who's gotta be paid *now* and who can wait awhile." Each time he lost a bet on the fights, the races, baseball, a presidential race, or gin rummy, he would darken visibly, then howl with rage, waiting like a wounded animal for someone to get him out of the trap he had fallen into—as if his wounds could be reached, as if I or my mother might be able to save him.

Like Claire, I was awed and terrified by my father. I, too, idealized him and did my best to turn him into a romantic legend that I might carry inside. So what if he didn't go to work or come home regularly, yelled so loudly the walls trembled, laughed wildly at his own jokes, and was not like any friend's father I knew. At least he painted beautiful murals, loved Pushkin, bellowed out arias along with the Sunday morning opera, and made up stories that enthralled the neighbors' children. If I needed something to applaud, I could celebrate these qualities and claim *that* for myself. So it was hard not to flinch when Claire told me that she could never look directly into her father's coal-black eyes; or that he sat in the living room in his pajama bottoms and refused to budge when she brought her boyfriends home, slicing them apart with sarcasm as soon as they left; or that he continually derided her ambitions, always with the same withering question: "What do you wanna do *that* for?"

Sometimes I wondered whose father she was talking about, hers or mine. By the time Claire turned away from her father, great chunks of him were already inside her: his pain, humor, wildness, talent, flare, but also his shame, grandiosity, morbidity, and violence. Because she saw herself, in her words, as "hopelessly inadequate" and therefore "marginalized" and "powerless," Claire compensated by becoming in her fantasies the muse to larger-than-life men— cultural icons like Bill Clinton or Hollywood power brokers like Jack Nicholson or Robert De Niro, who, like her father, had a mafia tinge about them, and whose power she wanted for her own.

IT IS ONE of the patriarchy's central paradoxes that fathers, good, bad, and indifferent, continue to rule the family nest, even when they remain in the background. A father need not literally disappear, as did Mary Gordon's; most fathers don't. Still, there are countless ways a father may be absent. The theme plays out in endless variations. Passive fathers, narcissistic fathers, seductive fathers, depressed fathers, absent fathers, bullying fathers—each in his own way humiliates and defeats the adolescent daughter's desire to forge her own identity; and the chronic feeling of "missing something" that she is left with inspires countless forms of acting out as she tries to replace absence with someone who holds the key to what she seeks for herself. When that fails, as it surely must, another kind of father surrogate—drugs, alcohol, sadomasochistic behavior—is likely to take his place. More often than not, the desperate aliveness of these choices serves, at least temporarily, to seal over the dead space inside her, or at least provide some momentary excitation, however bitter its aftertaste of self-doubt, shame, and worthlessness.

For all women who had a failed or lost father, abandonment fears can transform any experience of aloneness into one of overwhelming anxiety. Good fathers impart a sense of worth to their daughters that they hold in memory and metabolize internally to strengthen their capacity for aloneness. A father's love and support sanctions a daughter's creative expression of self—the ability to act and do and *be* in the world: it encourages her to appreciate and take her own life seriously. Women who are able to enjoy aloneness are more likely to choose partners who will complement them, being less encumbered by fantasies of someone who will "complete" them. They discover— with or without a partner—that being whole in themselves, they are already complete. The more we can accept—and even cherish— aloneness, the less needy we will be, no longer inclined to be a pawn of the culture or to lose ourselves to the will of others. In the whorl of adolescent change in particular, daughters depend on the solid anchoring such fathering offers.

THE JOYS AND SORROWS OF FRIENDSHIP

In adolescence, making friends and spending time with them takes on a particular urgency. It is why we spend hours e-mailing and phoning one another, virtually moving into one another's bedrooms. We are trying to figure out who we are—I am a math genius; I am a person who is funny and can make people laugh; I'm popular; I'm a loner; I'm none of the above—and we turn to our peers to tell us how we are doing. We can't help it; we've been torn loose from our moorings, the familiar sense of self that is rooted in parents and family.

Adolescent girls "try on" friendships for fit, and the friends we choose often reveal different aspects of ourselves. "Best friends" often hold parts of each other's unknown, or unclaimed, attributes, and they can be instrumental in helping us sort out different parts of our identity. Elise saw in her best friend, Lena, the free spirit Elise wanted to be; while Lena saw in Elise the sensitive, introspective artist Lena thought she wasn't.

In high school, my best friend was Karolin, an aspiring actor like myself, whose family life seemed to offer everything mine did not. Living in my Russian-Ukrainian family was like pitching a tent in a field of geysers where enormous jets of emotion—happy, sad, or angry, and everything in between—could, and did, erupt regularly. Karolin's parents had emigrated from Germany. Her father was a lawyer, and her mother was a homemaker and part-time social worker. They lived in a large, comfortable house with their four teenage daughters. How I loved the civility of their home—the tinkling bell that announced meals, the perfectly timed soft-boiled eggs served at breakfast, dinner-table conversations about books and music and politics that continued long after the meal was finished. For me, being there was like entering the peaceable kingdom; I could almost feel my mind coming alive.

As much as I loved the order of Karolin's family, she loved the chaos of mine. She never missed Sunday morning brunch at my home—the cornucopia of cheese, salads, salami, herrings, sturgeon, breads, and desserts, and everyone eating and talking at once. In no time, Karolin and I nestled into each other's lives. We were soul mates, going to the theater, reading poetry, listening to music, dreaming about boys, courting the Great Drama of Life together.

We were also each other's sounding board. Together, we helped each other navigate in and around cliques, or deal with a boyfriend's betrayal. We consoled each other when one or both of us wasn't invited to the "cool" party. We gossiped about the other kids, gave each other advice about how to get what we wanted out of our parents, how to say no when a boy wanted to make out with us, and, especially, when it would be okay to "go all the way."

The reciprocity that characterizes intimate friendship is a crucial form of validation for teenagers at a time when the wisdom of parents is apt to be undervalued. It is nearly impossible for a teenager to believe that an adult can understand her world. Parental wisdom seems old, out of date; our peers, on the other hand, are our fellow travelers. What a friend says is often less important than her presence at the other end of the line, *listening*. More important, she can drown out the voice of the adolescent girl's harshest critic—herself.

THE SHADOW-SIDE OF FRIENDSHIP

Jody and Charlotte had been inseparable since their freshman year of high school. From the first each felt she had found a soul mate in the other. But things started to change during their junior year, when Charlotte was chosen to play the lead in the school play. Jody knew she wouldn't be seeing much of her during the month of rehearsals, and, though she thought it a bit boastful, she was happy for Charlotte when she told her that the director had taken her aside and said she was "star material." On opening night, Jody brought a bouquet of roses to Charlotte's dressing room to celebrate, glad that their friendship would soon return to normal. But after the play, Charlotte started to pull away from Jody. They had always eaten lunch together and hung out after school, but now Charlotte stayed after to do improvs or rehearse with some of the kids in her scene-study class. They made plans to have lunch one Saturday, but at the last minute Charlotte called to say she forgot—she was supposed to go shopping with her mother. Later that afternoon, Jody went to the mall to buy a pair of sneakers and saw Charlotte walking out of the cineplex with a girl from her drama club. Jody couldn't believe it. She felt the blood rush to her face and wanted to duck into a store so they wouldn't see her, but it was too late. As they walked past Jody, talking and laughing about the movie, Charlotte nodded at Jody and kept walking.

After that, Jody and Charlotte saw less and less of each other. Jody was devastated. What made things worse was that there was no one Jody could talk to about her feelings. She kept wondering what went wrong—more specifically, what was wrong with her?—and played the image of Charlotte and her new friend over and over in her head. She felt humiliated knowing that everyone must have noticed they weren't friends anymore. How could she explain this estrangement to them when she couldn't understand it herself? The best Jody could come up with was that she was too much of a nerd for Charlotte, who seemed to relish her new popularity. She was also too ashamed to tell her mother what had happened, so she pretended things were fine and covered up her hurt.

At all times—but perhaps particularly in adolescence, when peer opinion is so important to us—a friend's betrayal can feel like the end of the world. Charlotte most likely did not fully understand the pain she had caused, but for a long time afterward her rejection undermined Jody's confidence in herself—so vulnerable is a young girl's forming self.

Belonging and betrayal, like Siamese twins, are congenitally united. The need to belong is intimately related to the need to please. Many girls are willing to sacrifice personal boundaries—and friendship boundaries—in order to be accepted. They will sleep with a boyfriend rather than risk losing him; "dis" a girlfriend to stay in the good graces of the clique's leader; or, like Charlotte, drop her after they move into greener social pastures. When yielding to social pressures means compromising one's sense of moral integrity, it is always a sacrificial act against the developing self.

"Adolescence is a beauty pageant," writes Rosalind Wiseman in *Queen Bees and Wannabes,* a book about the real-world politics of adolescence and the inspiration for the Hollywood film *Mean Girls.* "Even if your daughter doesn't want to be a contestant, others will look at her as if she is. In Girl World, everyone is automatically entered. How does a girl win? By being the best at appropriating our culture's definition of femininity. However, a girl can win by losing if being in the running means she has to sacrifice her individual identity."

Little girls are still resilient. The change comes about when they approach adolescence and absorb cultural messages that usurp their identity and substitute in its place the changeling identity of the "air-brushed material girl" in designer clothes put out there by advertisers and the media, whose only interest is profit. Never again are we quite so susceptible to the messages that undercut the self so effectively and so efficiently. In adolescence, we are sitting ducks. When the social self matters above all and girls need reassurance from one another that they look good, fit in, and are well liked, they have entered the depressurized cabin of self-doubt, where how they appear matters more than who they really are. It is why they endlessly compare themselves to one another, conform to the social standards, suffer envy attacks, and act out *against* one another, but, above all else, why they betray their selves.

THROUGH A GLASS DARKLY

Whereas it is normal in adolescence to feel doubt, the distressed teenage girl is the end product of all that has unlovingly been instilled in her. Sometimes a girl is so severely wounded that when she looks in the mirror, she sees only a broken, distorted image, its parts so fragmented that her self is not merely impoverished, it virtually disappears.

Girls fourteen to eighteen years of age have consistently higher rates of depression than do boys in the same age group. In addition to depression, many adolescent girls in this country suffer from other mood disorders that are serious enough to propel them into self-damaging and potentially isolating behaviors like bulimia, anorexia, hair pulling, cutting, burning, stealing, reckless sexuality, or drug addiction. The reasons a girl engages in such behaviors are complex and layered, but it is always the case that she has become self-*less,* and so out of touch with her feelings that she is rarely able to express them in words but instead acts them out. Her most painful feelings have dropped, like heavy stones, to the depths of her unconscious. Even so, their presence will have registered internally as the "*unthought known,*" to use psychologist Christopher Bollas's inspired phrase for an experience that is so unbearable, we cannot let ourselves bring it to consciousness. Instead, we dwell in pain. The young girl is also often angry, but, unable to acknowledge or express it, she turns it against herself—her body often becoming the primary site of attack. It is as if she is alone in a room with someone who wishes to hurt her, only that person is herself.

In the cycle of perpetual warfare that Tessa's parents were locked into, her alcoholic father flew into rages almost daily, and her mother was too weak to defend herself. Her way of getting back at him was by laying claim to their love. When her father was sober, Tessa saw another, gentle side of him; in such moments, she longed for his love, but his shifting moods frightened her, and she was afraid to reach out to him. Besides, she got her mother's message loud and clear that it wasn't okay for her to love him. Confused and unbearably lonely, Tessa grew moody and began to distance herself from both parents. At dinner, she barely touched her food, no matter how much her parents pleaded or threatened, and often refused to eat altogether, complaining that her stomach hurt. "It got so I just heard voices, as if the people blaring at me had disappeared. I felt frozen inside, detached from everything and everybody, like the life was being squeezed out of me." At age fifteen, Tessa was diagnosed with anorexia and hospitalized for nearly nine months. "Once I was there, I realized that it wasn't about putting things together, it was about removing myself from everybody and being where I wouldn't cause trouble." For the first several months, Tessa brooded in the purgatory of indecision, afraid of dying, yet unconvinced about living. Later, she described her hospital stay as a time of "perpetual winter." But it was also a relief to live in a structured and quiet environment with other young people like herself. While she was there, Tessa's father finally left her mother for another woman. Tessa went home six months later to an increasingly overwrought mother. "She was crying all the time and telling me what a bastard he was; she wanted me to hate him as much as she did." To escape her mother's emotional demands, Tessa stayed almost compulsively busy, like the girl in the fairy tale *The Red Shoes* who cannot stop dancing, even to save her life. When she was not doing schoolwork, she was practicing the piano, solving crossword puzzles, making costume jewelry, or taking daily five-mile walks. "I didn't want to think," she says, "and when I slowed down, I'd get horribly anxious. I felt like I had to live up to something . . . some picture they had of me." Who "they" were changed from day to day.

Finally, the burden of pushing herself so hard proved to be too much of an emotional strain, and just before her eighteenth birthday, Tessa once again retreated into herself. "I tried to stay out of my mother's way, but I also had no desire to see my friends." When they called to ask her to go shopping or to a movie, she said no. Her self-imposed isolation was a form of protection, preferable to going out into the world feeling so "raw, it was like I had no skin on my body." She went to school, worked on her projects, and, most of the time, stayed in her room, "feeling like I barely existed," she said. Then, in one of her darkest moments, Tessa saw an image of a young girl laughing and completely free, "and I knew it had to be me, locked up somewhere inside." That was when she decided that she could no longer bear to live this way. She had punished herself enough. It was time to move on. She began to make choices that supported that decision: eating healthy food, jogging, spending time with friends again, and, perhaps most important, taking a job as a veterinarian's assistant, where she could turn her attention toward suffering animals and away from herself. "I felt for them even more than for myself; to soothe them gave me strength; it actually made me feel joyous because I felt I could help them."

WHEN THE WORLD in which we live becomes too terrible to bear, sometimes our only defense is to turn away from it. Self-destructive behavior is one form of escape; addictions are another, as is becoming involved in harmful relationships. Any obsession, any desperate behavior, is a way of isolating ourselves and turning off or away from pain. Adolescent girls are adept at disguising their needs by trying to act normal. It can be a long time before parents realize their daughter leaves the table to vomit up her dinner before it gets digested, or is snorting coke with her friends, or is searching the Internet to find other secret cutters like herself. Yet even when these beleaguered teenagers engage in social interaction, the awareness of their inner distress amid the seeming normality of others—for remember that they literally feel "separate" from themselves—makes them feel even more markedly lonely and isolated.

"Suffering," Freud said, "is nothing else than sensation; it only exists in so far as we feel it." That is why we try to alter the chemistry of our bodies, using drugs to intoxicate and remove ourselves from the external world with pleasant sensations, as far as we are able. Adolescents are by nature thrill seekers, craving "pleasant sensations" almost as an art form. But when an adolescent's alienation is so extreme that, like Tessa, she barely feels that she exists, pain can tell her that she is, at least, alive. But pain is addictive; everything else loses importance next to its transporting power, and over time we need more and more of it not to feel numb. Only one thing has a stronger force: the deep yearning for wholeness that exists inside every human being and, when awakened, stretches past pain toward life. I have seen the power of this impulse countless times in the women I work with who, collectively, have engaged in virtually every possible destructive form of behavior, yet have unambiguously chosen the promise of life.

FOOTLOOSE (AND FANCY-FREE?)

Where am I? And who am I? Lily has just turned twenty-two. Until a few months ago, when she graduated from college, her life was still in the future tense, ahead of her, waiting while she prepared herself. Now the world is at her feet—she has only to click her stiletto heels together and claim it. But as she steps forth, fear suddenly spikes her. She turns back to watch the fading shapes of familiar figures. She wants to hold on to them, but she can't. The future is here, and she is in it.

Three weeks ago, Lily moved into a small studio apartment. She knows her parents will "freak" when they realize it's in the East Village, but she considers herself lucky to have found it; in Manhattan, cheap apartments are nearly extinct. Besides, she likes the idea of living alone—at least she did before moving in. Now she lies awake at night and worries about how to support herself.

Her parents send her a monthly stipend to cover her expenses, but the amount will be reduced by half in four months and altogether in eight, because, they keep reminding her—as if she could forget—they still have to put her two brothers through college. Lily thinks, somewhat ruefully, how much harder it is to luxuriate in fantasies of being independent now that she's entered the "real world," especially as she considers her options: $6.50 an hour as a part-time waitress—$0 so far as an actor. That's another thing, Lily thinks. Suppose I don't succeed? Then what? I've always wanted to act; it's who I am. I don't want to do anything else.

Each year, millions of young women, aged twenty-one and older, leave their families behind and step into that strange, disparate country called Adulthood, where they must assume the arduous task of trying to establish themselves in a job or a vocation and find out who they are. But despite being legally sanctioned as adults at twenty-one, young girls in their twenties hardly fit the conventional definition of one who is "fully developed and mature." In *Are You Somebody?: The Accidental Memoir of a Dublin Woman,* Nuala O'Faolain's memory of her own twenty-something self gets much closer to what we really are: "I faced into the future looking backwards. I was half a girl still."

Young adulthood can almost be defined by its unsettledness: it is a liminal state where we try things out—graduate school, jobs, relationships, new cities, sexual preferences, gender preferences, staying single or partnering—make lots of mistakes, and learn from them. Like Lily, who lies in bed worrying about money one moment and dreaming herself into stardom the next—vacillating between reality and her dreams of what reality should be. She has entered that stretch of time when we are, in O'Faolain's words, "rich in ignorance," meaning that our adolescent search for identity not only continues but intensifies. We will make many mistakes before we learn the difference between the kind of flame that warms the heart and the kind that can burn us, or discover that the same flame can do both. Each "false start" teaches us something we need to learn. "Now that I am thirty," wrote Elizabeth Wurtzel in *Bitch,* "I know for certain that there were things I did in my twenties that I needed to do. Perhaps I might have done them as a teenager or a college student, but I believe that I needed to do them as an adult, a free person, without a tour bus or a counselor or a parent or a roommate or some other guardian there to chaperone me through: *There just were things I needed to do absolutely alone* [my italics]."

It goes without saying that the force and direction of every young woman's needs vary: some feel urgent, others are more measured; some embrace the limitless world-is-my-oyster perspective, others are muted; some are romantic, others practical; some are outrageous, others modest. We may want to be in a committed relationship, travel to exotic places, make partner in a law firm, dye our hair blue and wear a tongue ring, sleep with lots of men or lots of women or both, become politically involved, learn to meditate, stay single, get married, have children, try celibacy, write a novel, learn to skydive.

To have such choices feels like freedom. But "free" is also a state of mind. Young women I've talked with tend to be too preoccupied with establishing themselves in the world to spend much time exploring their private selves.

Olga recently ran into a former boyfriend in a West Village café. At twenty-five, she thought she could marry him. Five years later, she isn't sure what was so appealing about him, "except his tremendous tenderness making love. I think I loved the idea that there was this great well of emotion I could tap into, which is more than I can say for lots of men." More that that, she loved the drama: that first meeting when he stood in her apartment and in an earnest voice told her "I really care about you"; the snatched moments of passionate lovemaking when he stole out of work midday; the titillating suggestion of "future plans," like the time he took her to meet his family in Rhode Island. But the relationship came to an abrupt end when he told Olga that he wasn't ready for a serious relationship. Shocked because there had been no warning, Olga took to bed for a week.

To be sure, Olga missed her boyfriend, but what she missed even more was the intoxicating state of infatuation that is part of falling in love—the extraordinary "high" of being possessed, claimed, taken over, lost to the self—but also the sense of possessing: claiming, cleaving, never letting go, with swirling fantasies that the person you want wants you back equally. Our earliest experiences of falling in love are almost always characterized by a desire to merge with the other person, the exhilarating fantasy—for fantasy is what it is—that two can become one. Later on, when we are older and wiser, we will fall in love again, but never with the same almost manic intensity.

Experiencing life is the climatic condition of young adulthood, related to the two major sources of our content—or discontent: Freud's love and work (*eros* and *arbeit*), which begin to exert great gravitational force during this time. By their mid-twenties, many young women will do astonishingly creative things; others will take longer to discover where their talents lie and to remove the obstructions that may hold them back—usually related to conflicting internalized voices about doing what is practical, fear of disappointing a parent's wishes, or of striking out on one's own. For just as the lure of infatuation and genuine love often have little in common, the same can be said for earning a living and finding the kind of work one really wants to do.

PLAY VERSUS PERFORMANCE

One thing is certain: whether in love or in work, women in their twenties must learn the difference between playacting and performance. By "playacting," I mean the kind of experimentation that begins in adolescence as we strive to figure out who we are in the world; it's part of the ongoing process of identity formation. Playacting incorporates "play," and always has an element of the spontaneous in it—the spark of our creativity. By "performance," I mean behaving in ways that constrict the self and obstruct its growth—putting on an act, a false front, trying to make people believe we're something we're not, and it is almost always about trying to shore up a shaky sense of self. Unlike the self that playacts, the performing self is far less free to be curious, spontaneous, exuberant, or courageous because it is always beholden to those we believe we must please.

Susan explains why she finally broke up with her first serious boyfriend, Josh. "He was always trying to change me, telling me I didn't use my mind enough," Susan told me. "I did use my mind; I just didn't want to write for the *Harvard Law Review* or go to meetings at the Council on Foreign Relations. I mean, I'm very glad he introduced me to all these things, but that's not who I am." Deciding she'd had enough, Susan was, as she put it, "back in singledom again."

But before long Susan started getting anxious about whether some guy or other was going to call a second or a third time—"because if you're in the bull pen, you may get picked and you may not." After waking up one too many mornings with a strange man in her bed—"guys who seemed wonderful at four A.M. but were complete jerks by day"—she just didn't think she had the stomach to start the whole process again. A frank letter from her friend Trudi jolted her into reality. "Susan, my darling," it began, "you are so gifted, so brilliant and witty, that it almost shocks me at times to see you move away from the real YOU to become the 'GOOD GIRL' who has to win over every guy. Why do you try so hard to please these clean-cut preppy guys who aren't worth a dab of the powder on your nose when they never are the ones you seem comfortable with anyhow?" Trudi's e-mail mentioned other ways Susan was "selling herself short" and urged her to "drop the PERFECT HOSTESS role and become who you really are." Feeling strangely calmed and satisfied, Susan closed her eyes and thought over what Trudi had written. She wished her friend was there. She wanted to tell her that she wrestled every day with the prodding voices inside her and that she knew she had lots of bad habits to relinquish. Then again, Trudi was living in Oregon, comfortably ensconced in a relationship, and the gratitude Susan felt soured a little.

"How can I live without being noticed? How can anyone?" Susan wondered. She thought about Nancy, her last roommate, blond and beautiful and a size 2. When they used to go to bars together, Nancy was the one men paid attention to. Susan said she "could be as witty as Beatrice with Benedict, and it wouldn't matter." Next to Nancy, she felt like a "cipher." Suddenly, all she could feel was shame, covering her like a moth-eaten blanket. She has actually begun to realize that when she felt like this, the only thing she wanted, the only thing that seemed to help, was *attention*. It almost didn't matter what kind or from whom—her boss at the Internet company, the people she parties with, the friends she lavishes attention on—as long as there was enough attention, Susan felt alive to herself. That's why going out has become a nightly performance piece that she has staged to get what she needs. "Early in the evening, it's for what I wear; after a few drinks, it's for the bon mots that stream from my mouth and make everyone at the table roar with laughter, and by two or three in the morning, it's for capturing some guy's attention and getting him to make love with me." When she reviews her own performance the next day, Susan's pleasure seems to depend entirely on how successfully she has "pitched" herself the night before. The problem is, Susan feels too fragile to take herself seriously, and the good feelings can never be sustained. "All it takes is one guy to lose interest, and I'll do almost anything to revive his attention. If I can't, I—well I get depressed." Susan knows she's living falsely to herself; she can feel the stress in her body that accompanies "dancing as fast as I can." And yet the fear of being alone—truly alone—is more than she can even think about. To her it means one thing only: she isn't worthy.

There is a script that adolescent girls naïvely follow when they begin to meet boys, date, hook up, or fall in love for the first time, a selection of ideas, notions, beliefs, "rules," and prescriptions gathered from a variety of sources—parents, teachers, and friends to instant-messaging from the media that guides their behavior. The problem is that as the ever-watchful, ego-ridden self is set in motion, criticizing, judging, finding fault, parts of this script become more deeply entrenched. By the time she has reached her twenties, the script has turned into a full-fledged ideology that defines her worldview, including critical thoughts about who she thinks she is. This makes a sad kind of sense. Our need to make our way in the world is real and urgent, and for this reason we often feel that "we are what we do"—even if we do it for all the wrong reasons.

What every adolescent girl and young woman wishes for herself is the freedom to stay true to herself and choose her own way. In real life, however, the psychological stakes of participating in so radical a choice are simply too high. In the compromises that follow, young women often begin to lose an active sense of their own agency. In the psychology of women, the costs are enormous: experiences of disconnection, difficulties speaking their mind, feeling they are not being listened to empathically, loss of self-confidence, and a failed sense of conveying—or even believing—their own experiences.

Even the most free-spirited young women are plagued by competing fantasies that quibble endlessly: singledom versus coupledom, work versus play, autonomy versus dependence, caution versus abandon, the ideal versus the real, and the playacting self versus the performing self. Added to this, today as never before, young women are beset by conflicting versions of what constitutes "happiness." Self-help books insist that women can have it all, while "rules" books issue unabashedly manipulative instructions on the performance aspects of getting—and holding on to—a partner. Symbolically and actually, young adulthood is a threshold space where deeper self-transformations can begin to take shape. In a developmental sense, women in their twenties are, so to speak, playacting themselves into reality, or at least should be. And reality—given our society's aggressively consumptive, hyper-speed, media-inflated stance; its war-locked posture toward other cultures; and its extraordinary insensitivity toward the needs of its own citizenry—is by no means easy to absorb. No one plays harder or faster than people in their twenties or are more in need of rituals and outlets for self-discovery. If a young woman doesn't play during this time, she will certainly do so, perhaps more recklessly, later on, or spill tears of regret and waste years wishing she had. For she is, almost by definition, self-absorbed, and her most urgent task—and greatest accomplishment—will be to begin sorting herself out from everyone around her and learn to be with herself as she is.

HOWEVER HARSHLY THEY might judge others, young women are much harder on themselves. Cultural and psychological currents overtake them before they are strong enough to withstand their effects. That's one reason why I enjoy working with them so much. The bittersweet irony is that I am able to be there for these women as I could never have done for myself. Their shields of bravado, sarcasm, arrogance, flightiness, dismissiveness, spaciness, and anxiety are necessary defenses against the crass insensitivities and coercions of the external world as well as their own internal drillmasters. Confused and abashed by the way they feel about themselves, they are seeking mirrors that offer them true reflections of who they are to relieve them of their terrible growing pains and self-doubt. We know that our cultural stereotyping and social expectations contribute to undermining the confidence of young girls. What we have yet to fully absorb is the sheer intensity and relentlessness of these forces just as the self is taking shape.

Very few girls get through adolescence without suffering a serious loss of self-esteem; far into our adult years, we carry the accumulated weight of shame, guilt, and anxiety that we internalized during this crucial period of development. Afraid of being at the mercy of these feelings, we compensate—for as long as we can get away with it—by embracing the culture's hydra-headed forms of diversion. But our self—our *true* self—continues to call out to us, letting us know in subtle and not so subtle ways that we are ignoring her.

Aloneness is a gift; it can return us to our self. Instead of avoiding it, we need to accept it wholeheartedly, even though we fear it. To rid ourselves of our fears, we first need to understand their source. As our fears diminish, we have a renewed opportunity to realize a life of our own. Each relationship in our lives is a teaching: a way to learn what we want and need for ourselves and what we are willing to give, or not give, in order to get it. In this sense, aloneness is a mirror wherein we may view ourselves more wholly and affirmatively.

Eventually, our vision clears. In the following chapters we see that we can go on living life as it is, or we can decide to live creatively— whether gardening, trading bonds, traveling, cooking, getting involved in politics, or (guiltlessly) doing nothing at all. The central issue for us will be to close the gap between knowing what we want for ourselves and actively living it. Our reflexive response will be to ponder what we did wrong and revert to the old, patterned responses that have kept us enthralled. But as we gain strength and determination, as we learn to intercept the life-denying voices inside us, we discover that each assertion helps us to find our own sovereignty.

Part III

SELF-POSSESSION

Chapter Six

BEFRIENDING ALONENESS

TRANSITIONING INTO ALONENESS

Hannah, a smart, self-assured pediatrician, called to tell me about an epiphany she had while eating a tuna sandwich at the local coffee shop. "I got it! He's having an affair," she said about her husband, Peter. Then, after a pause, she wondered, "Where have I been all this time?" Over the next few days, Hannah began piecing together the evidence she had only vaguely noticed before: the occasional hang-up calls at odd hours; the initials "JL" scripted on the title page of a novel her husband said he'd borrowed from a "friend"; his sudden enthusiasm for fado music; and, just three weeks earlier, a last-minute call explaining that he needed to extend his business trip another week. Now Hannah's curiosity moved into high gear. Setting scruples aside, she decided to read Peter's e-mails. "It was all there," she told me, "months and months worth of love letters between him and some singer named Francesca." That evening, Hannah confronted her husband. "At first he said he didn't know what I was talking about. But when I showed him the e-mails, he stopped trying to defend himself." For Hannah,

Peter's acquiescence was the worst moment of all: it meant he wouldn't fight to save their marriage.

Hannah had met Peter at a friend's dinner party. "From the moment I saw him, I knew I had to be with him. It felt like I had known him for a thousand lifetimes." Until this terminal crisis took place, they had been living together in Peter's apartment, and though he agreed that night to move into a hotel, Hannah decided she wanted to move out. "There was too much of him around. Besides, how do I know he didn't sleep with her here when I was away?" Hannah's outrage strengthened her resolve. She found an apartment and moved out three weeks later. Eager to make a fresh start, she did not yet realize that she was getting far ahead of herself. Soon she discovered that dismantling a nine-year-old marriage is layered with emotional complexity. Her anger yielded to attacks of self-blame and remorse, and she began to obsess mercilessly. "What did his leaving say about me? And who would ever want to be with me again?"

In the weeks that followed, Hannah couldn't stop thinking about the "other woman," her mind stuck on one thought: "Francesca's triumph." She created her own fantasy portrait of her husband's lover, embellishing it with superlatives no human being could possibly possess: Francesca was "a superb singer," "incredibly charming," "dazzlingly beautiful," "extraordinary in bed," and, of course, much younger than herself. Overcome with emotions she had never felt before, Hannah would complain bitterly. "I reek of envy and rage— it's like the smell of old, damp rags. I didn't know I had so much in me." When she calmed down again, she realized that deeper than her envy was the pain of betrayal: "I think his lies hurt most of all because they stripped down the possibility of belief. I guess that's what betrayal does."

Day by day, sometimes minute by minute, Hannah vacillated between anger toward Peter and against herself. She put in long hours at her office, scheduling evening appointments and staying to write up reports until eight or nine at night. She was doing her best to stave off the depression she was feeling as she faced the reality of being alone. She also continued to obsess, unable to stop thinking that *she* had almost single-handedly destroyed her marriage. "I was in love with Peter, but I also loved my work; maybe I took him for granted. I'm sure I didn't give him enough." "Did he give you enough?" I asked, to remind her that there had been two people, not one, in this marriage. But Hannah wasn't ready to relinquish the blame: "I still think if I'd tried harder I could have changed him."

Even after a relationship ends, it can be hard for a woman to give up the illusory idea that she had the power to change her partner, let alone the outcome. Clinging to this belief, obsessing about "should haves" and "if onlys," keeps us from moving forward with our lives. In time Hannah would realize that her marriage ended for reasons she could not foresee. For now she was in the midst of a major transition and, like all of us, had to find her own way through.

ONE OF MY most vivid memories of my second marriage is the emptiness I felt toward the end of it, as if my life consisted of endlessly receding points of gray, and that I would never stop walking its flat plain—the void inside me that revealed itself after I lost hope that my husband and I could recapture what we had lost. Among my foiled expectations, the hardest to give up was the idea that I would be with the man I married "until death do us part," and that my sons would grow up in the bosom of an intact, loving family. Anything less was to be a failure as a woman, a wife, and also a mother, and I berated myself soundly on each count. The day my husband and I told our children we were separating—they were nearing eleven and thirteen—still anguishes me when I remember the pained look on their faces and their bewildered silence.

I had practical concerns, too, and I learned that practical issues are freighted down with emotional content. About a year before the separation, we had moved back to Manhattan at my behest. I had lived in the city in my early twenties, and, after living in Princeton for fourteen years, it felt like coming home. But it also took us a while to adapt to city life, especially my sons, who needed all my support as they adjusted to a new school and made new friends.

There was also the deplorable state of my finances. I was accustomed to a comfortable standard of living. But my new job as president of a nonprofit artists' peace organization paid me only a modest income, scarcely enough to make ends meet. It didn't help that I had always kept myself in the dark about financial matters, as if not knowing how much I had in my bank account would magically keep me solvent. Now, for the first time in my life, I would have to address the dollar-and-cents concreteness of money issues and learn to live on a vastly reduced income. I rented out a spare room to a tenant, and did without. Later, I understood the fear behind my willful ignorance— taking control of my finances meant independence, which was in direct conflict with my wish to be taken care of. Many women, I've since learned, share this fear.

When couples separate, friendships are reconfigured, as old friends often take sides. At first, I felt surprised, shamed, and then desolate over the loss of people whose presence I had counted on, but I felt too shy and vulnerable to initiate calls, certain that, compared to my husband, I had far less to offer them. Now I know that in the face of another person's distress, it is human nature to put up a do-not-disturb sign. Many people simply cannot deal with a friend's suffering, for fear it will invade their lives.

I decided to become a clinical social worker; psychology had always fascinated me, and I had thought about becoming a psychotherapist for many years—but the shift back into the demands of academic life was unsettling. Suddenly I was navigating a landscape in which *everything* was new and untested, especially my self, and I felt wretchedly exposed and unprotected. What I desperately needed was some reassurance that I would get my life on a secure footing. Yet for the next two years, at least, there was no such security to be had.

I had been here once before, in my twenties, but then I lived in a bubble of romantic illusions, rushing into and then out of my first marriage, measuring my worth by the number of lovers I had, spending more money than I earned, and piling up debts under the assumption that some great man would sweep me off my feet and save me. My self never developed a strong musculature. Now, in my mid-forties, vibrations from the reality shocks of being on my own touched every insecure nerve and sinew in my body; there was no bubble to hide in, no fantasy of rescue to take the pressure off. I was a woman alone and a single mother with two children who needed me to be strong when inner fortitude was the last thing I felt. In this boot-camp phase of aloneness, I often felt exasperated by my sons' needs and angry that my own went untended, listened hungrily to stories about dinner parties other people went to, wondered endlessly about what makes life worth living and if I would ever find "it," tried to make sense of my marriage, needing to understand what can never be fully understood, brooded enviously about my husband's relative freedom from domestic cares and why he could get away with it when I couldn't, and dwelled too much in the past when there seemed to be no future. Shorn of all the things I'd taken for granted—social connections, financial security, the status and many perks that came with being married to a well-known professor—I felt, if possible, more invisible to myself than I ever had before.

Reminders of aloneness became a staple in my life. I envied couples, was disbelieving and sad when a friend's husband shamefacedly explained that his wife had stopped inviting me to her parties because singledom had converted me into a potential siren, and yet felt overwhelmed walking into a cocktail party full of strangers. My moods were shifting and prickly. I dreaded spending holidays alone while my sons visited their father, was angry and indignant when my new dentist's nurse automatically called me "Mrs.," and felt self-conscious shopping for one at a supermarket. But my worst moments came late at night, when loneliness filled me with self-pity and I knew for certain that I was destined for a life of boredom and misery. I didn't understand then that I had, in effect, committed perjury against my own imagination, consigning it to the old and rutted roads of bias. I had sworn falsely against the many unexplored possibilities aloneness offered, acting prejudicially—not only against myself but against all women alone.

Now I know with certainty that in the face of aloneness's inescapable visitations, we almost invariably undergo a major internal reorganization. But of course we don't always know *how*. Certainly, this was my own situation when, as a newly divorced woman, my inner confusion was reflected back to me in my dealings in the external world, for both seemed equally bleak. A man of wisdom named Adyashanti says that the world is a "duplicating machine," meaning that whatever issues we are going through in our inner lives will always reveal themselves in our outer circumstances. In terms of natural processes, such convergence is a universal constant, though we usually aren't aware of it, or are only dimly so, until circumstances set forth this knowledge in stark relief. There was nothing to be done but accept my situation. I had, after all, made the decision to find my own way.

When we are in a thriving relationship with another person, it is almost impossible to imagine being alone. Of course, this is less true if there are problems in the relationship, and more so if it is truly bad. But even in the best relationships we may feel twinges of regret for roads not taken—if we have to move to a new geographical location, interrupt our professional life to have children, take a job we don't like to earn money, or become the caretaker for a sick partner, child, or an elderly parent. The more we feel that we've sacrificed or that we are not living up to our potential, the more likely we are to dream of a substitute life unfettered by mundane concerns: "rescue" by a billionaire; lots of sex with gorgeous, virile partners; more money than we know what to do with; travel to faraway places; or, for many of us, just the time and space to be ourselves.

Such imaginings are almost always about freedom from our burdens or constraints. Rarely do they include the dust and cobwebs of reality that would inevitably collect in real life. When they do, when fears about being alone actually enter the pictures we create for ourselves, they often send us scuttling right back to the world we know, no matter how compromised we feel. But eventually there is a reckoning. Our false self cannot last.

For me, being on my own began to seem preferable to being alone and increasingly lonely in my marriage. Still, as much as I knew it would not last, the end of my marriage was a major loss, and I had to grieve. "We, in this culture, make the mistake of associating the experience of grief only with death," says Maria Housden, author of *Hannah's Gift* and founder of Grief in Action. "But grief is our very human response to any significant loss in our lives." In her book *On Death and Dying* (1969), Elisabeth Kübler-Ross defined grief as a process with identifiable stages: denial, anger, bargaining, depression, and acceptance. But for me, and for all women alone, acceptance is by no means the end point that signals the return to normal life. We must work through our feelings of loss, failure, and regret, and also contend with the shame that attends our new social status, as well as our all too real survival fears, and the sobering responsibility of raising our children alone—including the need to provide for them financially and emotionally while maintaining our own boundaries and giving time and care to self. Too many women opt out of this last concern. Child rearing is such a full-time occupation that it leaves us little time or energy to attend to our personal needs. And yet, this harried time is precisely when we need to make every effort to give ourselves pockets of solitude. The self feels too diminished otherwise.

When we are young, we often boldly imagine ourselves as strong, fierce, and independent, usually in fantasies where we cast ourselves in the starring roles—actor, doctor, physicist, opera singer, skydiver, rock climber. That our independence might also mean that we will be alone doesn't always figure into the picture. But, of course, this reality is exactly what we must accept—keeping faith when we feel least hopeful because the rewards for holding to our course are great. We need to remind ourselves—not once but many times—that unhappiness and fear in these beginning stages of aloneness are normal and natural; indeed, they are a necessary stage of our journey. It can be hard not to yield to the temptation to escape—whether by becoming workaholics, drinking or eating or going online too much, casting ourselves as eternal victims, or, alternatively, making harsh demands on ourselves to "get over it," denying our tears and our feelings, thinking we can get on with our lives when we aren't quite ready to do so. In due course we will arrive at the place we need to be.

As we move forward, even our seemingly small choices can matter. Michaela is a busy single mother who is working on a cookbook based on recipes she has gathered from family and friends. She began paying attention to her kitchen experiences and realized that she likes to cook only when everything around her is quiet and serene; as soon as any of her four young children flock into the kitchen to help, she gets anxious. "I want everything to turn out perfectly; and because I have no patience for their mistakes, I find myself taking the measuring cup or spoon and saying, 'I'll do it.' That's no good for anyone," she says. "It takes away all the fun." Her solution is to do most of the serious cooking while the children are in school, then do their favorite baking projects with them when they come home.

Annabelle, a divorced businesswoman in her early forties, says that while all the single women she knows "would love to have a man in their lives for companionship and sex, the lack of one doesn't hold anyone back. We aren't waiting for a knight in shining armor to swoop down and rescue us. We have our own lives, and we like them. My mother always told me that the man should buy you jewelry. Well, I want those pearl earrings, and, damn it, I can afford to buy them myself."

Women have nothing to lose and everything to gain from looking our fears straight in the eye and, instead of denying or avoiding them, staring them down. Change—genuine and organic change in our lives—doesn't happen in a blinding flash of insight, or when we wake up the next morning. Rather, it happens incrementally, in baby steps, and it arises out of multiple insights and our own granite willingness to persist. For many women, aloneness is what we need to begin our journey. Eventually, we will come to recognize it as a point of grace in our lives.

ACCEPTING ALONENESS

I learned slowly that aloneness has much to offer, almost despite myself. Many a midnight I sang and danced in my apartment to the blare of Middle Eastern or reggae music, something I could never do when I was married unless my husband was away on a trip. Many an early morning I sipped tea and drank in the silence, thankful for that hour of solitude before it was time to steer my sons and myself into the day. For several years after my divorce, having younger lovers served to remind me that I was still a desirable woman. But as I grew stronger and surer of myself, the differences in my life experiences and theirs eventually made aloneness seem the more welcome choice. Even the many hours I spent trying to find a way *out* of aloneness by filling up my free time in front of the TV or on the phone began giving me an existential hangover; such distractions were no longer enough to fill the need inside me for "something more." I had finished graduate school, my sons and I seemed to have weathered the worst of the emotional storms that accompanied the trauma of divorce, and we were busily adjusting to our new life. My psychotherapeutic practice was fulfilling and on solid footing; indeed, the more I listened to my patients' stories, the more I marveled at our human complexity. I was inspired by their courage, which often came through when one least expected it, and thrilled as I watched them learn to harvest their inner resources. I was finally earning enough income to support myself comfortably, and I was proud of that accomplishment. I was also making new friends—among them, other women alone who, satisfied with their lives, were exemplars of how I, too, could live well *on my own*. I saw occasional bravado— women facing difficult life situations and trying not to let it show— but the sincerity and aplomb of these women, not to mention their creative gusto, made a lasting impression on me.

OUT OF THE BLUE

Sometimes we find ourselves caught in a moment that is so against the grain of our desires, we would do almost anything to stop time. But it happens anyway. Often, a third party delivers the news: "Your husband has a tumor"; "I'm sorry to tell you this, but there's been a terrible accident"; or, lacking death's finality but just as shattering, "I'm leaving you." Each shock stuns us to the very ground of our being and strips us bare, forever altering the way we think about our- selves and the world. "Life changes fast. Life changes in the instant. You sit down to dinner and life as you know it ends." Those were the first words the writer Joan Didion wrote after her husband, the writer John Gregory Dunne, suffered a massive heart attack and died one evening as they sat down to the evening meal. We are awed by the ordinariness of the moment in which a cataclysmic event happens—in one instance, a man has a heart attack at the dinner table; in another, four airplanes fly through the clear blue skies of a perfect September 11 morning, shattering the American psyche. The psychoanalyst Leslie Farber once described such an encounter as the "perplexing pain of nothing" (no thing) when, stripped of one's role with all its identifying markers, a person becomes *no-thing*. The film *Blue* (1993), the first of Krzysztof Kieslowski's classic cinematic tril- ogy *Three Colours*, is a mythic rendering of loss and transformation in which a woman's life both ends and begins at exactly that zero point.

The movie opens with a horrific car crash, in which Julie, played by Juliette Binoche, is badly hurt. When she regains consciousness in a hospital bed, the doctor gives her the terrible news that the accident claimed the lives of her husband and young daughter. "I'm sorry to have to inform you . . ." he begins. In an instant, Julie is wife and mother no longer: the subtraction of her family transforms her into a woman alone.

At first, Julie cannot conceive of a single reason to go on living. But when she tries to swallow a bottle of sleeping pills, she gags and retches them up. "I can't," she tells her doctor, perplexed by her body's refusal to yield when everything inside her wishes to give up. She will go on living if she must, but it will be by default. She determines to do—and be—absolutely *nothing*. Julie's journey as a woman alone begins in the blindness of loss—without direction or understanding. "Before, I was happy," she tells her mother later. "Now I have nothing. . . . Now I have only one thing to do. Nothing. I don't want any belongings, any memories. No friends, no love. They are all traps." She moves to an empty flat in a working-class section of Paris, leaving behind everything from her former life, except for the blue crystal chandelier that had hung in her daughter's room. In the new flat, the chandelier sheds its blue light over all. One could say, in fact, that blue is the color of nothing. Or that it is transparency itself: an empty vessel waiting to be filled. Julie stays in the presence of the void, enduring emptiness, hoping for nothing, expecting nothing; instead, she lets the current of life move her at will and waits passively for whatever comes next.

But, one by one, the lessons Julie must learn come in forms she can recognize. She discovers that her husband had a mistress who is about to give birth to their child, that her mother preferred her sister to her, that she passively accepted being the unacknowledged composer of her husband's music, and, finally, that there is another man who loves her as deeply as her husband had loved his mistress and as she had once loved her husband. As these insights come, Julie goes for swims in a local pool, letting its blue baptismal waters—the same blue as her daughter's chandelier—wash over her, cleansing her of the pain of loss. And once she pays a midnight visit to Pigalle, the red-light district of Paris, its seedy quarters bathed in red light to signify descent into the underworld that is an element of every myth. Here Julie confronts the shadow-side of her existence, and it is less about shame-in-hiding than about the *self-in-hiding:* she has faced and accepted what it means to be human, including her basest emotions, thoughts, and desires. New truths reveal themselves to her, and Julie's past and future come together with clarity. Eventually, perhaps for the first time, she will truly become alive to herself and to others. She will become Julie, who, having made many stops along aloneness's vast spectrum—from isolation to alienation to emptiness to loneliness—eventually arrives in its haven of solitude. Here, Julie will learn to love herself enough to compose her own music, and she will be able to accept love from others and to love in return.

Blue brilliantly dramatizes the kind of major life crossing that every woman alone must make, sometimes more than once. In such instances, we enter a time of transition that is above and beyond our daily round of activities. Rarely do we pass through such crossings without experiencing great suffering, fear, and helplessness; nor are we able to recognize the profound teachings they offer other than by going through them, for when circumstances overtake us, we are forced to stop dead in our tracks.

Julie's experience, which begins in nothingness, makes it stunningly clear that aloneness isn't emptiness, though it may start out feeling like that. Julie is simply in communion with herself. She has accepted that aloneness is a basic condition of the human experience that is different from, but on a continuum with, being in relationship. It is the gateway leading us back to our self.

Loss of any kind throws us back on ourselves—into that psychic space where the self can break down before it begins to heal. Healing has its own rhythm and tempo—long pauses of inertia, when it feels like nothing is happening or ever will again. Like Julie, we are often obliged to abide in the inertial state of "no thing" before change can happen of its own accord.

As a young adult in her twenties, Inge lost her moorings. She had always wanted to be a nurse, and after she completed her training, she started to work in a large municipal hospital in San Francisco. There she fell in love with one of her patients, a woman who had been diagnosed with leukemia. Knowing that her prognosis was poor, the woman at first kept Inge at a distance; then she, too, yielded to the deeper feelings that had grown between them. Fully aware that they would probably have little time together, they decided to live together, come what may. When the woman died eight months later, Inge fell apart. As she put it, "I felt I had lost my soul mate . . . it was almost more than I could bear. I just knew something was broken inside." Inge decided she had to leave California and moved to New York. It took another two years before she was ready to go back into nursing. "Now," Inge says, "my passion is back—whatever broke got mended. Gratitude for the time we had together seemed to dissolve my anger for it being taken away. It's made me a different person— much stronger than I was before."

When she first realized that her need to be the perfect mother was causing her children considerable anxiety, Lara began to reassess her priorities. "I've been living this terribly robotic life, all because of my fear of losing control. It happens with everything," she said, "not just planning the week's menus and wiping up the counters but my work, my routines, everything." The week following her insight, Lara got up to make breakfast, but as soon as the children left for school, she felt overcome by depression and went back to bed. She did this again the next day, and the next. For the first time that she could remember, she allowed herself the luxury of disorder, and it brought her straight up against the reason for her aggressive assertion of control. She began to realize that since childhood it had been a way to stem the chaotic feelings inside her growing up with a demanding, alcoholic mother. "I'm beginning to understood that there are many things I have no answer for in my life," Lara says. What she now has to do is stay in her uncertainty, let her mind poke into spaces it could never go to before, and trust that insights will follow.

Donna, a single woman living on her own, did not learn that she was about to deliver a stillborn child until the day she went into labor. That was when her whole life changed. "None of the doctors told me anything right away. The nurses were prepping me, measuring the baby's heart rate. Then a resident comes in and scrutinizes the tape. And I just knew looking at her face that something was wrong, even before she said it. Then she left and more doctors came in. But they never talked to me, or even looked at me." After the delivery, Donna asked to see her dead child. "I couldn't lift my head for twenty-four hours because of the spinal, but I insisted on making the funeral arrangements myself. I needed to give myself closure, and I knew that unless I buried my baby, I'd never know he was dead." Afterward, Donna says, she "felt nuts for I don't know how long because life didn't feel the same." That was the starting point from which she began to pick up the pieces of her life, and she let herself tiptoe back into the world slowly.

On a Sunday afternoon in July, Joan and her husband, Max, were playing a relaxed game of croquet with friends. Joan thought Max seemed a little sluggish, but he was so clearly enjoying himself, she resisted saying anything. Still, she was concerned. The valve-replacement surgery he had had eight months earlier had taken its toll, and he had aged a lot. That evening, Max went upstairs to take a bath before dinner. After about thirty minutes, Joan called up to ask when he would be coming down. When he didn't answer, she went upstairs to find Max lying dead in the tub. He had finally succumbed to a heart attack.

When she thinks about that first year after Max's death, Joan isn't sure how she made it through—that stunning power of loss that made her lose her natural rhythm, slow down to such a pace that it felt as if she were tunneling through an endless day. Reflecting back two years later, what seems most significant to her is the power of the unanticipated: "The pain of losing Max was so complete; I would wander through the rooms of the house looking for him, completely numb. It was so sudden, so final, it derailed me." Even things as mundane as cooking a meal jarred her. "In the beginning, I couldn't even go into the kitchen except to make coffee. I certainly couldn't imagine making dinner for myself; we had always done that together, so instead I ate out." Joan relived their time together, the joy as well as the disappointments, and was haunted by questions about the relationship. "I would ask myself, Who was he? Who was I? And especially, Who was I with him? And Who am I without him?"

That first year, Joan spent a lot of time away from home, visiting different members of her family, especially around holidays, when memories of times she'd been with Max were simply too overwhelming to absorb. She also took comfort in the ongoing presence of her two cats, Diego and Romeo. "We didn't have children together," she says, laughing, "but we had our cats; they're still a tie to Max."

The process of releasing, imperceptible at first, began to take hold sometime near the end of the first year; by the second year, Joan knew it was firmly under way. "The firsts," she says, "are the hardest, like the first anniversary of Max's death, but it was true for all the holidays we spent together." There were also the first quiet days of "coming down to earth again," when Joan discovered that it was as important to spend time in her house as it had earlier been to be away. "I allowed myself to traverse all the steps that we took together, day in, day out. I think you have to go through that, and that if you leave too soon, you're just escaping the inevitable."

Joan has been learning who she is in revelations that come in the quiet hours before dawn, in the stillness of dusk, in long, winding evenings. "It's so painful—the idea that I'm no longer a wife with a husband. It's an amazing feeling when your whole direction, your whole forward-moving togetherness, is suddenly over. I'm not sure how to quantify it, I just know that it's completely different from being alone when I was with Max. I guess I'm talking about the big alone, and it still frightens me."

On good days, and there are beginning to be more of them, she is Joan Sayles, a woman with her own "strong opinions" and a "huge willpower" that she knows will propel her back into photography as she gets ready to resume her career. On the bad days, she is still "Mrs. Max Sayles," who goes to the movies too much because it's "safe." Joan says there is still one big battle she has left: getting over the feeling "that you have to have a man to be complete." She received that message so long ago, it settled inside her. "And I know if I release it— no, *as* I release it—it will free me up for something new to come in."

WHATEVER HAPPENED TO NORA?

In *A Doll's House,* Ibsen's masterful portrayal of a dutiful and orna- mental wife who becomes a sovereign and independent woman in her own right, Nora Helmer leaves her home, husband, and three young children, closing the door on the domestic world she never, even in her wildest dreams, imagined leaving. She does so because she finally understands that she has lived as a false self and needs to break free from the constricting mold in which her father, husband, and society have placed her. Ibsen wrote the play in 1879, eight years after he met Laura Petersen, the young Norwegian girl whose tragic story was the source of his inspiration.

Briefly, the "real" story goes like this: Laura married a Danish schoolmaster who subsequently contracted tuberculosis. Doctors pre- scribed recuperation in a warm climate, but because there was little money and the situation was urgent, Laura secretly arranged a loan, secured by a friend. The couple went to Italy, where the husband made a full recovery. But when the loan came due two years later, Laura couldn't repay it, nor could her friend, whose own fortunes had fallen. Terrified to tell her husband, Laura forged a check in a desperate attempt to pay off the loan. The forgery was discovered, and when the story came out, rather than show appreciation, Laura's husband treated her as a common criminal, declaring her an unfit wife and mother. She suffered a nervous breakdown, and he had her committed to a public asylum. Although Laura eventually persuaded her husband to take her back for their children's sake, he did so grudgingly and never forgave her. In his eyes, she remained a moral outcast.

Nora, too, worships her husband; she, too, sacrifices and shames herself to save him; and she, too, hopes vainly for the "miracle" of her husband's grace. But when Torvald fails to appreciate what she has done for him, she does not plead for forgiveness, or ask to be reinstated as wife and mother. Instead, staring at the face of her own complicity for having allowed herself to live as Torvald's "little skylark," a frivolous and pampered "plaything" in "a doll's house," just as she had been her father's "doll-child," Nora is shocked into wakefulness, and has a thought so heretical for her time that those around her might have easily mistaken it for madness: she realizes that she obeys a higher morality than the one father, husband, and society have taught her, and that her most "sacred" duty is to herself. She tells Torvald: "I believe that I am a human being, just as much as you are—or at least I will try to become one. I know most people would agree with you, Torvald. And books say things like that. *But I am not satisfied now with what most people say or with what it says in books. I need to think about these things for myself and find out about them* [my italics]." And so she does, fully aware she is plunging headlong into uncertainty.

Nora leaves her home for the last time later that evening, shutting the door with what George Bernard Shaw called "the door slam heard round the world"—and ushering in a new beginning for all women by reminding us that we have the power to "revision" our lives. Nora's act consummates her realization of what she does *not* want for herself, what is no longer right or possible for her. It is symbolic, as much about consciousness as about action. By no means am I suggesting that we should all be like Nora. Rather, Nora shows the growth of consciousness that precedes and stimulates action. Ibsen's heroine offers a vastly creative view of the sovereignty of a woman's self—reminding us that we are *all* Noras—whenever we venture forth into self-discovery.

From the moment *A Doll's House* first appeared, every actress worth her mettle—from Eleonora Duse to Claire Bloom to Jane Fonda—has vied for the chance to play Nora. One of the best was British actress Janet McTeer, who, like all of us, saw the Nora in herself. "The fit was perfect," she said, "because playing her was exactly the point of intersection where my life and Nora's converged." McTeer had left home at the age of sixteen, fully aware that it was "terrifying to walk out alone, hearing the echo of your own words, '*I don't even know what's going to happen to me.*'"

Stepping out is always just the beginning of the story, the visible tip of the transformational shift under way. When Nora leaves, she doesn't know where she is going. She doesn't have any practical skills. She doesn't know how she will support herself. Still, she leaves. Nora's worldview changed, and her intention became stronger than the voice of her husband or social convention. The integrity and strength of her choice made a vivid impression on McTeer. "Nora has a tremendous fighting spirit. It's carried her through eight years of sacrificing in secret for Torvald. Now she would apply that same fighting spirit to herself." For each new generation of women who see the play, Nora remains an archetype. Indeed, the Nora McTeer played onstage— from *inside* herself—is a stunning reminder of the core of strength and self-determination that lives in each of us—whether we are changing careers, leaving a lover, getting a divorce, coping with a disease, discovering widowhood, reaching old age, or finding our way into solitude.

"It's the survival instinct that kept Nora going," McTeer said finally. "That and making choices. I'm a straight woman who has chosen to be an actor, and not to have children or be married, thank you very much . . . because that's what I've chosen." Then she paused and looked directly at me. "As for Nora, I think she'll be fine." So will the rest of us, if we do what we have to do.

PINNED ABOVE MY desk is a *New Yorker* cartoon by BEK that nips playfully at the theme of stepping out. It shows a woman sitting alone on her sofa, telling her phone mate, "I'm still a work-in-hiding." Meanwhile, it is likely that she ducks for cover; hugs her living room sofa for dear life; sits behind her office desk as another month, or year, rolls around; stays in a bad relationship because she's afraid to be alone; tolerates her friend's envy; and so on. The crucial question is: How might this woman emerge from her hiding place—step out and beyond her old self?

One of the hardest challenges women alone face is deciding not to hide but to step forth into our lives, knowing that there will always be more work to do. For we human beings are like dissonant notes that refuse to allow fixed and permanent harmonic resolutions. We might call this natural *dis*harmony in our nature *ambiguity* and, however reluctantly, give it room inside ourselves. We do this because we must: because life teaches us that nothing stays the same; because we hold opposite feelings simultaneously—joy with sadness, the bitter with the sweet, even hate with love; and because there will always be eddies running against our primary emotional current. Like a room with windows open to different weathers, ambiguity adds a poignant richness to our lives.

In *The Beauty of the Husband,* the writer Anne Carson speaks of marriage as "that swaying place," to convey the ambiguous feelings that are bound to arise as we travel its path. There are, however, many swaying places in life, since many states give rise to ambiguous feelings—being in love, motherhood, autonomy, work, creativity, aging, and aloneness among them. "It's just me pushing against my habit of sadness," says Sally, one of the women I work with, as she learns to navigate through the fog of ambiguity that sometimes settles over her. But who exactly is doing the pushing? Isn't it more accurate to say that the life force inside us—consciousness itself—thrusts us forward, propelling us to be and to act, sculpting the self anew so that it may evolve? We push on with our lives because at heart we are love and beauty bound. Sometimes we call this force resilience, knowing that its mobilizing potential is at the heart of any recovery, but, in truth, its power lies beyond any name.

Though our journey as women alone begins in fear, it ends, hopefully, in renewal. Befriending aloneness, we learn the creative potential of solitude, wherein we can recover, reclaim, and learn to express self. But we must be willing to allow the process of discovery to occur naturally. This means that we must sit with, not run from, the discomforting feelings of shame, guilt, self-blame, and more that sometimes afflict us. For it is a truism that as we confront our fears, by acting in spite of and *through* them, tentatively at first, then with increasing confidence, we begin to recover the integrity of self that we so yearn for. Integrity refers to an inner wholeness, wherein a person is not divided from herself by shame or low self-esteem. We know then that we have crossed the line away from ignorance and toward our own innate wisdom.

SELF-POSSESSION

In my work as a psychotherapist, I have seen a succession of women trying to reclaim the self. They come seeking relief from the pain of something that has gone awry in their lives, which could be anything from breaking up with a boyfriend to marriage wounds to a hypercritical boss to some undefined but persistent angst. But as soon as that pain has abated just a little, and they begin to listen to their inner feelings, they discover that they are far more severe on themselves than anything the outside world has to offer. That's when they begin to get in touch with the fears that have been holding the self in thralldom.

Yet, sooner or later, the self will appear. It has gone into hiding because it was too raw and vulnerable to survive otherwise, or, in writer Peggy Orenstein's words, because it has experienced "things too tender to tell." For to whom does a woman tell her painful truths when she feels *unseen*? To feel invisible is to believe that we are with out worth, and nothing sends the self into hiding faster. Such loss of self often reveals itself in a woman's dreams. A woman whose energy is blocked might, for example, dream of herself as a large mammal— a stallion brought to its knees; an ape trapped behind bars; a caged panther endlessly circling; a white porpoise lashed to a ship's mast, desperately trying to breathe out of its element. A woman suffering neglect might be more likely to conjure up images of smaller aban- doned creatures—a starving kitten or puppy or an infant alone in her carriage, forgotten. Or the identity of a self might be splayed, as in one patient's dream of a half-human, half-fishlike creature that slipped out of her mother's body. But as we begin to get in touch with these feelings and acknowledge the "tender things" we carry inside, little by little the self dares to show itself. The stallion gallops, the ape is uncaged, the panther sprints, the porpoise swims in its natural ele- ment; these creatures are, after all, descriptions of energy that is now free to help the self assume its true dimensions.

SELF-BLESSING

There is still a missing piece we need to set in place before we are ready to step out. This is the blessing that consecrates the self and sets it in motion, and which the poet Galway Kinnell has written about in "Saint Francis and the Sow" with deep, heartfelt wisdom: "The bud/stands for all things,/even for those things that don't flower,/for everything flowers, from within, of self-blessing." The word *blessing* is one of the richest, most confluent in our language. From its

English roots, *blessing* carries the meaning of consecration and holiness, but also of the mark of blood. From French, the verb *blesser*—to wound—bespeaks the blood wound that makes every blessing sacred and holy. A blessing, then, is an act of reverence that bestows protection, holiness, and love on the benefactor. But Kinnell is also saying that the deepest blessing is the one you bestow upon yourself.

Sometimes, as Kinnell also reminds us, our capacity for self-blessing must be awakened from without: for "sometimes it is necessary to reteach a thing its loveliness, put a hand on the brow of the flower and retell it in words and in touch it is lovely." The "hand on the brow" is the offering of one human being toward another. It may come from parental or companionate love, the compassionate caring of a minister toward her flock or of a therapist toward her patient, or the healing energy of certain family members, friends, or communities. What matters above all is that the touch of this hand be as full of affirmation as it is free of self-interest. Then it can help the woman to gather her own strength so that she does not have to lean on another.

Blessing is also an initiation. The path of a woman's journey reaches, after all, far beyond her passage from girlhood to womanhood, which means that we will need not one, but many, ritual markers to help us find our way from one life-crossing to the next. Each threshold, each divide between crossings, marks a real moment in time. It also has profound mythic and symbolic content. Both need to be recognized.

Think of all the markers in your own life when something happened to change you, when you realized in a simple but defined way that you were different than before. Think of the blessing you gave yourself—or received from others. Or did not. And know that it is never too late.

Chapter Seven

STEPPING OUT

REVISIONING OUR STORIES

nce upon a time ... my story begins. But where is the beginning? Does it start with my parents or theirs? Does it include my habit of sleeping until the last possible minute, my nervous laugh, my fears of inadequacy, or of germs, my cat allergy, or the friends I choose?

Once upon a time ... I insert a story into my life, which becomes part of my life. So which part is true, and which is false? And does it really matter?

Once upon a time ... I become my story's ruthless editor, willing to go to great lengths to create a seamless version of myself. I exaggerate, distort, and censor information, sometimes deliberately, but sometimes without meaning to.

Once upon a time ... the story I tell myself starts to break down. First, small pieces splinter off, then chunks fall away, and, finally, my vision clears. I catch a glimpse of what I might be like without my false story. That's when I find a small wedge of faith—some heart opening that wasn't there before—and I pick it up and use it as my walking stick to keep on going.

THE RHYTHMS OF CHANGE

In the Green Mountains of Vermont, it's not much fun driving at night on a rutted back road when the fog is so thick you can't see two feet beyond the windshield and there's nothing to do but slow down, try to stay calm, and bump patiently along. Change is just like this foggy back road: we are heading somewhere but can't see what lies ahead. And because we live in a fog of unknowing—able to imagine a future based only on what we have already experienced—we often imagine the worst and opt for the status quo. We crave change; we are afraid of change; but, most of all, we are afraid *to* change. So we stay stuck in our old story, hoping for the best but not really sure it can happen. For stepping out to begin, we need faith and the articles of faith: patience and a willingness to respect and be gentle to ourselves. This is how change happens.

IN HER ILLUMINATING work *Faith: Trusting Your Own Deepest Experience,* author and meditation teacher Sharon Salzberg examines the cycle of fear and hope that kept her in a prison of despair until she realized that she had mistakenly bound her hope to fear rather than to faith. As a child, Sharon was convinced that the reason things never seemed to change for the better was because she "didn't deserve to be happy." Harsh circumstances in her childhood gave her plenty of reasons to believe this. At the age of four, her adored father suddenly disappeared and she and her mother moved in to live with her aunt and uncle. One night, she and her mother were alone watching a favorite TV program together. Her mother was recovering from surgery and seemed to be doing fine. Suddenly, she started to bleed profusely. Before an ambulance rushed her to the hospital, Sharon's mother told her to call her grandmother, whom she barely knew, to come get her. She never saw her mother alive again. Sharon was nine. Two years later, her father returned home a broken man; within weeks, he overdosed on sleeping pills and spent the rest of his life in an institution. Sharon continued to live with her grandparents, but was devastated by their ironclad silence around these terrible losses and uprootings. She turned her grief and anger inward in the form of a profound lassitude. This was her way to distance herself from the world.

"Faith," says the Bible, "is the substance of things hoped for, the evidence of things not seen": it is the grounding place of hope (Hebrews 11:1). Having grown up with no control over the cataclysmic events that robbed her of her childhood, Sharon voided her desires, and told herself that nothing mattered. At sixteen, she entered college and was obliged to choose a field of academic study—that is, to move in one direction or another. She chose philosophy and enrolled in a Buddhism course. For the first time, she sensed that things could be different. This "glimmer of possibility" is the beginning of faith.

Through her own suffering, she eventually realized that fear had deadened her life force by holding her apart from herself—and from other people. To reengage in a different way, she knew that she would have to stop trying to control what life might bring and instead put her trust in the one place it had the capacity to flourish: her heart.

That's when hope began to turn into faith. Fear didn't vanish from Sharon's life; yet, tempered by this intuitive, transcendent knowledge, it loosened its terrible hold on her. She began to understand that change is always frightening, and that some quotient of fear would accompany her—as indeed it does all of us as we begin letting go of our false story and journey forward. As she expressed it, "Faith enables us, despite our fear, to get as close as possible to the truth of the present moment, so that we can offer our hearts fully to it, with integrity." Faith is what allows us to step into what we don't know and can't control: the Unknown. In the words of an old Chinese proverb: "If I keep the green bough in my heart, then the singing bird will come." Faith transcends logic, reason, and intellect, for it is the bough and the bird and the heart.

A woman alone often has a particularly hard time revisioning her story. The more we begin to remake our lives, the more strenuously the voices of shame and fear will try to bully us back into inertia. If we listen to them, the tracks of our storytelling imagination will peter out in a vast desert of loneliness. These are the voices that belong to our old life, the ones that tried to persuade us that things aren't as bad as we think they are, that whisper in our ears: you'll never make it on your own; you're thirty, by now you should be married and starting a family; it's selfish to have a child on your own; divorce is failure; you can't leave him, it's better to be with someone—*any*one—than to be alone; no one wants you, what a loser; and, finally, the clincher—you are nothing without a man.

What women alone need to hear is the voice that refutes these assumptions, that implores us to honor ourselves, that reassures us that change is possible, that says we are fully capable of making our own choices. This voice is in each one of us. It's the voice of the young girl we once knew, exulted in, and then lost track of—or, like Sharon, buried—the best friend we haven't seen in thirty years or more. *This* voice speaks up. When we are making love with our partners, it is not shy about telling them what we like. It allows us to say to our children, "I love you, but this is *my* time to myself." It asks for help when we are overworked and stressed. It doesn't hesitate to ask the boss for the raise we know we deserve.

We learn to know the sound of this voice because it belongs to us. Its words do not continue to divide us from ourselves but rather begin to make us feel whole. It is the voice of our authentic self, and, for most of us, its sound has been muffled for so long that when we do begin to hear it, it can sound too loud and rude: it says things a good girl doesn't say, even if we blush and try to tone it down.

Many women sadly tell me their own authentic voice sounds "too large," "too overbearing," "too demanding," or "too powerful." Ironically, although we may feel great entitlement in our professional lives, have no qualms about spending a lot of money on clothes or taking a vacation, the decibel level of our voice is out of hearing range when it comes to the places deep inside us that wait to be awakened.

Women have a long history of knowing how to survive, how to get by, how to fashion an acceptable life for ourselves, but when it comes to our own bone-deep nourishment, to even *knowing* what we truly want and need, too many of us wrestle with the feeling that we don't deserve this kind of care. We still cover up and compensate for the deep unworthiness we feel. And if we don't feel powerful in our own right, choice feels risky. Many women are afraid to make any decision to change their lives, for fear they might make the wrong one, even though doing nothing is itself a choice. Choice means assertion; it's a dynamic thrust carrying the force of our intention behind it—not a boss's, a friend's, a husband's, or a child's—and that can feel inherently dangerous. "I want to know my own will and move with it," says a woman who is still on the fence, fantasizing about a new life, but is not yet ready to act. But waiting, too, is part of the process. Right now, she is looking for her own walking stick. When she finds it, she'll move on.

We, who are so schooled in the art of listening to the voices of others, can often hear our own voice only when we are alone, safely away from the noisy demands of children or partners or work. For many women, the first choice, then, is to give ourselves the necessary time and space in which to renew our acquaintance with our lost voice, to learn to recognize it, and to rejoice as we hear it express our truth. For women who already spend more time alone than they want to, that same choice means staying with the uncomfortable feelings that might arise, trying not to block them out or deny them, and having the faith that when we do, our true voice will eventually cut its way, beat a path, trudge through all the static we hear inside and outside ourselves and the muffled, compensatory sounds we utter back. We will listen as it answers our most persistent questions, "Who am I—as woman, creator, mother, child, lover, partner, human being?" Its answers do not continue to divide us from ourselves but rather begin to make us feel whole.

In *The Naked Voice,* Chloe Goodchild, a singer and teacher who lives and works in England, writes:

> *I had an "inner voice" which spoke to me in dreams and in my work. This inner voice was my life-line, and I trusted it more than my own life, although it did not make life any easier for me. It even disrupted my personal life, requiring me to make decisions that were often very painful to bear. Still I listened to it—I had to. This voice was as dear to me as my own heart-beat. It would not let me rest until I came face-to-face with freedom. Then, at last, a mirror shone with undeniable clarity in my face, reflecting back to me the deepest ground of my being. The loneliness disappeared.*

Events happen quickly—earthquakes, getting lost, twisting an ankle, graduating from college—but change does not. We do a perfect swan dive off a twenty-foot high board, hear the cheers, and revel in the moment. Only we know how much practice and how many belly flops went into it. We know from experience that change is hard work. We also know that it is never linear. We love taking a giant step forward, but lose heart having to move two steps back until we're ready for the next giant step. When we confront our fears, what we need most of all is to have faith both in ourselves and in the process. Then we can trust that there will be more forks in the road, that any setback paves the way for more opportunities than we have ever dreamed of. Such turning places grow visible as we *practice,* sometimes over and over, repeating the same steps until we get it right.

That is all we can do. What happens beyond that is out of our hands. For while the self is always in flux, the grounded sense of our own being—its felt presence—emits a vibration of well-being. That is what we must listen for, and we always know when we are getting close. Sometimes it will feel as if an eternity passes before the right note is struck. This is when faith matters most. Faith is our tuning fork, just as patience is our guide, teaching us to persist until we can sound out what we feel intuitively and live accordingly.

Most of us are feverishly impatient. In fact, we are socialized to be overstimulated. Modern life virtually demands impatience, forever reminding us about all the things we should hurry up about or miss out on: things we should buy, how we should look, what we should have for ourselves, and how to get it—fast. We are amped up emotionally, overworked and overloaded with tasks that shrink time and subtract it from our personal lives. Time is always at our back, dogging us, making us anxious. So we shift our impatience onto things—jars or medicine vials that don't pop open, spilled coffee grounds, missed taxis, late planes, electronic phone menus, a frozen computer. The doctor or hairdresser who keeps us waiting, a friend who's always late, a dawdling child, can drive us crazy, eating up precious seconds we have allocated for the next urgent task. We are so terrified of not getting the job done, or of losing out, that we resist every opportunity to stay quiet, alone, and in communion with ourselves. In fact, we often interpret quiescence as a sign that we are failing, falling short by not living our lives to the hilt. And yet, when we finally let ourselves get there, solitude is the only place we can relax, take stock, and silence the chattering of our hyperactive minds and still-restless bodies.

To be in solitude requires patience. Patience allows us to stay in the present without knowing or trying to rush or control the outcome. Patience allows time for reflection and change, but also for error, backsliding, and even relapse, before we are ready to start again.

"I need to know it's okay to fail," says Dora, a gifted and energetic graduate student who has just completed her master's in journalism and whose old story about what constitutes "success" interferes with revisioning her new one. Dora's parents are both successful writers, so it is no wonder that her need to measure up to them had nearly drowned out her own voice. Every time she sat down to write, she drew a blank. "I imagine my parents looking at what I'm writing and shaking their heads. How do I get rid of them?" she asks. "What about telling them to quit looking over your shoulder?" I suggest. "That's good, but it's not enough," Dora answers. "I think I'll tell them to get a life." Dora has recently made it her practice to write an entire draft before she edits herself. When the censoring voices show up, she tells them to leave. She is learning that the most important thing is to show up for herself—over and over again—and keep on going.

Patience teaches us to fall and get back up again: to try again when we falter, as often as it takes. A firm, steadfast, yet gentle energy, patience stills the turbulence around us so that we may develop focus, concentrate, and persevere. Never awed by the passage of time, patience understands that we reach plateaus, where it can feel like nothing is happening, and sometimes we even backslide. Cervantes said, "Have patience, and shuffle your cards." Given that we have only one deck to play with, we need to heed this advice.

IN *START WHERE You Are,* the Tibetan Buddhist teacher and author Pema Chodron writes about the starting point for the self-exploration that eventually leads to change: "You may be the most violent person in the world—that's a fine place to start. That's a very rich place to start—juicy, smelly. You might be the most depressed person in the world, the most addicted person in the world, the most jealous person in the world. You might think that there are no others on the planet who hate themselves as much as you do. All of that is a good place to start. Just where you are—that's the place to start." Chodron is talking about Tonglen meditation practice, but her advice applies just as readily to any effort we make to change.

Begin, then, where you are, *not* where you want to be. Begin stuck in the doldrums of your false story—if that is where you are. Begin there because, in truth, there is no other place to start from. Tell yourself that you are going to listen for the sound of your own voice—and remind yourself when you forget. And you will forget, over and over again. Use as your beacon any glimpse you have ever had, or may have, of another, preferred way to be, and act in this world. Shun stereotypes in whatever mouths they appear: strangers, parents, friends, lovers, partners, broadcasters, film stars, politicians. Question every *should* and *ought* that crosses your path by listening to how it makes you feel—in your throat, chest, solar plexus, stomach, navel, groin. Know that you are on the right path—your path—whenever you feel your own voice kicking inside you like a babe in the womb. Expect that it will be weak and trembling for a long time and keep exercising it, just as you would any other muscle in your body. Gradually, it will grow clear and sturdy and you will learn to distinguish its sound from all others because it carries the warm tones of your heart. If you feel disembodied, breathe slowly and evenly to pull yourself back down into your body again. Your voice will follow.

Above all, remember to let your story unfold according to its natural rhythms. This is tricky, since you will try to get a step, then two, then even more, ahead of yourself. And when things don't work out according to plan, clear the way and leave room for open endings. Often, you will think you're out of step with everyone else. You will forget that there is no such thing as a generically "correct" sequence of growing into yourself; there is only *your* sequence. This will be disappointing and even alarming at times, especially in moments when you want to be with someone and the right person isn't there;

or you reach perimenopause and want to have a child; or if right after you have a child your partner leaves you. There will be times when you get the very thing you wanted and it turns sour on you; or you get something you don't want instead. For most people, flexibility and resilience are skills we left back in childhood. Your own story depends on both; otherwise, it will dry up like kindling. Know that your story is never finished. Nor would you want it to be. The Unknown always rides with change; if you fear it, it will seem like a tsunami heading in your direction. As your fear diminishes, it will simply be the next thing that comes into your life.

Change often enters our lives when we least expect it. Kennedy Fraser was about to begin writing *Ornament and Silence: Essays on Women's Lives* when a small but significant personal event occurred. "A man of my own age, with whom I was talking at a party, withdrew his attention from me to look hungrily over my shoulder at a pretty young woman many years my junior. As a younger woman I had relied on the attention of older men and depended on their approval. I saw very clearly, in that instant when the man's gaze shifted, that one kind of power had passed from me. The time had come to develop other resources."

At fifty-one, just weeks after she and her lover parted ways, Frieda, as she describes it, "entered menopause. It changed everything. It was similar to the way I felt as a teenager starting to menstruate—the strange sense that your body, the house you inhabit, is no longer the house you know—and it was weird and disorienting. I think I'm going to have to rearrange my perception of what 'sexiness' is."

Candice, in her mid-sixties and recently married to her companion of eight years, told me that she and her husband could go for weeks without sex. "My libido will never be as it was." She sighs. She is giving up her femme-fatale image of herself, timeless in one sense, very much belonging to age thirty-five or fortyish in another.

Lena, a trim brunette in her mid-forties, has been wondering aloud, What path should I be on? In real life, the word *unattainable* stayed in

Lena's head like an old refrain, coloring every goal she imagined for herself. She had been a screenwriter for years and sold a number of scripts that had never been made into movies. Thus she had never achieved her neon-lit version of success—"the 180 degrees between 'coming close' and 'making it.'" To Lena, selling a script wasn't enough. "I want A to Z—the hit movie, the Academy Award, me on stage in my Prada gown remembering who to thank— all the razzle-dazzle!"

Eventually, Lena decided to give up screenwriting. But if she wasn't a screenwriter, who was she? "I'm inadequate," was her instant answer, "a mediocre screenwriter and an inadequate human being." Lena spent the next few years waitressing at a posh Beverly Hills restaurant and, as she expressed it, "marking time in purgatory," before she began to pay attention to "a crazy idea for a novel that had always been dancing in my head and dared to play around with it." That period was the loneliest of her life. "I just sat there with every dream, every idea of success I'd ever had, every idea about who *I* was, and watched myself letting them go, one by one. Even with less money than I'd ever had in my life, I wasn't in that desperate place of feeling like a failure any longer." In fits and starts, Lena started writing "a lot of gibberish. It was terrifying. On any given day I didn't know if something or nothing would come out." Many days, Lena simply stayed in bed, trying to shrug off negative judgments with the realization, "I guess that's what babies do—go limp. Something was telling me not to fight what was happening." Besides, in fits and starts, something *was* coming through, pages were stacking up, and she was writing again. She attributed her doggedness to "some part of me which keeps me going when there is everything *but* certainty." About this time, Lena dreamed that she was visiting a place called "the Newell Company." The "new well" of Lena's dream is the source of Lena's burgeoning faith, patience, and self-respect. She had indeed stepped out of her old story, and the book she once shrugged off is coming through.

CREATIVE LIVING

In *A Life of One's Own,* the British psychoanalyst, writer, and painter Marion Milner (using the pseudonym Joanna Field), describes how, at twenty-six, feeling a vague but pressing discontent with her life, she began to keep a diary to see if she could find out what "kinds of experiences made me happy" and what she really wanted out of life. To all outward appearances, things couldn't have been better. She had received a First Class Honors Degree in psychology and was earning a good living doing research and lecturing. She had plenty of friends and lovers, and enough leisure time to enjoy them. Still, Milner sensed that something fundamental was missing from her life— some "gap between knowing and living" that she ardently wished to close. Rather than rely on her intellect, as she had always done, she decided she would try to learn from her senses—or, as she put it, through "the whole of my body." To do so, she began to pay close attention to the way she lived each moment, noticing how one thought, and then another, like stones thrown into water, agitated her mind and disturbed the currents of her experience.

What she discovered—something many of us may know intellec-tually but rarely allow ourselves to assimilate as "felt thought"—was that she had two ways of seeing: one was the narrow path of reason, which helped her gather, order, and sort information; the other was the wide-angle path of intuition, which allowed her to gain under-standing through all her senses and, more important, made her feel she was living life to the fullest. Yet, as thrilling as this felt, Milner soon found herself beset by old, unconscious, and very much ingrained ten-dencies that repeatedly led her to disregard her intuitive choices in favor of rational thinking. She realized how much she had let herself be influenced by values that her friends, family, and colleagues accepted uncritically: "being good at one's job, pleasing people, being popular, not missing things, doing what's expected of one, not letting people down, helping people, being happy." But this version of "being happy" belonged to others; Milner wanted her own. Her list of wants included the time and leisure to selectively "get at things" of her own choosing—like living "among things that grow—a child; a garden, and quietness"; lots of laughter; and a chance to play for the sheer purposeless joy of it. And she marveled at how difficult it was to give herself these things. In short, what Milner came up against in herself some seventy-odd years ago are the same doubts and conflicts that continue to beset women today as we try to fit ourselves into mass-produced values rather than discovering, and living by, our own.

Not to be deterred, Milner vowed to herself that she would pursue her own way, trying not to censor herself even if it meant going against the verdict of her harshest internal judgment: that she was *selfish*. For if *selfish* meant finding out what made her feel alive, well, then, selfish she would be. This was far easier said than done, of course, but Milner continued her exploration for personal satisfaction for the next seven years. In the fourth year, she began to write *A Life of One's Own,* which, based on her diary entries, was to become a classic for its depth of observation, clarity of expression, and almost ruthless candor in revealing her personal thoughts and feelings.

Milner had a great appetite for life—walking on a country road at twilight could make her laugh until the tears came for the sheer pleasure of being alive, but so did talking to strangers in a café, making love, taking in her surroundings, playing a musical instrument, buying pretty clothes, and, always, studying the behavior of her fellow human beings. Yet her quest for happiness is what touches us most; for as time passed, and as she allowed herself the solitude to watch, to take in, to simply be that is so necessary for such an undertaking—all the while living an active life—she discovered, to her great surprise, that the "best things" in her life had nothing to do with "successes, either in friendships or work or play," but were related to "very small moments" when she let her rational mind fall away and was able to take in the world intuitively.

In this pursuit, her "worst sin" was to let herself be pulled blindly in all directions so that she had no vitality left for needs that belonged to her personal self. Sorting out her personal preferences from others, Milner writes: "[They] assume that what happens is what matters, where you go, what you do, things that happen, the good time that you have. But often I believe it's none of these things, it's the times between, the long days when nothing happens, the odd moments, perhaps when you open a letter, or sit alone in a restaurant, or exchange the time of day with a stranger." Soon after she completed her book, Milner decided to become a psychoanalyst. Altogether, she continued her diary for twenty-five years. Her pioneering exploration of our need for a truly personal life and her awareness that this pursuit is itself an art form is the legacy she leaves to us.

Consciously or not, we all want to live our personal lives. We would then be in our original home, so to speak, and comfortable enough to live creatively. "Creative living"—as Winnicott termed it—does not mean only the creative life of the artist. To make art is wondrous, enriching, and indispensable. But it is just as essential to enjoy the freedom to live creatively whatever we may be doing, whether it's slicing carrots, cutting flowers, trading bonds, baking bread, taking a walk, drawing a breath, riding a bus—or—writing poems, symphonies, or novels. The portrait of the artist is really about the creative spark that exists in each of us, young, old, and in between, that is enlivened by solitude. When that spark is ignited, our lives feel rich and meaningful; when it stays buried, we go about the business of living ready-made, compliant, rule-dominated lives, wondering what went wrong and how to change it.

Infants and toddlers whose early environments do not offer enough comfort and security often can't access the creative freedom inherent in play because it is harder for them to feel spontaneous and free. Watch any young child at play and see how she withdraws her attention from the outer world, choosing and manipulating objects like blocks, sand, and playdough in service to some inner, dreamlike, private imagining. But the child can only play when she is relaxed and unguarded—that is, when she can trust the space she inhabits and the mothering figure who attends her. Play is a creative act, Winnicott reminds us, because it is both satisfying and exciting and also involves the body. But when children who don't play become women who can't play, we must learn to grant ourselves the opportunity by daring to confront our lurking fear of ending up alone in the playpen. Play is, in fact, the central organizing feature of creative living—what all life-affirming creatures do. Animals play. So do humans. We do so because, as Johan Huizinga says in *Homo Ludens,* "All play means something." The creative impulse of play moves artists to produce their works. But the creative impulse resides just as emphatically in our moment-to-moment experience of living. It is present in our fantasies, the make-believe worlds we create, and the delight and spontaneity we so often find, even in the most ordinary of occasions. To be playful with ourselves is a kind of self-acceptance. To laugh at ourselves lightens our spirit—and can actually help to heal our wounds. The precious balm of play is, in fact, one of the most influential forces in our lives.

Years ago, I worked with a Jungian analyst named Christopher Whitmont, a small man with twinkling eyes who knew the value of play. He sometimes role-played with me, asking me to act out different characters from my dreams and, in true method-acting style, encouraged me to assume the posture or stance a feeling might invoke as a way to bring it into consciousness. Occasionally, if I was stuck, he would hand me his worn copy of *The I Ching or Book of Changes,* an ancient Chinese text of divination, to see whether it might shed light on my dilemma.

One day, Christopher suggested that I join one of his therapy groups. I balked. To engage in play therapy was one thing; to be part of a group and lose my sense of specialness was quite another. "Well, then," Christopher advised, "let's consult *The I Ching.*" Reluctantly, I threw the six coins and drew the hexagram called Preponderance of the Small, whose meaning, according to Confucian wisdom, signifies that "one should not strive after lofty things but hold to lowly things"—or, in plain language, the ordinary. This seemed to argue in favor of joining. I was mortified. Not only was my special status being challenged, but all my airborne fantasies as well; henceforth, I would just be an ordinary person leading an ordinary life.

No matter how gently and patiently Christopher explained that life was an accumulation of mostly ordinary moments, I could see no way to reconcile "lowly things" with the ecstatic or the sublime—the mountaintop I wanted to live on—always. Another year went by before I agreed to try the group, six months more before I deigned to take an active place among its members. Once I'd made the transition, however, the rewards were great. Seven more "players" not only meant seven more mirrors but seven times seven new ways of seeing. It also meant coming down from the magic mountain to be with ordinary mortals with whom, I was to discover, I had a great deal in common.

Since then, I've learned this lesson anew every day—that what we call ordinary includes odd moments, dull moments, hard-work moments, light moments, and, yes, even rapturous moments of the sort that the two mountaineers Joe Simpson and Simon Yates sought after and describe in their book and film *Touching the Void,* which documents their perilous quest to reach the summit of Siula Grand in Peru. Or like the hypnotic experience of watching, for hours at a time, penguins parading across Antarctic ice floes that Diane Ackerman describes in her poetic study *Deep Play,* about the creative and transcendent experiences achieved through heightened forms of play. Such a moment is thereafter framed in our memory. Explorers, mountain climbers, deep-sea divers, adventurers, search these moments out to pitch their lives to higher frequencies. But moments of rapture and ecstasy also arrive quietly and take hold in us silently. Once, when I was in my late-forties, I stroked the throat of a giant Galapagos tortoise and felt a soft blush of ecstasy that propelled me backward in time like a fish swimming into the prehuman seas. The memory of that moment has stirred my consciousness many times since.

But I am also grateful for the countless seemingly ordinary moments that reside somewhere in my personal storage file: the tired, muscular pleasure of hard work, physical or mental; the communal pleasure of breaking bread with friends and feeling their support; the silly pleasure of giggling uncontrollably at zany things; the moaning pleasure of lovemaking; the awed pleasure of hallowed spots or certain kinds of music; the bittersweet pleasure of certain memories, of people lost to my life and sometimes objects or places as well; the distilled pleasure of mastery, especially in triumphing over fearful things; the relief pleasure of getting over a stomach flu or a cold or guilt; the fleeting pleasure of buying a new sweater or pair of shoes; the quiet pleasure of making soup, puttering, or watching a patient grow strong in her awareness; the deep pleasure of giving but also of learning when not to; the proud but worried pleasure for the destiny of my own children, which lies beyond a mother's protection; the keen yet lamentable pleasure of time passing; the wake-up pleasure of spring after its long absence; the fatigued pleasure of too-muchness; the frantic pleasure of not enough, never enough; the hopeful pleasure of "well, maybe"; the fierce pleasure when "good" seems to "win" over "evil"; the surrendering pleasure of learning that I have no control over what happens in the universe—but that I will also act with vigor and persistence "*as if*" I do. All these and so many more.

As we develop a sense of play, we discover that what we have called ordinary resonates with meaning, except that we have overlooked or stereotyped it, dumping it on the disposal heap of so-called "boring," "so what," and "who cares?" kinds of things. Our perspective shifts: the half empty glass becomes half full, and because we have allowed it into consciousness, the unthinkable loses its power over us. Maurice Sendak's classic children's book *Where the Wild Things Are* tells the story of mischievous young Max, who, exiled to his room for misbehaving, escapes into a fantasy world inhabited by a host of wild creatures. The point of Sendak's story, of course, is that a child's own "wilder" thoughts and feelings—her anger, guilt, fears of rejection or the unknown—have a life of their own and will come knocking on the door until they are admitted. Still, it is astonishing how hard it is—for children *and* adults—to absorb this knowledge, since we seem to see "wild things" everywhere but in ourselves. Milner expresses the same idea in more adult language: "no idea can be safely shut out of the mind, least of all those that the deliberate self would like to disparage." *No* idea. Not any.

"Do I contradict myself?/Very well then I contradict myself,/ (I am large, I contain multitudes.)" Walt Whitman said. Miles Davis put it this way: "If I ever feel I am getting to the point where I'm playing it safe, I'll stop. That's all I can tell you about how I plan for the future." In our inner world, censorship and the creative impulse make terrible roommates. You can live according to established rules, or you can make your own. But it's hard, if not impossible, to live both ways simultaneously. Creativity is about play, play is ultimately concerned with the quest for meaning, and quests by their very nature are subversive. They involve adventure, perseverance, and the willingness to experiment—to break molds and recast rules. For women especially, creative living is about the secret life of the self, and, most especially, our deep need for self-expression in whatever satisfying form it may take.

Describing what turning forty felt like, the writer Maria Housden explained her own process: "I have spent a lifetime trying to 'get better,' 'be nicer,' mooring myself to my relationships with other people while mostly overlooking my relationship to myself. When I turned forty last summer, I realized, 'NO MORE!' From now on, this is as good as it gets; *I am as good as I get.* No longer immersed in a neverending process of self-improvement, my energy is now poured into the life I want to live. It's not that I am no longer interested in participating or in contributing to mutually satisfying relationships...

it's simply that I have reoriented my center of gravity in relationship. Now, it is *first* about me and what is true for me—and what a relief that is."

Maria Housden was forty when she had this insight; some exceedingly fortunate women learn to trust their feelings even earlier; others—most of us—mellow into themselves much more slowly. Yet, in truth, what matters is to start listening to our own desires at *every* age, according to our own rhythms.

Julia, in her mid-fifties and widowed, had, by all conventional standards, lived the signature "good life"—a long marriage to a man widely recognized to be brilliant, charming, handsome, and wealthy; loving friends and family; travel to exotic places. Then Julia's husband was diagnosed with cancer. She nursed him devotedly for two years before he died, and came to see me about six months afterward in a state of deep depression. At first our work was entirely devoted to Julia's need to give herself permission to grieve. When she did, Julia discovered, to her astonishment, that even though she had "everything she could ever need," she didn't want to return to the life she had. She started to pay attention to a secret wish that had languished in a forgotten corner of her soul: her desire to live in the country and cultivate a small herb farm. The more she listened, the more this wish grated against what Julia now called "my old superficial life," with its rounds of cocktail parties, dinner parties, and other seemingly important social occasions. A year later, Julia sold her Manhattan apartment and moved to her dream house in the Berkshires. She is now a member of an organic-farm collective that sells its produce to New York restaurants.

I once reminded a patient who had stopped dancing years earlier due to a foot injury of her infinite capacity for creativity. She reported to me a week later that "the word kept coming through—infinite, infinite, infinite—and instead of me feeling closed, empty, dried up, squeezing myself, like the last bit out of a tube of toothpaste, all of a sudden I felt like I could think of something else, and something else and something else." "Possibly," Milner says, "the thing that matters, that you are looking for, is like the root of plants, hidden and happening in the gaps of your knowledge."

That is why some of the humbler forms of creative living are so satisfying: they are embedded in the soil (the *humus*) of life. Take puttering, for example. Webster defines puttering as moving or acting aimlessly or idly, though that's hardly the whole of it. For one thing, puttering is private, not something you do in front of others. And though its design seems random, it is also preparatory, sometimes spilling over into purposefulness, like a gentle nudge that helps you take a step in the right direction. Even when it leads to nothing, a certain amount of puttering is necessary. Puttering is a comma, a breathing space that can anticipate, or break up, the marching rhythms of the day—a light distraction that lets us acknowledge things around us and enter a companionable relationship with them. Watering the plants, stacking magazines, opening the window, moving things from here to there, making a second cup of tea—any series of small acts strung together this way constitutes puttering. Puttering, above all, is a pretext, a game of pretense. While I'm plumping the pillows, my mind is already limbering up. It doesn't always work, but when it does, puttering is the way I catch up with myself and set the coordinates for whatever comes *after.*

In a reading of her poetry at the 92nd Street Y in New York City, a member of the audience asked Mary Oliver to describe her creative process. But what she had to say transcended the realm of poetry. In essence, her words went something like this: Pay attention to the whole world. Don't go to sleep on it but seek out its meaning by observing, bearing witness. Above all, remain devoted. Otherwise, you will be dealing with the outer crust of yourselves—the individual persona that is programmed to respond to the world and survive in it but is only the outer crust. Remain devoted. Until you and the world become seen (again), tasted (again), revered (again), lived (again).

MAKING CHOICES

One perfect day in August, I take the largest bowl I can find and head for the blueberry bushes in my friend Gail's Vermont garden. Several full bowls already line the kitchen counter, but friends are coming to dinner, and I know from experience that everyone will want seconds of her cold blueberry soup. The sun is high, the bees have been roaming their blue bounty for hours, and I am a circle of one. Starting low on a bush, I reach as far inside as its branches allow and nudge the velvety midnight-blue balls into my open palm. On the stem a few small, hard green knots wait for the sun to soak color and plumpness into them. The ripe berries yield gently, but the green cling tightly to the vine. It is a lesson in timing and readiness, a reminder that the unfolding of any living thing cannot be forced or rushed. The moment will come when it is ready to drop from the vine. Just as you will know, according to the natural law of your own ripening, when you are ready to step out.

Stepping out is an act, *a self-assertion,* a movement beyond whatever steps you have taken before. It means something different to each of us, but the process that leads up to it is always the same: you don't know exactly how or why, but you find yourself ready to be, or act, in a way you were unable to just moments before. Its force is unstoppable, and there are bound to be consequences. You are moving into larger quarters, leaving your constricted, interior space for a more generous, expansive one, and the change can be frightening. But with faith and patience to help quell the tremors inside you and keep you flexible and resilient, persistence will carry you through. What matters is that we make choices with faith that we will survive the consequences, so that forever afterward we will hold the knowledge that our choices were stronger than the fear that held us back. Another thing: as the circle turns, and new situations present themselves, our longings will mutate; we will step out again—and again.

Such moments—and opportunities—will continue throughout our lives.

Here are just a few examples of the choices a woman alone might make. When any one of these signifies a movement toward her full potential, she is stepping out:

> *to have a child without a partner*
> *to not have children*
> *to stop caring what other people think*
> *to say no and mean it*
> *to say yes and mean it*
> *to buy a vibrator*
> *to be celibate*
> *to have sex with whomever you choose*
> *to befriend aloneness*
> *to stop abusing alcohol*
> *to take scuba lessons*
> *to leave a failed marriage*
> *to enter a loving relationship*
> *to befriend your body*
> *to leave an abusive partner*
> *to get a tattoo*
> *to stop trying to "do it all"*
> *to take charge of finances*
> *to switch careers*
> *to start a business*
> *to get a physical exam*
> *to keep going after loss or failure*
> *to go back to school*

Maureen was, as a child and an adolescent, a sublimely good girl. Since both parents worked, Maureen took on domestic responsibilities. She would go straight home as soon as school let out to babysit her younger siblings, straighten up the house, and set the table for dinner. Then she went upstairs to do her homework, studying hard to get straight A's so as never to disappoint either parents or teachers. She never had time to play with children her own age, and, with underdeveloped social skills, Maureen became an extraordinarily shy and self-conscious adolescent. Once only did she dare to ask her parents for permission to go to a high school dance; when they refused, she never asked again. At eighteen, Maureen left home to become a novitiate in a religious order. After taking vows, she studied for her doctorate in anthropology and taught at a local college.

When we started working together, Maureen was in her mid-fifties, a sad, soft-spoken woman with pale silver-blond hair. She had left the religious order after twenty years because its cloistered world felt cut off from the "real world," and lived alone in a small apartment. But her "quiet, orderly life," as she described it, was also her bane; whatever she did—teach, visit friends, clean her apartment, even read and listen to music—she did dutifully, and with a desire to please. Everything felt like an obligation, nothing gave her pleasure, nothing tasted of self. In time, the quiet distress that had always shadowed her began spiraling downward into depression and despair.

Before Maureen could begin to imagine something new and different for herself, she needed to take a long, hard look at her lonely, joyless childhood and adolescence, and understand the price that always being "good" had cost her, how it choked her spontaneity and narrowed her imagination, lest it dare play outside its cramped quarters—or even worse—grow to enjoy its new freedom. Then one day an image came to her full-blown. She saw herself standing in a field, dressed in bright red and orange silk threaded with gold— "like a sari." Close by was a large tree with a huge, leafy bower. Maureen wanted to walk through the field, but stayed beneath the tree, where she felt "closed in by the shadow it cast, and separated from the green field." The meaning was as clear as sunlight. She would have to step out from beneath the bower into her own true colors—

a frightening yet oddly comforting thought, since she now realized that her self-in-hiding was vibrant with color. Like Milner, Maureen gave herself the liberty of finding out what made her happy. This was easier said than done, however, since she knew that acting on her desires first would feel risky, even dangerous. Eventually, Maureen was ready to make her first free "choice": she resigned as chairperson of the faculty search committee, something she had wanted to do for years, but she'd stayed on because she didn't want to let the other members down. After much internal debate and many sleepless nights, she sent her letter of resignation to the college president. It was one of the most difficult, but liberating, acts of her adult life.

WE WILL STEP out not once but many times during our lives. In my early twenties, I was an out-of-work actress living with a man I didn't love but clung to, having parked in his life because it felt like there was nowhere else to go. I got pregnant, and I panicked, knowing that I could no more mother a child than myself. Mark had absolutely no paternal ambitions. This was the early sixties; abortions were illegal, but it was easy enough to tap into underground sources. The morning of the abortion, Mark dropped me off in front of a respectable-looking building on Manhattan's Upper West Side. I entered the lobby alone, and took the elevator to the eighth floor, where a stone-faced doctor let me into a dingy apartment. Handing him the payment in advance (cash, of course), I felt furtive and ashamed, and when he did the procedure without any anesthetic, I cried out in pain. He refused to acknowledge me. By the time it was over, I felt raw, violated, punished, victimized, resentful, and relieved all at once. Mark, who had waited for me across the street in his Volkswagen, tried to be kind, but the fact that, as a man, he was exempt from the experience I had just gone through broadened the distance between us even further, and from then on we lived on different planets. A few months later, my younger brother contracted spinal meningitis and died within the week. It was almost more than I could bear. I remember spending my days in a rocking chair near the window, staring at the street four stories below, while the news hummed on a radio in the background. Never before, or since, have I felt so out of touch with myself or the world.

One late fall weekend, I gathered my courage, left the city, and took a room by myself in a small B&B in Provincetown, Massachusetts. The room had a balcony facing the ocean, where I sat for hours, watching the waves strike the shore and fall away. A friend had given me Doris Lessing's novel *The Golden Notebook,* the story of Anna Wulf, a writer and single woman who is struggling to integrate the many fragmented parts of herself that make her life unbearably painful. From the moment I met crazy, insecure Anna, who was full of self-rebuke and whose emotions spilled all over the place, I knew I was no longer alone. Being an emotional wreck at the time, I loved when she asked, "What's wrong with living emotionally from hand-to-mouth in a world that's changing as rapidly as it is?" And because I was alone and terrified of it, I rejoiced when she said to herself, "Why do I always have this awful need to make other people see things as I do? It's childish, why should they? What it amounts to is that *I'm scared of being alone in what I feel* [my italics]." It was through Anna's necessary madness that I could finally begin to understand my own state of mind. A few weeks later, I left Mark and found my breath again.

WOMEN AT THE CROSSROADS

In *A Room of One's Own,* Virginia Woolf wrote that "books have a way of influencing each other." So, too, do all our stories, freely thought and told as we gain the "habit of freedom" Woolf so eloquently describes. Inevitably, we must earn our freedom through our own lived experiences; yet it is also true that other women's stories can help ripen us on the vine just a little bit faster—as Doris

Lessing's story of Anna, whose struggles mirrored my own and with whom I could identify, helped me. What follows are just a few such vignettes of the myriad ways women navigate through their life cycle and face the prospect of being on their own, in both an actual and an emotional sense. I selected them out of literally hundreds of interviews I had with women facing aloneness, either by choice or by necessity.

GINA, A TENURED professor of English at a major university, is nine weeks pregnant, unmarried, and without a partner, male or female. At forty, she threw the dice once and for all and decided to have a child. Not that she thinks of herself as a victim; she is, in fact, robustly independent. During her twenties, Gina partied her way from one monogamous relationship to the next. In her thirties, her heart already broken a number of times, she realized that she had been making the same relationship mistake over and over and decided that the "two-by-two Noah's Ark model wasn't working." She started going out less and spending more time alone; eventually, she stopped dating altogether, "until I can get it right." But by then, Gina could hear her body clock ticking louder and louder and knew the time left to have a child was running out. At thirty-nine, Gina decided to put more effort into finding the right "someone." She soon discovered that "the whole concept of 'Hello, how do you do, I'm about to try and conceive, and would you like to join me' doesn't really work. Not only was I not meeting anybody, but it was becoming clear to me that my heart wasn't in the whole Grail Quest for the Other. I'd lost interest in the model that said my life was incomplete until I found my other half. I'm not a half. I'm a whole."

With her fortieth birthday looming, Gina knew she had reached a turning point. She considered asking one of her male friends to father

her child, but fearing that the repercussions of tying lives together might exceed the boundaries of the friendship, decided against it. As she put it, "I didn't want to put my child through a divorce." Nor did getting pregnant "accidentally" seem like a morally viable option either. Instead, Gina decided to use a sperm bank. She started doing research and decided upon the California Cryobank, where Web site donors are listed by number according to basic physical traits—height, weight, even eye and hair color—but also by race, ethnicity, religion, and education, including areas of study and the number of years spent in school. Gina chose to sort by education, paid the fee, and received profiles of prospective donors, which she narrowed down to ten. Alone during her winter break, ten became three, then two. "And then I realized, This is the one. I have just chosen the father of my child."

That was in mid-January, and the rest happened within a few weeks. On the day it appeared that the egg was ready to burst through the ovum, the doctor injected sperm into Gina's uterus. "I started to cry," Gina said. "It felt like a kind of magical moment. I was praying and meditating on being open, and I was silently calling to the child—I've created the doorway. Come."

"It's a very interesting experience being pregnant alone," Gina says two months later, reflecting on an unfolding new life inside her, as yet only dimly aware that she, too, has walked through a "doorway." She says that if she had a partner, she would expect him to be interested and involved and listen to everything she is going through. "So I need to be my own partner," she adds firmly. "I want to know I can rely on myself. If I can't, my child can't rely on me. I need to know that I can be the solid tree." What gives her strength is the certainty that she wants this baby. "Who knows? I might decide at some point to have a partner. Meanwhile, I've built a life up so that I don't have to answer to anybody. It's one of the reasons why I'm single," she continues unapologetically. "I'm alone because I'm not good at making compromises that allow you to live with a partner. I like doing things my own way." Sometimes she worries about what it's going to be like to share a home with a child, though she senses that she will have "the courage to offer my child the mirror to become the person she or he was meant to be." Her journal is her private confessional where she tries to talk through her doubts and fears—like how she will one day explain her decision to her child, or what it will be like in the beginning when she is at home with her baby. Right now, Gina's goal is to create a larger community, and she is grateful to be living at a time "when there are lots of alternative kinds of families. Unmarried women used to get swept off to some secret place . . . I get nothing but support."

FROM THE TIME she was in her early twenties, Bronwyn, aged thirty-five, knew, as she put it, that she wanted to be "child-*free*—not child-*less*," shifting the emphasis to a choice she has freely made and feels none the less for. One of three girls and two boys born to a second-generation Irish Catholic mother and an English father, Bronwyn grew up in a close-knit, extended family. In seventh grade, her father changed jobs, and the family moved to a small suburban New Jersey town. But the move was difficult for Bronwyn. She had trouble making friends and felt ostracized and lonely.

The following year her status changed dramatically when she joined her school's cross-country running team and proved to be their strongest member. Suddenly, she had an identity, having earned her schoolmates' respect and the nickname "Brawny." At the same time, she was keenly aware that her athletic abilities were responsible for her dramatic change of status. Being a runner, she discovered, became the tag by which others defined her, and by senior year, her name, together with its squelched identity, had outlived its usefulness. "You see this continuing through a life," Bronwyn muses philosophically. "People define you in a certain way and then you have to break out of it. I think it's why I had to get away from running." Once she stopped, she stopped for good.

In college, Bronwyn made a conscious choice to continue to break the mold. Willing herself to be less shy, she vowed "not to be so freaked out by interacting with people." Living on the small, friendly campus helped, and she began to participate in student life. She also began to pursue her serious interest in art history. After graduation, she got a job in a New York gallery where, given the number of like-minded souls, Bronwyn says, she never has a sense of feeling isolated for her beliefs. Indeed, the need to find her own way has been one of the central themes of her life—including her decisions to remain single and child-free, both made while she was still in her twenties. Bronwyn is clear that her experiences of being one of five children, growing up in suburbia, and her early ostracism were critical factors. In high school, she remembers being "freaked out by the idea of getting pregnant and getting stuck in New Jersey and my life ending. I still felt like that in college. I guess I equated marriage and family with loss of freedom."

But what made Bronwyn's choices decisive was the validation she received from her mother during conversations they had after she was diagnosed with breast cancer. "My mother was already very ill when I asked her a strong question: If things were the other way around and it was Dad who was going to die, do you think you would get married again? Her answer was 'Absolutely not. I would definitely be alone.' And when I told her I couldn't see myself getting married and having children, she said, 'Well, you know, I love you kids, but I really think I could have been, if not more happy, then equally happy, alone.' She didn't put her marriage down," Bronwyn adds, "but she surely imagined going in another direction. She saw another life for herself, and she had never expressed that before."

Her mother's avowal resonated deeply with Bronwyn; not only did it support her own desires, it also reinforced them. While family meant everything to both parents, they also encouraged all their children to do whatever they wanted to, no matter how impractical the world might find it. Now Bronwyn's mother was letting her know that, given the chance, *she* would have done things differently— including *not* having children. I ask Bronwyn how she interpreted her mother's remarks. To her, the intended meaning was transparent. "She was saying 'Don't get married'—that's how I internalized it in my twenties." "Don't get married, or don't have kids?" I asked. "Both," she assures me, "because the only reason to get married is to have kids—that's the contract."

While working at the gallery, Bronwyn met Lincoln, her first serious boyfriend, and soon she was putting all her energies into helping him open a bookstore in New York. "I never had a boyfriend before, and I thought I really should make this thing work. It wasn't marriage I wanted; it was a good working relationship. So I put my own dreams on hold to help him achieve his." Before long, however, the relationship ran into trouble. Lincoln's constant criticism started chipping away at her self-esteem. Then, when she found out that he was sleeping with other women, she finally told him to leave. She felt sad and disappointed, but the experience renewed her deepest convictions about being independent.

At twenty-eight, Bronwyn opened her own gallery on lower Broadway. Afraid that financial constraints might impinge on her choice of artists, she also started a small PR company with the idea that it would give her the cushion she needed. Her plan proved so successful that Bronwyn has been free ever since to make the aesthetic choices that feel right to her. One of them was to work with more women artists. In gendered terms, the gallery has always been fifty-fifty, but Bronwyn is convinced that "it is always the women artists who took what I was doing seriously. Most of them have second jobs, so they tend to be more understanding and don't demand that you create all the income for them. Or maybe they just think that way naturally. Their art is the center of all things, so they took my work just as seriously."

Nowadays, Bronwyn is living a life that feels right to her. She has always made it clear to the men in her life that she does not want to marry or have children, and she is careful to act conscientiously. The solitariness of her pursuits as well as her decision to be child-free have liberated her—securing the way for her to continue making her own choices. Not only has she created an alternate community of people, but, as a gallerist nurturing the work of women artists, she is "a mother of sorts" as well. At the same time, Bronwyn is very clear that the decisions she has made, and continues to renew, are hers alone—and not a *cause célèbre*. "I have a friend who wants the traditional thing—to find the right guy, have a child, you know, follow the rules—all the kind of stuff I find utterly perplexing. But I encourage her because that's what *she* wants."

WITH SHORT BROWN hair and alert blue eyes, Martha is a successful career woman who for twenty years has headed up the editorial department of a leading New York brokerage firm. Like many unmarried women in their late thirties and early forties, Martha says it is as if she "forgot" about marriage—until she realized one day that "a major boat had been missed. I wasn't a nester," she says. "I was somewhat uncomfortable with domesticity. If I had an epiphanic moment in my life, it was that I didn't want to be in any way restricted." She had boyfriends, but never one with whom she felt prepared to enter marriage, and, happy in her work, she poured her energy into her career. By her late thirties, Martha's priorities had changed. The missing piece was less marriage than the more urgent wish to have her own biological child. But at the time, she was in a relationship with an older man who had children from former marriages and wasn't interested in fathering more. Eventually, the relationship foundered, and Martha for the first time thought seriously about in vitro fertilization.

Then suddenly all such ideas were put on hold. At forty, Martha was diagnosed with Hodgkin's disease. Her doctor was optimistic about her chances for recovery, but said that chemotherapy would send her into early menopause. Martha asked him about the possibility of freezing some of her eggs. "Why?" he asked. "You don't even have a boyfriend." His rude dismissal was "so offensive, I wanted to fly at him." But a fertility specialist she consulted agreed that it wouldn't be a good idea. It would mean delaying chemotherapy treatments until after her next menstrual cycle, and the doctors told her she was too ill to wait.

Martha spent the next year on chemotherapy and another full year recovering. "Simply getting through each day was such a project, I couldn't think beyond," she says. But as soon as she was well again, Martha's desire for a child returned. "The feeling was so strong, it took me by surprise. At first, I put up every rational argument why it wouldn't work. I was too old. I was used to my own routine. What if I changed my mind afterward? What if the child didn't like me? But no matter what kind of obstacle I put up, the longing just got stronger. One evening I just said to hell with it—I was going to adopt a child and that was that."

Once she made her decision, the process began in earnest. A friend put her in touch with a California adoption agency, and within a year, Martha, then forty-six, was the mother of a thirteen-month-old Chinese baby girl. "I was thrilled, but the adjustment was weird at first."

Martha describes her daughter, Pearl, as "an incredibly happy, healthy, outgoing little girl." She says her worst parenting moments came right after she brought Pearl home. "For a while, I felt like I was babysitting. I wasn't sure I was bonding because I actually felt thrilled whenever I had a few hours to myself." But Martha fell a little bit more in love with her daughter each passing day, and gradually relaxed into the rhythms of motherhood. She feels very differently about her life since becoming a single mother. "I thought it would be like a continuing sense of ecstasy, but it's not like that." Instead, the word she chooses to describe the shift inside her is *contentment*: "I feel complete, as if the missing piece of a puzzle has fallen at long last into place."

HARPER MET DON at her friend's house. Eight years older and divorced, he was bright, seductive, and made her feel special. She fell head over heels in love. They got married six months later. Harper was twenty. In the early days of the marriage, Harper's friends came over to visit. Don was a self-employed car mechanic, and around a lot, and he would eavesdrop on their conversations, always grilling Harper for more information after they left. When Harper protested that she didn't want to betray their confidence, he insisted that married couples shouldn't have secrets, and she went along with it. But when he began insulting her friends to their faces—telling one of them that she was fatter than her fat husband, and another that he would bet crows love to nest in her hairdo—the situation became so uncomfortable that Harper stopped seeing them. Her parents, who had liked Don at first, became more and more wary of him and said so to Harper whenever they saw her. Harper knew on some level that they were right; Don, perhaps sensing her distance, began discouraging her from having contact with her family, and in this, too, she complied.

Don's behavior turned into abuse when, one day, he accused Harper of having a sexual relationship with her best friend. When she denied it, Don hit her across the face. Harper almost left that time, but he was so apologetic that she stayed. Besides, she still loved him, and when he made love to her, she felt sure everything would be all right. Soon, Don became more violent. "He would get right up close to my face and shout at me, or push me against the wall, or grab my wrist so hard, I thought my hand would come off. But I was completely isolated from my family and friends; Don was the only one I could talk to, and sometimes he treated me really nicely."

Harper worked at a beauty salon as a hair colorist a few miles from their home. Looking like a devoted husband, Don would drive her to work in the morning and pick her up at the end of the day. But the truth was Don had started driving her Pinto after his own car died, and Harper was afraid to ask if she could drive to work herself for fear he would become abusive. When her license expired, she didn't bother to renew it. "It was a subtle surrender. To make peace, to make the yelling stop, I would agree to things out of intimidation. So now I didn't drive, I had no friends; it got to the point that I was afraid to leave the house by myself."

The violence escalated. After one fight, Don threw Harper out of their apartment in her underclothes. She banged on the door to be let back in, then called the police from a neighbor's apartment. But when they got there, Harper backed off and told them it was just a "small disagreement. The way they looked at me, then Don, I could see they didn't believe me, but there wasn't anything they could do, so they left."

One evening, after a particularly severe beating, Harper decided it was time to leave. "Something just clicked, and I knew that if I didn't get away from him, I could end up dead. It was like a door had opened inside and I could walk out." She told Don that her sister was having marital problems and that they were going to a diner to talk. Instead, they went to an ER, where a doctor examined her bruises and entered them into her medical record. Then Harper checked herself into the nearest shelter for battered women. For the first time, she was with a heterogeneous community of women who were immensely supportive of one another—and of her. In the next few months, no longer under Don's influence, Harper was able to feel pain and grief for herself and gained insight and perspective. She described herself as a victim of "gaslighting," a term that entered our vocabulary after the scheming husband in George Cukor's 1944 film *Gaslight* almost succeeds in persuading his innocent young wife that she is losing her mind. "I knew that I was a battered woman, I had a language for it, I knew that what had happened to me was abuse, and I knew it was wrong. Going to those support groups was probably the single most healing thing I've ever done." From personal experience, Harper knows that one's partner can destroy whatever vestige of a woman's self remains by using the power of illusion, which makes the batterer sound convincing as the observer who names what is happening to the victim, rather than as the perpetrator *who stages* and enacts the whole process.

Recently, Harper enrolled at a local community college to study accounting. She also leads a group meeting at the shelter several evenings a week and has become well-versed in the long list of reasons women stay with their abusers, including the fear of being blackmailed, or stalked, or killed, or losing social status, or of themselves repeating the same pattern with another partner, especially if they've been abused before. "The truth is, with money or without, most stay because their abuser and the culture tell them they're to blame and they feel belittled enough to agree."

Harper took the giant step of leaving her abuser and is on her way to feeling "like a real person." She lives by herself with her cat, Olive, and likes it that way. "I can do what I want whenever I want. I can read, keep the TV on all night, go out with my friends—it's a whole new life."

In every woman, there is a place of fear, no matter how courageous we may be, or how many times we step out. Photojournalist Paula Allen travels all over the world documenting the stories of courageous women whose struggles against violence and oppression would otherwise remain invisible, like those in a safe house in Kenya where young women have escaped female genital mutilation; or in a Kosovo village in which only women and children survived the war; or in Asia, where "comfort women" spoke about their enforced sexual slavery by the Japanese military during World War II; or in Calama, in northern Chile, where female villagers have spent more than twenty years combing the vast Atacama Desert with shovels to find the bodies of their loved ones, twenty-six men who were among thousands of *los desaparecidos* (the disappeared) murdered by the Pinochet junta after they seized control of the government in 1973. Often traveling alone through extremely dangerous and violence-prone settings, Paula was not prepared for the fear she felt spending "recovery time" alone in her Adirondack cabin.

Toward dusk on the third night she was there, the skies became overcast. Soon the moon disappeared, leaving a wake of darkness. Paula began to feel the creeping stealth of fear, and, as the night deepened, unadulterated terror. "I went to bed surrounded by every kind of thought—not the kind of dark fantasies where you tell yourself to stop and they melt away—these were more about the immediacy of drunk or crazy men coming to attack me because they knew I was alone." At first, she tried to convince herself that nothing had changed, that, except for the darkness, this night was exactly like the others, her experience just as pleasurable, her desire to be there just as strong. "But I couldn't talk my way out of it *because the possibility existed,*" she said.

Paula put on every piece of clothing she had brought. Then she equipped herself with a hatchet and a flashlight and lay down in bed. By midnight, the terror was overwhelming. It kept coming, wave upon wave. Paula made a conscious decision. She knew she had to go into it, so she let herself go deeper and deeper, admitting entrance to every horrible thought in her head until daybreak, when she managed to fall asleep.

A few weeks later, Paula decided it was time to spend another few days at the cabin. This time, she didn't experience the direct assault of terror, though she was certainly aware of its hulking presence. "Had I stayed another night, I would have gone through it again," she says with certainty. "It builds up . . . not the first day, not the second, but . . ." Appropriately, the sentence is left unfinished, for Paula, who travels into the world's danger zones, has become aware of the irony of her own untold story—or, rather, the story that belongs to her and to all women: freedom *includes* fear. It is there because we carry it in our collective unconscious, because its spell weaves into the immediacy of our daily lives, and because it is a concrete experience in most of our lives.

SOMETIMES, WE DARE ourselves to step out, and, lo and behold, we do. Eva, the head librarian of a prestigious law firm, is glamorous, sophisticated, and sixty. Nathan, who began working at the firm several months earlier, is thirty-six. One morning he noticed Eva walking through the library on the way to her office and was impressed. On the pretext of needing help to find a legal document, he knocked on Eva's door. A week later, they made love for the first time. Eva has been obsessed with him ever since. "Until then, I expected nothing out of life," she tells me. "I was just going through the motions, but I didn't feel anything. I wasn't even interested in romance. Those feelings seemed so far from my reality, and I felt all right about that. I had my work, my Pilates classes, a few good friends. We went to the theater, to concerts. And I traveled a lot, which I love." In short, everything about Eva's life was ordered, tidy, and in place; there were no surprises, nor was she expecting any.

For the next few months, Eva saw Nathan once a week, either at her apartment or at his, and yet their lovemaking was hardly rapturous. Nathan was sexually impatient—"like a baby drunk on mother's milk," Eva laughed a bit self-consciously—which left her feeling unsatisfied yet far too shy to express her newly aroused sexual desires. Nor did he hold her in his arms or talk to her after they had finished making love. Eva was convinced Nathan was just using her. She wanted to stop seeing him, but what she could no longer hide from herself, nor wished to, was the strength of her sexual passion, which had come fully alive for the first time in years.

That summer Eva went to Spain for a month's vacation. She thought about sending Nathan a postcard but decided against it, "in case," she says, "he had forgotten me." When she returned, she waited for Nathan to come to her office, but he never did. Eva was miserable; she blamed herself for going away, for being a bad lover, and, most of all, for not being able to think about anything but him. Then she ran into him in the hallway. He was talking with some lawyers and didn't seem to notice her, so she simply glanced his way and kept walking. The next morning, Nathan came to Eva's office. "Why didn't you say hello when you saw me?" he asked, staring hard at her. "I didn't think it mattered to you," she replied. Nathan didn't say a word. Instead, he closed and locked the office door and started walking toward her. Eva watched him, struck still by his boldness. "You must be crazy," she murmured. "You're crazy," she repeated, unable to believe that she was falling out of control. They made love on the beige carpet, while outside, Eva's two assistants—oblivious to what was happening behind closed doors—cataloged law-journal articles into their computers.

A few days later, Nathan came into Eva's office to let her know he was free that evening. "He stood there with his head averted, pretending to look at some journals that were on my desk," she says. "But I, too, pretended. I didn't want him to think he had become so important to me." That was two months ago. Since then, Eva hasn't seen him, and he hasn't called. Eva sounds anguished. "I made a terrible error because I had an opportunity, and I missed it." "What opportunity was that?" I ask. Eva smiles at my question. She wants nothing more than to talk about her obsession. "For Nathan to be my lover. He was not a good lover, you see, but perhaps he could have been if I had been . . . *kinder* to him"; she leans on the word as if it solved a mystery.

For a while, Eva comes to see me every few weeks. She tells me that once she saw Nathan walk by her office, and that several times they have passed each other by like strangers. "I want him so much," she says, her desire as fierce as the pack of yelping dogs that appeared in one of her recent dreams.

The last time I see Eva she is wearing a red wool jacket and a black knee-length skirt. Her nails and lipstick match the color of the jacket exactly and her eyes are shining. "I've seen him again. Last week we made love in his apartment. Only this time, it was different than before. He was very anxious, very tired, because of course he works all the time. When we were in bed I held him in my arms for a while. Then he fell asleep. When he woke up"—she blushes like a young girl—"he performed . . . cunnilingus." It is painful for her to say the word aloud. Still, her lover has attended to her, and she is stunned with gratitude. "Even if there is pain, at least I'm alive again. I can feel myself. Nathan woke me up." Whatever happens, Eva wants me to know it will have been worth it.

At ninety-three, Kitty Carlisle Hart, widow of the playwright and director Moss Hart, told me about a revelation she had twenty years after her husband died. "I was at the piano practicing scales, and I suddenly stood up. I had always felt until then that I had been a caretaker for Moss's things. I had gone straight from my mother's hands to Moss's hands, and did whatever they told me to do. Now I said, 'Everything in his apartment belongs to me, and I can throw it all out the window if I want.' I felt liberated. The inside changed. I was my own person for the first time." From that moment on, Kitty Hart never stopped singing or working tirelessly to get funding for the performing arts. And though she's had plenty of beaux, she never remarried. "Do you think you wanted to preserve your freedom without realizing it?" I asked. Kitty Hart smiled at me as if she'd just been given an award. "I never thought about that. You've given me a gift," she answered.

IT IS HARD to appreciate the amount of work we do before being ready to step out. Most of it is invisible, building up underground, like the alluvial deposits that slowly accrete until they form a delta. It is always a confluence of things: meditation, art, dreams, the support of caring friends, "mistakes" repeated ad nauseum, hating ourselves until we grow tired of it, therapists, ministers, mentors, one crisis (and then another), getting sage advice at the right moment, a chance remark falling on open ears, insights, vows to change (after oh so many before), effort, failure, renewed determination. Then the *eureka!* moment comes, and we call our attorney to file for divorce, announce to our family that we are going back to school, move to Montana, change careers, work against violence toward women, and on and on. In this alchemical process, there is always suffering—at times a veritable wasteland of it; even so, the article of faith that has entered our lives holds fast until we have gathered enough strength to push open the door.

Chapter Eight

REAPING THE HARVEST: SOLITUDE, THE SACRED, AND THE REDISCOVERY OF THE SELF

SOLITUDE

In *Journal of a Solitude,* the poet May Sarton returns to her Vermont home after weeks of social engagements and rejoices to be, once again, in solitude: "I am here alone for the first time in weeks, to take up my 'real' life again at last. That is what is strange—that friends, even passionate love, are not my real life unless there is time alone in which to explore and to discover what is happening or has happened." Sarton finds the social world she left behind "nourishing" but also "maddening"; fulfilling but also depleting, *unless* she can balance it with time alone to gain contact with what she calls her "deep self." She has learned that both solitude and a social life are essential for the quality of depth that belongs to her "real life," which is always about trying to find a balance between retreat and return.

One of the great boons of solitude is peace, a state of inner quiet and emotional harmony that seems less available and, consequently, more precious than ever before in our fraught world. So I understand why Sarton found that the peace of solitude always "rests in the natural world, in feeling myself a part of it, even in a small way." For me, the unhurried experiences of watching tidal pools along La Jolla's coast, hunt-and-pecking for shells on Sanibel Island, or walking barefoot along the fern path to my favorite Vermont lake are moments I prize for their incorruptible value. Yet I also appreciate Louise Bogan's hard-won "quiet of the heart," as its "provincialism"—its demand for "objects"—fell away: "Now a room with sun in it, a half day's leisure, a fire, cigarettes, unlimited books, a piano and some music, a clean bed and a garden in the summer seem all the materials necessary for my life."

In such solitude, we almost feel ourselves stretch into timelessness. Animated by the living pulse of the moment, the dailiness of our lives drops away, small preoccupations withdraw from center stage, the droning ego is hushed, even our nagging concern for the people in our lives is temporarily suspended. This is a state of plenitude, and there are no intermediaries between the self and the surrounding stillness. We have reached a clearing where there is nothing to obstruct our sight lines. Thoughts play but without clouding our vision; things are simply what they are. And for as long as the winds don't change and we are able to hold our balance, we ride the wave of solitude to shore.

"Only when one is connected to one's own core is one connected to others, I am beginning to discover. And, for me, the core, the inner spring, can best be refound through solitude," writes Anne Morrow Lindbergh in *Gift from the Sea*. On the continuum of aloneness, solitude is our end point: the space that truly belongs to the deepest part of self, and that we would spend time in were it not for the fear we carry. Yet, as I have tried to show throughout this book, because we have too often mistakenly come to view ourselves in terms of how other people think and feel about us, defining ourselves *away* from our selves—and from the very ground of our being—in the process, solitude always at first raises special alarms.

This is why Megan, a painter nearing her sixties, halts at the door to her studio. Shouldn't she first make the phone call to her doctor? Go food shopping? Meet a friend for lunch who may be insulted if she chooses not to? Her longing for solitude feels selfish and indulgent. It also entails the risk of missing out on something *better,* or, worse, discovering that she's only a mediocre artist after all. "Sometimes it seems that everyone knows what they want . . . are purposeful except me. I worry that I have no ideas. Or only banal ones."

Such doubts move Megan's desire for a more purposeful solitude to last place on the short list of gifts she will grant herself. If she could, she would clone herself into several separate selves—each running off to do something else—rather than spend several undisturbed hours alone in her studio. And yet denying herself studio time always makes her feel empty and a bit dry. Knowing this, Megan pushes open the studio door. The obstructing voices clamor for attention, but in the end the voice she listens to is the one that urges her to pick up her brush, and paint.

Active Solitude

Solitude is sustenance: food for the deprived self. We enter solitude for many reasons: to rest, to nurse our grief, to ease the strain of giving to others more than to ourselves, to hear the sound of our voice, to nurture our creative energies, or, for some, as part of a spiritual practice. We move into solitude to satisfy our longing for meaning, both personal and transcendent.

As a young woman, Marie Claire traveled through Europe, taking odd jobs to support herself. Eventually, she ended up in Neuchâtel, Switzerland, where she found work on a dairy farm. Her job was to tend the heifers on the upper plateaus of the Alps. She lived by herself in a small cabin, and, except for her occasional trips to the village, or the times the local people visited her, bringing food and home-baked bread, she was entirely alone. But each night, after the sun went down, Marie Claire could not stop herself from crying. "Living with the darkness felt tremendously frightening to me. To be alone in the cabin was like returning to my childhood. My father, you see, would catch me in the bedroom and seduce me, or my mother would trap me and beat me, so to be in an enclosed dark space was terrifying."

To assuage her terror, Marie Claire decided to sleep among the cows instead, so she took her sleeping bag and moved outdoors. Cows are gentle, curious animals, with sweetly slow, lumbering movements. When she lay down in the fields at night, they would form a protective circle around her. "I'd look up at their faces with those full lips and soulful eyes and feel quieted; and sometimes they'd sniff my body. But they don't move fast. I never got the feeling, as with horses, that they might step on me. Cows don't try to hurt anyone." In this way, Marie Claire began to feel a renewed kinship with the familiar, only this time, the familiar was becoming safe and trustworthy and healing. So, too, was the immensity of the silence, which to this day is Marie Claire's "favorite sound."

There is freedom *from* and freedom *toward*. What we each long for, often without realizing it, is the freedom of a silence so vast, so permeable, so full of peace, that we need only stay still to discover it, moving neither away nor toward. Perhaps this is what we mean by thriving, a state of flourishing that is quantum leaps ahead of "getting by" or "making do." Indeed, thriving is overflow, the sap that flows from the peace of stillness at our center. Under the night sky and its canopy of stars, and in the animal world that protected her, Marie Claire sought freedom from her fear and found it by moving toward the freedom of solitude. "Some part of me," she says, "knew that was exactly where I had to be."

WHEN MARTA, A businesswoman, was diagnosed with inflammatory breast cancer at the age of fifty-two, her oncologist and surgeon mapped out the conventional protocol: chemotherapy, followed by a mastectomy, more chemotherapy, and, finally, two months of daily radiation treatments. Marta listened carefully to what the doctors had to say. Not completely convinced they were right, she began researching on her own and realized that the sheer magnitude of information available, some of it contradictory, made it difficult to arrive at clear choices. "What did make sense—the only thing I could do—was to search deep within myself," Marta says. At home in the early morning quiet, on walks around the Central Park reservoir, she let herself examine questions and possibilities, weighing them against her fears and doubts, listening for an answer that made sense to her. In the end, Marta decided she would undergo chemotherapy and radiation, but would not have the mastectomy, except as a very last resort. "If nothing else, I needed to be in control of what might be my final decision. That was the compromise I made with myself."

After eight months of chemotherapy, Marta began radiation treatments. To endure the treatments, Marta engaged in a kind of willful dissociation from what was happening to her body. "I tried to ignore what the technicians were doing. I tried to look inside, to just keep thinking, There's much more of me than this. The only way I could do that was to go into a very deep solitude. And when I did that, there came a kind of self-revelation that I can only describe as a feeling of inner peace. I'm not sure it was about God, as such, but it felt like I was connecting to some divine spark. I felt calm. The people around me picked that up, and that made the atmosphere very relaxed. I thought about all sorts of things, trying to concentrate on peaceful, beautiful images, like the sea and birds flying or pelicans diving into it. But I also thought about the most prosaic things, like what I would eat for dinner, or whether my dog had his afternoon walk, or the clothes I needed to bring to the cleaner . . . until my mind went to places I didn't want to go, which I couldn't always help. During the treatments, I felt totally alone. My challenge was not to let this experience break my spirit; had I not entered solitude, it might have."

SPENDING TIME ALONE in nature is Diane Haug's way of finding, and holding on to, her own internal rhythm. Trained as a mental-health professional and now a transpersonal psychotherapist and holistic Breathwork practitioner in New Mexico, the years Haug spent working with the dying taught her that life was too precious to postpone her own excursions into solitude. In her twenties, she "made the conscious step of taking on the practice of being alone in the natural world." In all weathers, under moonlight or in darkness, Haug took long walks on the prairie land that adjoined her house in Austin, Texas, until her nocturnal habit of solitude grew into a necessity. Even in "deepest states of grief or exhaustion," Haug listened to her body. "I just knew I had to get my body on the ground, belly to belly, and let the tears flow to release my sorrow or bring me joy and calm." In this way, the solitude she experienced in the natural world taught her to experience the many weather systems in herself.

When women alone learn that aloneness means simply being present with oneself, we are ready to engage in active solitude. This is aloneness's great gift. It is the *prerequisite* for active solitude. And the more we practice solitude, the sooner we will discover that it is an all-weather companion. Many of us already know the pleasures of a casual kind of solitude—the time-off-for-good-behavior indulgences like taking a few minutes to flip through a magazine, paint one's toe-nails, take an extra-long shower, arrange flowers, or curl up in bed with a stack of videos. What we have yet to claim for ourselves is the solitude of fullness so that we may live our lives creatively and well.

At its most benign, solitude is like a gift of grace washing over us—a blessing that smoothes the brow and settles our composure. But as Haug, Sarton, and most of us discover, the climate of solitude is changeable. "That, of course," says writer Gail Caldwell, as she traces the map of her own solitude, "is the good news and the bad." But it is also what makes our entrance into solitude an essential part of the "*art*" of being on our own. Solitude has to be thought about and cultivated. It is not a passive state, and it takes a lot of *practice* to be there. Even if at first we enter to rid ourselves of distractions, we must do so consciously and with intention, or risk losing its benefits. The point is to choose to be in solitude because we need and want something from it.

Freya Stark gratefully acknowledged how much her inner preparation depended on her "habit of solitude, which . . . is to the spirit what a private room is to the mind, giving it space to grow." For Stark, time apart would turn her into one of the twentieth century's great women travelers and explorers; for many of us, it may well be about hearing our own voice and finding our own center. Yet for this benefit, solitude makes its own demands. Each time May Sarton returned to the state of solitude, she had to prepare herself anew. "The ambience here is order and beauty. That is what frightens me when I am first alone again. I feel inadequate. I have made an open place, a place for meditation. What if I cannot find myself in it?" Sarton's words echo common fears. For in our first excursions into solitude, we inevitably come up against what she calls "the huge empty silence." This is why we must practice being in solitude until it does indeed become a "habit," a natural part of our lives that we willingly make room for. As solitude begins to feel open, not empty, we will be able to partake of its many offerings. For some of us, finding freedom from distractions will be reward enough. Others among us will gain satisfaction in being able to write in our journal, bake a loaf of bread, or solve a mathematical problem. Still others will choose to pursue that elusive *something more* that we call the sacred.

THE SACRED

It is mid-December, and, along with thirty or forty other guests, I am sitting in the Bombay apartment of Ramesh Balsekar, a distinguished, frail-looking man in his eighties. Born in Bombay, Ramesh is a teacher, or guru, and former president of the Bank of India. After his mandatory retirement at age sixty, Ramesh met his teacher and was, in the vernacular of the mystics, "awakened." Thereafter, he began to share his insights with seekers who arrive from all over the world daily to see him. Although he was born into the Hindu religion, Ramesh claims not to espouse any particular belief system. He describes himself simply as a teacher of Advaita, which is not a religion but a philosophy of nonduality that teaches that the One, by whatever name we call it, is manifested in the universe, and in all beings, as the transcendent Self. In other words, we already are the "god" we are seeking outside ourselves.

As he does every morning, 365 days of the year, Ramesh is holding a courteous two-hour dialogue—*darshan* in Sanskrit—about the meaning of existence. If there is any goal to these discussions, it is simply to remind his guests to go beyond their mind, or ego, where, free from all concepts, memories, and conditioned feelings, it is possible to awaken to the knowledge of being One.

"What are you looking for?" Ramesh gently asks the young man sitting next to me, listening carefully as the man explains that he is an architect from the Netherlands who has come because, although he is successful, he is not content. "I've thought for a long time that there is something more to life than what I've found . . ." he says. In the coming weeks I will hear the same question and some variation of this response repeated again and again, as each new visitor searches inside to try to describe what she or he is seeking. The one-syllable answer: peace. Peace of mind. Peace of heart. Peace as the still point at the center.

It is my turn. "I'm here," I tell Ramesh, "because of a longing to bring the sacred into my life." Briefly, I explain that my Ukrainian mother was Russian Orthodox, my father the son of a Russian Orthodox mother and a Jewish father. Although my parents did not practice any religion, as a child I often wished at times to "belong" to one faith or the other, albeit mostly on the days my friends left school early for catechism classes or Hebrew lessons. I did, however, pray every night to a god who was, in my imagining, a Force of staggering power whom I needed to appease so that nothing dreadful would happen to me or my parents. As I got older, I lost interest in this "god," my prayers ended, and whatever spiritual longing I might have felt went underground.

It resurfaced in my twenties, when I began sampling different spiritual paths. I was particularly drawn to Sufism, the esoteric tradition of Islam, because it, too, speaks of the human heart as the actual dwelling place of the godhead, or what Sufis call the "Beloved." I read a lot, had encounters with gurus from various esoteric traditions, went on retreats, and meditated. But it is also true that, depending on what was going on in my life, my interest waxed and waned, and sometimes—for example, when I was absorbed in romance or career issues—it seemed to disappear entirely. It wasn't until I became a woman alone, had gotten my professional and creative life in order, and had had my share of relationships that my longing for "something more" returned.

I come to *darshan* every day of the month I spend in India, listen to people's questions and Ramesh's answers, then leave and spend the rest of the day sightseeing, meeting friends, and enjoying my leisure time. Nothing measurable has changed. True, I feel a calming self-containment, my buzzing ego is slightly less noisy than when I arrived, and my faith in god, as spirit or impersonal consciousness, feels a bit more secure. Back home, I meditate most mornings; as I do, I notice that my daily routine seems easier, and when I start seeing patients again, the feeling in the room seems lighter. I don't think I could have arrived at this place had I not befriended aloneness and engaged in solitude. My life is no less busy than when I was married and bringing up children, but I feel an inner spaciousness that wasn't there before, or, more accurately, that had been obscured by too much inner static. Much less of my energy gets caught up in spirals of self-doubt or the kind of dire "what if" fantasies that used to plague me.

It has become easier to see what is important, to sort what matters more from what matters less, and to decide what my priorities should be. Living in these perilous times, some measure of solitude has begun to feel absolutely crucial to my well-being. It is with a great measure of satisfaction that I realize that aloneness in *all* its forms has been an integral dimension of this deeper search of mine.

The word *sacred* comes from the Latin *sacrare:* to set apart as holy. To set *ourselves* apart and move into aloneness suggests that we have come a great distance from the needs or desires that otherwise occupy us, and which may have, in fact, kept us from experiencing the many satisfactions and privileges of aloneness. For aloneness in this "sacred" sense embraces not only the search we are on but our own holiness as well as that of everything around us.

But it usually takes us a long while to come to this knowledge. When the self is undernourished in its need for love, it tries desperately to "pleasure" itself with one thing or another. Only after long experience do we begin to realize that "things" are poor substitutes for love and yield only temporary satisfaction. You could even say that addiction is the search for pleasure gone awry, or, more poignant yet, the search for a spiritual life that has been aborted. To recognize the sacred in all things—not as an intellectual idea but as felt truth—means that the hunger of the ego has been satisfied enough for the self to become attuned to holiness: we have achieved a higher integration of consciousness.

Women have been attuned to elemental life rhythms—its cycles of birth and death—since prehistory. When life's sacred mystery touches us—whether in the form of a sunset, a seashell, a vision, a meditation—it is as if the wings of an angel have brushed against our shoulder. "Our life," says Annie Dillard in *Pilgrim at Tinker's Creek,* "is a faint tracing on the surface of mystery, like the idle, curved tunnels of leaf miners on the face of a leaf." And so we revel in this mystery of what we do not know and call it longing. For in its final incarnation, longing is about our search for a spiritual life—for something that is set apart—whatever that may mean to each of us individually. Feeling somehow incomplete, we each seek our own form of the sacred. For women alone, the acceptance of solitude allows us to hear, and respond to, our spiritual longing. Indeed, the wondrous paradox is that in solitude we learn how to abide in genuine and intimate relationship to ourselves, and then to our partners, our children, our friends, and things in the world around us.

Katherine Kurs, who holds a Master of Divinity from the Harvard Divinity School and has a private practice as a spiritual/pastoral counselor in New York City, says that as an only child growing up with parents who "had a terrible marriage," she found great comfort and freedom in hours of solitary meditation and silent contemplation of God. It wasn't until she was in her thirties, however, that she realized her work was "to stay passionately engaged with God and also passionately engaged in and with the world." In her counseling office and in her writing, Kurs talks about the spiritual practice of "learning to live here," integrating the transcendent, mountaintop experience with the quotidian world.

The mountaintop is the place of the theophany: revelation, illumination, spiritual insight, profound connection, and transformation—sometimes even transfiguration. "One makes the ascent alone to face the awesome presence of God," says Kurs. But, she points out, you cannot remain on the mountaintop indefinitely, as ecstatic as that experience may be. "The spiritual work truly begins when you come down from the mountain. Otherwise, such experiences can ultimately end up isolating us, alienating us from other people and the world around us."

Yet to find the sacred, we sometimes deliberately remove ourselves—moving into solitude so as to stop time and go within. All religious traditions honor periods of formal retreat. When Kathleen Norris realized that the writing career she embarked on in her twenties was "essentially a religious quest," she chose to honor this deeper understanding by becoming a resident for two nine-month periods at a Benedictine monastery. In *The Cloister Walk*, Norris describes how, as a member of a celibate community, she spent her days reading and reciting psalms, praying, and doing chores, far removed from the routines of her daily life in South Dakota where she lives with her husband, poet David Dwyer. During this self-imposed "wilderness time" Norris faces her deepest torment: she realizes that while she has been able to be a good friend to her husband, her heart had been shut against the "true intimacy" of marriage. "The goal of a monastic life," Norris writes, "is to let oneself be changed by community ritual, ceremony, and the repetition of the psalms, until, in the words of one hymn, our lives *become* a psalm in praise of the glory of God's name." Having surrendered to such "change," Norris returns to South Dakota to find every aspect of her life, including its centerpiece—her marriage—profoundly enriched.

Michaela Ozelsel was born in Germany, raised for years in Turkey, and received her bachelor's and master's degrees in clinical psychology from the University of North Carolina and her doctorate at the Goethe University in Frankfurt, Germany, where she also lives and works. In *Forty Days: The Diary of a Traditional Solitary Sufi Retreat*, she recounts in vivid detail her solitary forty-day Sufi retreat, called the *halvet* ("the solitude" in Turkish). Ozelsel, who has large, light-giving eyes, a ravishing smile, and a head of moving blond curls, explains that she chose the austerity of the *halvet* to work against her accustomed reliance on cognitive processes and let herself be guided by prayers and meditation in the presence of Allah. By opening herself this way, her hope was that she might, as the Sufis say, remove some of the "rust of the heart" and perhaps do some "polishing" as well. Before starting, she was also reminded by her teacher that the intention of such temporary retreats is to bring people to their deeper purpose of serving the community once they leave.

Like Norris, Ozelsel was careful to observe the rituals associated with the *halvet* as the way to reach a higher goal. Although she was entirely alone, she made sure to wear her head scarf and to repeat the

Zhikrs (mantras) her teacher gave her exactly as they are meant to be sounded. At times, she could literally "see" her rational mind, and her various personal anxieties, holding fast, like dirt beneath one's fingernails. Certain Zhikrs, she also discovered, had the force of a "scouring brush," cleansing and emptying her in preparation for the deep internal heart transformation that had already begun to root itself within her and would continue long after the *halvet* was over. As the days progressed, the intensity of Ozelsel's shifting emotional states brought her face-to-face with the meaning behind her own personal suffering: the awareness that true freedom was possible only as she could transcend every last particle of neediness toward the worldly things in her life, including, in her case, whatever feelings remained about the sad dissolution of her marriage. As she recounted it: "from the beginning I have been prepared to feel a deep longing. My whole life long my *ney* has been singing its song of yearning. How can one be made ready for that most basic longing of humankind, longing for the presence of Allah, if not by 'practicing longing' with worldly things?" Eventually, Ozelsel understood that what arose in her "over and over again as deep pain" was a preparation for her life-changing relationship to the One, which would reach deeper than any she could have ever thought possible.

Sometimes it seems that we don't really seek the sacred as much as the sacred seeks us. Either way, the door can open. Nature, presenting us with endless instances of creation, is one of the great unifiers. "On the planet the winds are blowing: the polar easterlies, the westerlies, the northeast and southeast trades . . . Lick a finger, feel the now," writes Annie Dillard. And so we do, walking, trout-fishing, kayaking, lying on the grass, sitting against a tree, breathing in the scent of mown grass, stepping into the woods or a cave, scaling a cliff. Some of us venture even further into the natural world. In the last of seven years spent in a remote corner of southwest New Mexico, Diane Haug purchased a yurt and lived in it alone for six months, without electricity or running water. "The yurt," she says, "is like a membrane between you and the outside. You can hear the first raindrop that falls on it, the first brush of a breeze against it. It also has a skylight, so that lying alone at night and watching the stars is truly amazing. I was living with the sun and the moon, and up at daybreak. I heated my space with wood, so I created a very strong relationship with fire. Ah, it was a sweet experience. I felt intimately connected with nature," Haug recalls.

If we go "inside," we find the candle is already lit. "I have had the experience of what I call the beloved and which everyone calls by a different name . . . a sense of the loving awareness that is my nature and what I belong to. And that is *everywhere*," says Tara Brach, author of *Radical Acceptance: Embracing Your Life with the Heart of a Buddha*. "There is an infinite field of compassion in the universe, and when I'm feeling very small, the yearning and the hurting become a prayer to connect and be held by it. In a way, it's the small self calling out for the mother of the universe to embrace me, and I actually imagine this field of energy around me. But what happens immediately is that the separation dissolves and I become that field. So in a sense I'm the radiant awareness that loves and also the vulnerable self that is being held. There really is a process of feeling separate, reaching out, and then becoming the one I'm reaching out to."

Each of us has a different way of finding the sacred; each of us has her own language for the "beloved"; each of us will be drawn to it by different sounds. Yet whatever that language sounds like—even its silence—we are always speaking about the language of *solitude*— a movement apart that, paradoxically, can open us to receive and become part of the transcendent. A woman I work with, who because of a rare blood disease must spend almost all of her time in bed, told me: "In my darkest moments, I place my hands over my ears and listen to the hum of my bloodstream. It reminds me that Life still courses through me and has its plans." A friend rattles off the sounds that intoxicate her: "Gulls, flowing water of all kinds, the Brahms

Requiem." In *Terra Incognita,* the travel writer Sara Wheeler, who, along with the American painter Lucia deLeiris, lived for weeks in a tent in Antarctica, describes the mystical and synesthetic quality of this experience: "The dignity of the landscape infused our minds like a symphony; I heard another music in those days."

To find our own language—a language we understand and that "speaks" to us—there are sitting practices (*zazen,* Vipassana, yoga, silent prayer) as well as movement practices (walking, spinning, turning). Both nonmotion and motion are forms of meditation; both teach us to be fully alert, which in itself is a form of ecstasy; and both bring us to the same goal of stillness. A woman I work with says that sometimes "I lift my arms up in a V formation and fly into awe like migrating birds." Another goes hiking by herself in the mountains to remind herself that she is "only one kind of life among the many."

"Like the moth drawn instinctively to the flame, we are irresistibly pulled to the source of our existence," writes Shakina Reinhertz. Her book *Women Called to the Path of Rumi* is about the practice of turning, which the followers of Rumi, the Mevlevis, formalized into a ritual that has passed down intact for six hundred years. "Turning, like drumming, belongs to all of humanity," Shakina says. The practice of turning is a natural and organic way of experiencing ecstasy that goes back to the original Paleolithic campfires of our ancestors. Artifacts from the same period have also revealed the frame drum, so it is likely that sophisticated rhythmic movements were already in play. What could be more natural than to imitate the circular motion of life that is revealed on all levels? Little children put one foot in front of the other to turn. Tibetan Buddhists form a circle for the New Year God dance, the members turning on their own axes. Shakers turn until they "come out right." Turning is a form of sacred prayer. Shakina, who has been turning for twenty years, talks about the formal practice. "First, the concentration is in the feet, then the body, the arms, then to the people on each side of you, then to an awareness of all the people turning in the room. Everyday thoughts drop aside. There is no thinking; you enter a new consciousness. In time, the mind expands, becoming lucid but emptied of the ordinary. With each revolution you are saying Allah in your heart, so the practice becomes a powerful group prayer. Then there comes a point—*Inshallah!* (god willing!)—when it moves from turning to being turned; when you disappear and are with god."

The participating presence of others offers powerful encouragement to seekers. The Buddha actually spoke of community (the *sangha*) as one of the Three Refuges. But in fact all sacred traditions agree that community—the meeting, sharing, and interreliance—is a central foundation of spiritual practice. Such an ingathering of people is called the fellowship in Christianity, the minyan in Judaism, and the *sohbet* in Sufism: a style of informal investigation and an intimate conversation regarding spiritual matters among those who are on the path.

Sacred words and ritual—regardless of their tradition—are heart openers: in the inner stillness they inspire, they actually free the fixated mind and tyrannical ego from the habit of self-absorption. In effect, they encourage us *not* to take things personally but instead to gain what William James in *The Varieties of Religious Experience* called "oversight" and the Vipassana teacher Christina Feldman refers to as the "long view . . . a sense of spaciousness and openness around oneself." This is, of course, a view framed not by our hindered minds but by discovering through gentle persistence with these practices that our own consciousness holds the gift of deep and penetrating insight—insight not obscured by the tight grip of a narrow "me" focus. In *Faith,* Sharon Salzberg speaks about the *ishta dev,* which in Hinduism is the personal deity to whom you offer your heart, chosen for the qualities you most wish to emulate. For one person it might be the Virgin Mary; for another, Kali, the Hindu goddess of Creation and Destruction. Sharon's *ishta dev* is the Statue of Liberty, "because she seems as enduring as the freedom she symbolizes."

THE SACRED, THEN, is about our inherent need to find openings onto the spaciousness of the transcendent as it may be personally discovered and experienced, and as it moves, quickens, and enlivens the spirit. So it is very much about time given over to solitude and a quality of sharing that often moves beyond one's relationships with other people. Yet satisfying this need may just as easily be about going fishing or gardening or watching birds build their nests or listening to music or to silence. It may also be about holding one's awareness while waiting for the light to change or sitting on a bus. And it may be about prayer, or meditation, or going into a cloistered space. Whatever "it" is, assuredly it is that thing that lifts us out of ourselves, fills a dark room with light, stills the droning mind, quiets us.

Often the most ordinary choices can bring us to the sacred. Toinette Lippe, whose book *Nothing Left Over* describes the joys of living well in a state of simplicity, discovered that something as simple as changing the form of the bread she bakes gives her a "different view of things" and even "changes the outcome": "Sometimes I make a long loaf, and sometimes I make rolls. When I take the bread out of the oven, the texture and the taste are different, depending on the shape and size. This never fails to surprise me."

ONE ORDINARY MORNING Anna wakes up with a queasy stomach and does all the right things for herself. She drinks water, herbal tea, and ginger ale; sends herself healing energy; tries to forget how she feels; and hopes the sour feeling will go away. When it persists, Anna wonders whether a walk would help. It's early afternoon; the rain has stopped. A walk down Lexington Avenue might do her good. Should she? Shouldn't she? Anna decides she should.

Even so, the debate continues. Going down the elevator, she sees her own image before her, resting comfortably on the living room couch and slyly beckoning her to return. Now there are two Annas, or, rather, one Anna in *two* places: one is walking out the front door but tempted to go back; the other is walking out the front door determined to continue her walk. Before she even reaches the corner, Anna's thoughts have shifted into a minor key where baleful regrets tug one way ("I can't wait to get home"), and then the other ("I'll take a very *short* walk"). She spirals back to last night's dinner, where she ate too much. Her father used to tell her: "Your eyes are too big for your stomach. You'll never learn." Anna's stomach is staying sour. "When will you ever learn?" she asks herself.

Anna turns the corner and is halfway down the block before a realization stops her short. Here she is, caught once again in the same old "self-centered dream," and she has sleepwalked the whole way: without seeing people, stores, or traffic; without hearing their sounds; without smelling the compost of city life around her; without being exactly where she is and no place else. And for the hundred-millionth time she recognizes that she has gotten completely lost in her thoughts—blaming herself and making judgments about not feeling well. Anna breathes a sigh of relief. She realizes that if she reenters the present and stays aware, responding moment by moment to whatever *is,* but no longer getting caught in judgment, she can rescue her ego from being trapped in old conditioning. The choosing, picking mind is quieted; in this way of seeing, one thing isn't better than the other; there is no preferred vision; nothing is special and everything is special.

My JOY AS a psychotherapist is in seeing people move from need to desire, and, sometimes, even to the higher frequencies of deep longing. The mystic and poet Rumi expressed it this way: "Little by little, wean yourself. This is the gist of what I have to say. From an embryo, whose nourishment comes in the blood, Move to an infant drinking milk, To a child on solid food, To a searcher after wisdom, To a hunter of more invisible game." In this pursuit, fullness comes, and with it a generosity of spirit that many of us have never known before. We have become free enough to find the sacred in all of life—beginning with the hallowed ground of one's own self. What better preparation can there be to enter—or renew—our relationships—whether with loved ones, friends, the communities we are in or choose to become part of—than by having spent time in solitude. This fullness of self is the offering we can bring to others.

Chapter Nine

ALONENESS AND RELATIONSHIP

As much as I have talked about how aloneness inspires self-sovereignty, creative living, and even a sense of the sacred, we cannot bring our new—and, hopefully, satisfying—connection to aloneness into fruition unless we are prepared to take what we have learned into the heart of our relationships with other people. That would be like spending hours alone in the kitchen cooking a splendid six-course meal and then forgetting to invite the guests.

The truth is that, seasoned by solitude, we're ready to welcome others to our table, having more of ourselves to offer and share. But because it can be hard to feel sure of this, we postpone invitations for fear the guests won't show up. Before we can resolve this very real dilemma, we need to answer this question: "If I embrace solitude, and if I accept being a woman alone, does that mean that I'm consigned to a life without an intimate relationship?" The answer is both "No" and "Maybe, but that's okay." "No," because at any age and stage of our lives, it is possible to meet a person who becomes, if not our dream lover, then a wonderful friend and companion. And "Maybe," because no matter what friends, family, dreams, astrologers, or soothsayers may say about our future, we have no way of knowing what will happen to us in the next hour, let alone the rest of our lives. This doesn't mean we can't take charge of our lives. In fact, the more responsibly we care for ourselves, the greater our chances of improving the quality of our lives and of those we love, sometimes to astonishing degrees. But this is much more about our willingness to collaborate with destiny than it is to try to determine destiny's course. And if, by chance, we don't find that romantic relationship we yearn for, we surely have other enriching possibilities—lovers, family members, the friends we make, old and new, and the communities we belong to, or become part of, can enrich our lives immeasurably—as long as we stay open and receptive.

Hardest of all, it seems, is simply to surrender to what feels to us intuitively right, even though this will be what our deepest self is telling us to do. Beyond that, we need to accept that being alone is where we're at, and that where we're at is okay. The point—and I can't stress this emphatically enough—is that we want always to speak and act through an informed heart. And there is no better way to arrive at the wisdom of the informed heart than by embracing solitude instead of trying to escape it. By doing so, we make a commitment to self that allows us to get in touch with our own worthiness. No matter whether we are alone or not, that is the battle worth fighting. The rest is about fighting windmills, and it's all uphill.

LISA REDUX

Five years after her breakup with Sam, Lisa, whom we met in chapter 1, is doing well. Soon after Sam left, her career as a set designer started to take off when the set she created for a successful off-Broadway play caught the attention of a well-known Broadway director, who hired her to design the sets for his next play. That was the turning point, and she has been working steadily ever since.

Finding a close and satisfying relationship, however, took longer. After Sam left, Lisa was wary of men. She kept the apartment she had shared with Sam, living alone, mourning her loss, thinking a lot about what had gone wrong between them, and wrestling with concern that the breakup had been her fault. "The first six months were terrible. Being alone in the apartment stirred up all sorts of painful feelings, and I hated going home. Thank god my work kept me busy. I'd get home so late each night that all I could do was turn on the news and get ready for bed. Sleep was never a problem. I was exhausted." Eventually her pain subsided and Lisa began to appreciate the time she spent alone in her apartment. "Once I could think clearly again, I kept wondering why I had been so undone by the end of a relationship that I *knew* had gone bad. It's amazing when I think about it," she says now, "some part of me wanted out as much as Sam did, but I was afraid to let go." Lisa realizes that she had been smitten by Sam's glamour and charisma, even though it was a double-edged sword. On the one hand, she basked in his aura, feeling like the chosen one; on the other hand, she worried about whether every attractive woman in the room might steal him away from her. "I thought about that a lot—how I could have believed that my own life counted for less without him, but, even worse, how I could feel that as a person *I* was worthless. I wasn't going to let that happen again, if I could help it, so I just decided to be on my own for a while." So Lisa took time for herself, devoting herself to her work, and enjoying the company of her close friends, and for a long time that was what she needed. "I got to know myself in ways I never could when I was in a relationship because I was too self-conscious, more concerned about what others thought about me than about living according to my own values."

Lisa's biggest worry was "having no sex drive whatsoever," but her best friend, Sabrina, who had gone through a similar breakup and was in the middle of a hot new romance, assured her it was temporary. "Don't worry, love," Sabrina said in her breezy English accent. "Sex is like a river; sometimes it just goes underground awhile and you can't hear it. It'll splash up to the surface again, you'll see."

Then, at the opera one night, Lisa met Alex, tall, athletic, prematurely gray, and handsome. He took his seat beside her just as the curtain was going up, and something about him set off small seismic quakes inside her. They started a conversation during intermission, and by the time it was over, they had exchanged phone numbers. Over dinner a few days later, Lisa learned that in addition to being a music lover, Alex was an environmental lawyer, a gourmet cook, and a passionate bicyclist who had pedaled his way through the south of France and planned to buy a house there one day. That was the good news. The bad news was that he was fifty-five, going through his second divorce, and had a twelve-year-old daughter from marriage number one. Still, Lisa was attracted to Alex, and it didn't take long for her libido to return in full force. "You're right, Sabrina," she said, laughing, after their first night together, "it's back, and it's a geyser." "Congratulations. Have fun," Sabrina told her.

Lisa's friend Katherine was less enthusiastic. "I don't trust him," she said. "He's a little too perfect, or should I say slick." Lisa had just spent a weekend at Alex's house in the Berkshires, where, she couldn't help notice, photographs of Alex's wives were still on display. She was becoming aware that she had fallen for a somewhat older incarnation of Sam—the same charm, charisma, and unreliability— so she took Katherine's words to heart. She noticed how often Alex broke their dates at the last moment, pleading a heavy workload or some emergency with his daughter. A few months later, Alex left for a bicycling trip up the northern California coast, telling Lisa he would call as soon as he arrived at the San Francisco airport. When a week passed and she hadn't heard from him, she knew that what had barely begun was already over. When he finally did call, Lisa overrode Alex's apology. "You're six days out of my life, and I prefer it that way." During the next year, Lisa had a few more "encounters," as she liked to call them, because she knew they wouldn't amount to anything, and sometimes she and her friend Matthew would spend the night together and, by mutual consent, make love "for the sheer friendly comfort of giving each other bodily pleasure." But most of the time, Lisa found to her surprise that she was perfectly content being by herself. "When you're celibate, is it okay to use a vibrator?" she asked Sabrina, only partly joking. "It's okay to use anything except a man," Sabrina said, laughing.

Then Lisa met Simon. They ran into each other at the farmers market, and though Lisa couldn't place him, Simon reminded her that they had met before—he was the jewelry designer who had designed the bracelet she was wearing—a gift from Sam. Simon smiled at her. His eyes, she noticed, were large and kind. They talked for a while, decided to go for lattes, and talked some more. In the following months, they moved, very slowly, from lattes to sharing meals together or going to the movies. The night they first made love surprised them, for both its ease and its tenderness. What continues to astonish Lisa is that Simon is nothing like any of the men she's been drawn to. "He's shy, he's an introvert, he doesn't care a whit about his appearance, and he couldn't care less about making a name for himself. So why am I with him?" she asks her friends. "That's exactly why," they remind her. "He's real, and he's a real man. You can't do better than that."

Eventually, Simon asked Lisa if she ever thought about living together. "Well, yes, but no . . . I mean, I've been living alone so long," she heard herself saying, "I'm not sure I want to give up my freedom." Lisa's growing intimacy with Simon enabled her to measure her progress since separating from Sam and to ask herself probing questions about what she wants from a relationship. She now realizes that being with Sam was largely about her own unfulfilled needs. Still, she has no regrets; she knows that love affairs, for all the pain and dislocation they may cause, are part of our initiation into selfhood. As Lisa began to take back her own power, the needs and dependencies she fed on have turned into strengths. Now she can ask the kinds of questions she would have been too afraid to address before: If I am a woman alone, do I want to stay that way? If so, why? And if not, why not? Can I be a woman alone and still have an intimate relationship with a man? And if I do decide to have children, does that mean I should get married first?

Lisa is not yet sure about what her answers will be, and she is grateful that Simon isn't pressing her. In the interim, however, she decided to send him a letter, describing what her life was like before, what it is like now, and what she requires for herself: "time to work, to meditate, to be with my friends, and to just be alone. Please let me know if you can agree to this." Once again, Lisa was surprised. Simon seemed comfortable with everything she wanted for herself. In *Love in the Western World,* Denis De Rougemont says: "*To be in love is not necessarily to love.* To be in love is a state; to love, an act." Lovers teach us the difference between excitation and love. They can also help demystify the oldest romantic myth of all: that one plus one equals a whole. Lisa knows that she is a whole; that Simon is a very different whole; and that while they don't "fit" together in all respects, they don't need to. As long as they have the staying power of mutual admiration, fondness, and respect that evolve primarily out of our own sense of self-worth, they have the necessary ingredients for a genuine relationship. How different this is from the pinched, cramped search to find what is missing in ourselves in another person, as Lisa did with Sam—as we all do when we're just beginning to learn about ourselves.

The other day, Lisa looked at me and burst out laughing. We had been recalling the terror-stricken version of herself and the distance she has come in gaining perspective and wisdom as a woman alone. "Can you imagine me being with Simon six or seven years ago? We would have killed each other," she says. "Maybe," I answer, "but you would have had to notice him first." Lisa thinks a moment. "It's true," she says. "Not for a minute could I have ever imagined him in my life." I look at the woman sitting across from me, growing so solidly into the fullness of self, and feel gratified, for I know with heartwarming certainty that she will find the right answers for herself.

ELLEN AND ROBERT

Ellen was twenty-two the summer she married Robert. In a way, their union was inevitable. Their parents were good friends and, because the two families lived within blocks of each other in the Boston suburb of Lexington, Ellen and Robert virtually grew up together. Ellen says she fell in love with Robert at fifteen, listening to him debate the need to preserve the rain forests; she thought he was smart and cute and perfect. As for shy, bookish Robert, he would probably say he had never thought romantically about anyone else. Ellen was lively and extroverted; what's more, from the time they were children, she seemed to have a talent for drawing him out. Robert proposed when they were both in college. Ellen couldn't imagine a better idea.

They got married right after graduation. Robert was about to start graduate school in anthropology at Harvard, and Ellen was beginning her second year as a substitute elementary-school teacher. Money was very tight, so they moved in with Robert's parents. One evening after dinner, Ellen was feeling antsy, impatient with a conversation between Robert and his father about species of butterflies. She decided to go for a long walk by herself. It was, she said, her earliest memory of discontent; she had just found out she was pregnant with her first child, Robert was absorbed in his studies, her own family had moved to Arizona the year before, and she had begun to feel enmeshed in the Clarks' household. "I wanted to live with my husband and just be our own family. The Clarks were very kind, but they were always around. We never really had the chance to be together as a couple." By the time Robert began writing his doctoral dissertation a few years later, Ellen was taking care of their first child, Sophie, and expecting another. Life felt rigidly circumscribed, and she couldn't wait to have her own home. She and Robert started looking that spring. They had always wanted to live in the country, and when they found a small farmhouse in northern Massachusetts with several acres of land, they bought it.

For a while it seemed that Ellen had gotten everything she wanted. But there were new realities to deal with. Robert took a job as a teaching assistant at Harvard, staying in Cambridge during the week and coming home only on the weekends. When he was home, he was often grading papers or working on his dissertation, and Ellen began to resent the fact that she was the designated caregiver, while Robert felt free to come and go as he pleased. To make matters worse, they were mostly living on money borrowed from Robert's parents, so there was no room in the budget for babysitters. With no time to herself and only Robert for adult companionship, Ellen began to depend on his company. The more needy she felt, the further Robert withdrew emotionally. He wondered what happened to the vivacious woman he had married. Ellen, hurt by Robert's lack of attention, felt more and more disillusioned with their marriage.

Ellen had always been a dutiful daughter; now she'd become a dutiful wife and mother as well. She had assumed that she would get married one day and raise a family, and her career ambitions had never reached beyond being an elementary-school teacher. She automatically deferred to Robert. "He was my authority for everything because he knows so darn much—even now, the level and scope of his knowledge amazes me—and I'm sure I saw myself very much through him."

But in the politicized atmosphere of the late sixties and early seventies, a time when women were beginning to raise questions about their roles and their identities, Ellen was beginning to realize that there might be more to life than a heap of failed-marriage dreams. Her girls were both in school all day, and when some of her new friends urged her to join their women's group, she agreed. Soon she was reading the works of de Beauvoir, Betty Friedan, Germaine Greer, and others, and having long conversations about them with members of the group; it was only a matter of time before she would begin to feel the stirrings of her discounted self.

"In my group someone would ask a question, say, about how children should be raised. I would say, 'Well, Robert says,' and they would respond, 'Yes, but what do *you* think?'" Slowly, Ellen began to separate out her own voice from Robert's, and, as she did so, gained confidence in her own ideas. But when she began talking to Robert about them, like believing they should share responsibility for child rearing and household tasks and keep a common kitty for expenses, he became defensive, and their discussions quickly escalated into full-fledged fights. "Robert's standard line was, 'You have no idea how heavy it is to grow up as a man and have the expectation that you will support a family.' Mine was, 'You don't know how diminishing it is for no one to expect anything from you.'" Neither could accept that they were both right, and their battles were ongoing. To make matters more complex, Ellen had agreed to do the administrative work for Robert's newly established center for the study of science and religion, but she soon started to feel that the academics who formed the core of the center's operations treated her more like a secretary than an equal. "We took the center to bed with us at night and got up with it in the morning, trying to make a go of it." The problem, of course, was that they had no time or energy left over to be a couple, or for Ellen to explore what she wanted for herself.

As their marriage started to disintegrate, Robert continued to escape into his work. Feeling lonely and lost, Ellen decided to seek a psychotherapist. "The work I started to do on myself was crucial. It allowed me to begin to separate myself out from Robert's life." Her first act of assertion was to resign from the center. She found a job as a student adviser at the local community college, counseling young people about their educational goals and helping them plan their courses and schedules. She soon discovered that she loved this work; it suited her helping, caring personality perfectly; moreover, her supervisors saw her talent and acknowledged it. At thirty-nine, she decided to go back to school for a master's degree in education.

Then Ellen found a note Robert had written to a close friend of hers, and began to suspect they were having an affair. "I was destroyed. It felt as though the center of me had been pulled out, leaving this enormous hole," she says. Robert insisted that Ellen had misconstrued the relationship. But to Ellen it didn't matter. "The emotional connection between them was there without me. It was everything I hadn't been getting from Robert in our marriage. She got it all." Ellen filed for divorce.

But the shattering impact of her realization also catalyzed Ellen's search for self. Not only had she made the choice to be a woman alone, she also understood that her whole life was now open for exploration. As she describes it: "Nothing I had ever thought or felt or believed made sense anymore. And I was very aware that what I had to protect and get to the heart of was this very vulnerable core of *me*."

No woman who has been through the breakup of a marriage, especially when there is another woman involved, likes to remember the early painful days of separation. We cope as best we can because we must, but at a slow pace, like automatons, not like women seeking freedom for themselves. Instead, we are thrust back on ourselves, and the self is still too fragile to bear the weight. It is even harder when, for all our grievances, our anger and frustration, we know in our hearts that we still love the person we are leaving. Yet sometimes the leave-taking still needs to happen.

Neither Robert nor Ellen had stopped loving each other. But their love was encrusted with the residue of neglected, spurned, and unheeded feelings that could find no natural outlet in the company of the other. Indeed, in their worst moments, they could barely feel the other's suffering at all; their own had taken over all the emotional space inside them; as for the good feelings, the loving feelings, those energies had been unlovingly spent.

The girls would now stay with Ellen during the week and with their father on the weekends. Because Robert had begun to earn a decent income, he also paid for child support. Otherwise, Ellen was on her own—"uprooted," as she described herself—and had to endure the growing pains of separation and loss, but also of anger and hurt, which are part of the reclamation of self. As for Robert, he was "stunned" by the reality of the actual separation and felt sad and disappointed at the rupture of his family. Yet he accepted that as one of two people in the relationship, he was partially responsible for what went wrong and aware that he had a great deal of personal exploration to do.

As a woman alone, Ellen worked part-time to complete her master's degree, stayed loyal to her women's group, and continued therapy; she also made some new friends, dated other men, and became active in her church. Gradually, as she could begin to measure her accomplishments and see that she could shape her own life without depending on Robert, Ellen started to feel more resilient and self-assured. "Still, I would be very aware of being alone, and sometimes I felt so lonely. I wanted an intimacy, a deep emotional connection to someone, like I'd once had with Robert. Then I would look at other people's marriages and I would think, Well, how many people really have that? and so my inner dialogue would continue. Many nights I just cried. I'm not the despairing type, I just think I was healing."

After the girls went to bed at night, or when they were at Robert's, Ellen also spent a lot of time in solitude. In the warm weather, she took long walks by herself in the woods, baked bread, and canned fruits and vegetables; during the long winters, she wrote in her journal and took up knitting in earnest; as her fingers knitted and purled, she could feel herself relax. For that was when her mind came to rest, her body grew quiet, and she could tune into the frequencies of her own sonorous self as it began to emerge.

Seven years passed this way, while Ellen and Robert created new lives and relationships. Still, when Ellen heard a rumor that Robert was getting married again, she felt a pang of loss and regret whose intensity surprised her. She called to congratulate him, and was even more surprised at her relief when he told her it wasn't true. They caught up with each other during the call, and soon were talking regularly on the phone and occasionally meeting for dinner. Sometimes they took walks in the countryside, bringing a picnic basket with them. "We didn't think about what was happening," Ellen said. "It wasn't a matter of 'let's get back together,' it was about lots of real talking, having good times together, and rekindling our friendship." To their surprise, romance once again flourished between them.

In the years since the divorce, Ellen had been building herself up inside and out; having questioned her assumptions, conditioning, and ingrained expectations about who she was and what she wanted as a woman, her false self had fallen away. She felt sure of herself, no longer threatened by Robert's intellectual confidence, or angry and frustrated about what he couldn't give her, and the love that had always been there between them began to flow again. As Ellen puts it: "They say that the cells in our body renew themselves every seven years. I guess we had to be completely 'new' before this could happen."

An established, or renewed, sense of self allows each person in a relationship to see, and accept, the other as they are. But relationships that are negatively reinforced by one person's needs inevitably obscure the reality of who the other is by superimposing—projecting—who he or she "should" be. Given the high failure ratio of such an enterprise, it is no wonder that idealization turns into contempt, criticism, defensiveness, and, eventually, alienation: the ultimate withdrawal, not only of one's affection but of one's active and responsive *presence* from the other. When we reach that level of erosion—as happened in the first part of Ellen and Robert's story—we have left behind the possibility of a genuine relationship. "I hold this to be the highest task of a bond between two people: that each should stand guard over the solitude of the other," wrote the poet Rainer Maria Rilke, expressing a love that is evolved enough to allow both people "a wonderful living side by side" but does not rob either of their personal freedom. Love of this kind is shorn of neediness yet based on the individual needs of each person as well as what each needs from the other. What in fact "saved" Ellen and Robert, and indeed turned their story around, was their willingness not only to be alone but to surrender to the power of solitude as a way to transmute need into self-sovereignty. Only then could each begin to truly see the other—this time without the screen of projection.

Eventually, both Ellen and Robert came to the realization that they might be able to get what they had been seeking all along—a true partnership—and on Valentine's Day of the following year, they remarried in a private ceremony.

NOT ALL STORIES between couples end this satisfactorily. It is sometimes best to separate, or divorce ourselves, from the person we are with and the life we have been living. Should that moment arise, however, the question is: What will we do to help ourselves *afterward?* Do we rush headlong into the next person's waiting arms? Or decry our fate because no such person is waiting in the wings? Or do we take the time we need through intervals of solitude to learn about ourselves, our needs, our very self, so that we are sufficiently grounded in our own being to enter whatever relationship may come next?

Throughout this book, I have tried to make clear that to be a woman alone is not the end of the story, or the end of the line, but a beginning, a state of unexplored potential alive with possibilities. Yet it would be foolish to pretend that we enter aloneness with this knowledge securely rooted in our minds and hearts. As most of us know only too well, we need to befriend aloneness before this can happen—a process that takes time and patience. Even if we want, and have every right, to ask What comes next? each of us will still have to find our own answers as well as our own rewards. At no time is this more difficult than when a relationship ends in separation, divorce, or widowhood—especially when it comes to imagining a future for ourselves without a partner, without sex, or without both. In each case the same question applies: What are we going to do about it?

WHAT ABOUT SEX?

Regarding sex, it goes without saying that younger women are the most fortunate—and younger, educated women even more so, as author Paula Kamen indicates in *Her Way: Young Women Remake the Sexual Revolution,* citing a range of studies to show that their sex lives are more varied, and better, than ever. The rest of us, say, forty-five and above, have our options as well, even if they aren't quite what we might have hoped for ourselves. For while Gail Sheehy's *Sex and the Seasoned Woman: Pursuing the Passionate Life* may be overly optimistic about the sexual boom for women over fifty, Daphne Merkin's killjoy assessment in *The New York Times Magazine* article "What's So Hot About Fifty?" that most women over forty-five are left sexually adrift may be too large a dose of "corrective reality" than the situation warrants. The question is whether we are willing to go outside the box of more traditional thinking and be more sexually adventurous. I'm not suggesting that we try turning ourselves into reincarnations of Mae West, who could toss off a line like "Why don't you come on up and see me sometime . . . when I've got nothin' on but the radio" and mean it. Or (unless it sounds right for us) that we try to assert our sexual desires with the assertive aplomb of sixty-six-year-old Jane Juska, whose sexual memoir, *A Round-Heeled Woman,* describes how her sexual and romantic life started to take off right after she placed her personal ad in the *New York Review of Books:* "Before I turn 67—next March—I would like to have a lot of sex with a man I like. If you want to talk first, Trollope works for me." But that shouldn't stop the rest of us from, say, placing our own style of ad in the personals column; going to an Internet dating service; alerting every friend and then some that we are looking, not just for a partner but for a sexual partner; going as a party of one to more sedate but upscale restaurants; spending the night with a sexually available friend; or any combination of these. In the meanwhile, there is also the vibrator and a panoply of sex toys at our disposal, as well as a new and expanding oeuvre of "herotica," including videos and Internet sites, in which women are free, at least in fantasy, to express, and partake of, the same set of desires as a man. For those among us who prefer not to think about a sex life unless it's with an actual partner, or who prefer not to bother with sex at all, there's also celibacy. What matters most is that we try to the best of our abilities to find our own form of sexual gratification—always remembering that in the time of AIDS, we take great care to keep our bodies safe.

As regards new relationships, once again, depending on our outlook, taste, and degree of openness, life offers us many opportunities. Many women alone, both hetero- and homosexual, look for partners who are much younger, or older, than themselves. Other women, who have lived in heterosexual relationships through marriage and child rearing, often find deep satisfaction with same-gendered partners; still others create new communal-living situations for themselves, especially as they draw toward retirement age. If all else fails and there is no one on the horizon, we really do need to accept the reality that that's okay, or risk being unnecessarily miserable. For what we do have, or surely can give ourselves, is the fruit of our own creative lives as well as the deeply comforting, and reciprocally rewarding, embrace of family—even those of our own making—friends, and community.

WIDENING CIRCLES

FRIENDS

Think of the safe harbors in your life, and you will quickly realize that friendship is among the precious few. We share our joys and sorrows, hopes and aspirations, fears and desires, with friends, and, through this sharing, feel *mutually seen*. For women alone—especially single mothers, women newly divorced or widowed, middle-aged women caring for failing elderly parents, or "roleless" elderly women— friendship can serve as a life-affirming means of connection. Among women, friendship, at its best, offers the compelling *I Know Just What You Mean* response that is the title of a book by two lifelong friends, Ellen Goodman and Patricia O'Brien, who have always regarded each other with recognition and appreciation: "I know just what you mean" actually originates with "I know how you're made, how your body behaves, and what many of the issues are that you and I, as women, have faced in the past and will probably face in the future."

"Women's friendship," says Lithe Sebesta, "is like slipping into another skin. It's not freighted with sexual tension, so it can feel incredibly intimate." Friendships between women are structured for intimacy. In part, this is a legacy from our cave-dwelling days and the different gender experiences that were already being established, as well as our long history of being treated, and, over time, experiencing ourselves, as the subdominant gender. But the fact remains that the differences between men and women—and, consequently, the stylistic differences in how we communicate—is real and needs to be taken into account. As linguistics professor Deborah Tannen writes in *You Just Don't Understand: Women and Men in Conversation,* "many frictions arise because boys and girls grow up in what are essentially different cultures, so talk between women and men is cross-cultural communication." Men tend to engage in the world as individuals in a hierarchical social order and "try to achieve and maintain the upper hand" so as to preserve their independence as much as possible. Women approach the world as individuals who are part of "networks of connections" and negotiate for closeness by trying to "seek and give confirmation and support, and to reach consensus." Women actually struggle to preserve intimacy so that community can be maintained and isolation avoided.

The language of women is about caring, noticing, listening, and hearing; it has the capacity to extend beyond words to gesture and even silence. Barbara Graham, who has written about women's friendship in "The End of the (Friendship) Affair," says that among the many things she can share with her husband, "emotional body level sharing," which characterizes her relationships with her close women friends, isn't one of them. Sometimes, in fact, the stimulation, ego support, and self-affirmation that a friendship provides seems to have as much to do with the connection we *sense* through our conversations as with their content. Psychotherapist Stephanie Hanks puts it this way: "As women, we're *used* to communicating with each other. There's almost a shorthand language that develops between friends. When men listen, they don't really get what's going on, and women don't realize how much men really don't get it."

In Steve Martin's novel and film *Shopgirl,* this disconnect is set forth succinctly, and repeatedly, by Ray Porter, a successful businessman played by Martin, who starts an affair with the attractive and much younger Mirabelle, played by Claire Danes, who works in the glove department of a fashionable L.A. department store. After several dates, Ray tells Mirabelle, "I don't think I'm ready for a real relationship right now . . . [but] I love seeing you and I want to keep seeing you." What he means is that he's not prepared to commit to her or anyone else. But Mirabelle thinks this is his way of saying that he is falling in love with her. Eventually, their conflicting goals—her desire for intimacy with sex and his for sex with no intimacy—stalemate their relationship. Ray continues having affairs, while Mirabelle grows into herself as an artist and eventually finds a true relationship of the heart with her old friend Jeremy.

In friendship, we take turns being the nurtured and the nurturer. Friends are mirrors who remind us who we are and cheer us on to becoming more. In turn, we listen to their problems, offer advice when they ask for it, stand by them in their need, and take delight in what brings them pleasure. Friendship is a prism; turned one way, then the other, it teaches us about ourselves, bringing facets of ourselves to light that might otherwise remain dormant. For years, Beatrize, aged fifty, kept saying she wanted to leave the city, but she did nothing about it. One day, a close friend reflected back to her that she "came alive" whenever she spoke about the six months she had lived in New Mexico. "Don't you see?" her friend said. "There's nothing to keep you here. It's time for you to go where you want to be." Stunned, at first by her friend's frank counsel but also by her own reflexive inertia, Beatrize barricaded herself behind a dozen reasons why she couldn't leave. Her friend remained firm. "Just think about it," she suggested. In the following weeks, Beatrize came to the realization that her friend was right; lapsing into old story patterns about why she couldn't have what she wanted, she had almost forfeited her deepest desire. Six months after their conversation, Beatrize boarded a plane for Albuquerque and began a new—and life-affirming—chapter in her life.

Clara, a single woman with a gift for friendship, says her women friends help her maintain her relationship with her boyfriend by offering clarity. "For example, if I were to say, 'Guess what? He forgot my birthday again,' they'd probably say something like, 'Well, and what did you tell him? When this kind of thing happens, don't just accept it; bring it to his attention.' This is their way of letting me know, 'Yes, you've been discounted, but you have the power to change that.'" For Clara, that kind of frankness not only provides a much needed reality test, it has also emboldened her to stand up for herself. "Before, I didn't realize I was being discounted; now, I notice it a lot, and when I do, I say it loud and clear because by now there's no fear left."

As traditional family relationships shift over time, friends—women *and* men—can be a consciously chosen family. This is especially true for the millions of women who are already alone or who are transitioning into aloneness. Women's friendships are based on shared feelings and confidences; as such, they have the power to validate, heal, and transform, and are as essential to our mental and physical health as are good nutrition and exercise. Friends who share our interests, our passions, and at least some of our values and goals are intuitively aware that their potentiality—and ours—will be enhanced through such relationships. They are ready to cherish what is special about us and to offer, according to need, courage, consolation, common sense, and just plain presence.

"I have lost friends, some by death—others through sheer inability to cross the street," Virginia Woolf once poignantly confessed. "Crossing the street" is of course a metaphor for making the effort, and sometimes the extra effort, to be a good friend, especially if we have withdrawn because of wounded feelings or our own defensive hard-core inertia. Meaningful friendships are bound at times to stir up painful feelings. Sometimes a friend doesn't call when she says she will, or listen empathically enough to our story, or rough-rides our story with her own. If we accept these kinds of oversights as inevitable facts of human nature, rushed lives, or a friend's momentary self-preoccupation, then, as needed, we will open up a space to meet and talk and may even become closer for the effort. As we gain a stronger sense of self, we also grow more discriminating in choosing friends. As one woman told me, "I think you can sense early on whether it will be an uphill battle and you will always have to be smart, competitive, and careful, or whether there will be a flow back and forth."

Not all friendships are rose-colored. I have heard many women bemoan their lack of friends, the experience of the other's envy, jealousy, and betrayal, of being used or judged, and the pain of exclusion from one magic circle or other. Women also talk about the disheartening self-consciousness that often accompanies their need to please their friends at all costs, lest they lose them. Friendships on the brink can cause them almost as much suffering as unraveling romantic relationships; and sometimes—depending on how lonely or needy a person feels—even more. Instances of negligence, or worse— betrayal—inevitably stir up unresolved childhood disappointment, loss, and frustration. Sometimes we unconsciously choose friends whose behavior bears resemblance to our early painful experiences. On such occasions, one of the most mature acts we can take is to leave behind a friendship that makes us feel as if we always have to measure up to some kind of unattainable gold standard of what friendship is supposed to be. Wherever possible, the best course is honesty—a forthright statement that you might not be the kind of person your friend has been seeking, or that it's best at this time to go your separate ways.

Women today suffer a backlash for having been liberated from the narrow corridors of domestic space. Not only do we move more easily in the public realm than ever before in our history, but we are also beleaguered by the consequences and responsibilities that such freedom entails—including the stress that accrues with less personal time, more work, and highly compartmentalized lives. When a simple phone call to have a refrigerator repaired, fix a stalled computer, make a train reservation, or get Medicare benefits can take up to an hour, trapping us in the virtual reality of automated voice-mail responses, not only do we feel more stress but we have also lost valuable time for ourselves and our friendships.

Modern lives have become so fragmented, the pace of living so accelerated, that we can scarcely find time to shop for dinner, let alone have time left over for emotional or physical intimacy. Yet it's precisely when life rushes through our fingers so quickly that we need to set aside quality time for friendships to evolve. In an era of shifting personal relationships, friendship between women—particularly women alone—may well be our most reliable form of personal connection.

MENTORS AND ROLE MODELS

Almost every one of us needs a mentor at some point in our lives, someone who guides and protects, who embodies an as yet unrealized dimension of our being. A mentor lights a fire under our imagination, and stirs the embers of our languishing or lapsed longings, inspiring us to be who and what we want to be, and sometimes more than we imagined we could be. A certain body of knowledge gives the mentor—be it a woman or a man—the authority to counsel someone of lesser experience and wisdom. For women alone, especially those who are stepping out into various stages of becoming who they want to be, a mentor who has learned to prize the gift of solitude can be an invaluable guide and resource. Mentors enter our lives to set an example—and standard—of excellence. The mentor is unchafed by the rub of daily contact, real and unreal expectations, and the excess weight of too personal an investment in outcome, as, say, one's parent might be. In this sense, the mentor's status is that of a kind of fairy godmother, or godfather, whose occasional appearances grace and enrich our lives when we need them most.

My high school English teacher was one of my first mentors. Miss Doran never raised her voice. She didn't have to, so firmly centered was her quiet authority over us. We kids respected her, and her daily lessons held us, almost literally, spellbound, giving us no choice but to learn. Her classroom was as neat and orderly as a drawer full of old linens; by the end of the year no student left it without having learned the fundamentals of grammar; more than a few of us carried away an abiding love for literature as well. When Miss Doran told me I was college material, I believed her, even though there was no precedent in my family for pursuing a higher education. I felt seen by her, noticed but not judged, and the sheer newness and luxury of that feeling helped me begin to take myself seriously.

Mentors are usually older than we are, often by a decade or more. This is natural, since as neophytes we are just beginning our search for some knowledge or truth our mentor has already discovered. My friend Barbara was "saved" by a mentor after having been sexually abused by an older woman from the ages of eleven to fourteen. Starved of nurturing as a child by her own narcissistic mother, Barbara had been ripe for love of any kind, and for those three years a counselor at the camp where she spent her summers took full advantage of her innocence and need. Three years after the abuse ended, at age seventeen, Barbara was asked to babysit by a young wife and mother of two. Carmelita welcomed her into their household with warmth, affection, and, for the first time in her life, Barbara felt accepted. Equally important, Carmelita served as an example of the kind of mothering Barbara would emulate in her own life. Carmelita was the first person to whom Barbara disclosed the story of her seduction: "Because she was entirely without judgment, she taught me how to transform my wound into a sword of healing by telling my story to others, first in play form, and, more recently, as a personal memoir. She was the first person who taught me to be more fully myself, which is something I simply had not known before, and it had a very corrective effect on me."

Mentors are actual guides in one-on-one personal relationships. Role models need not be. In fact, most of the role models in my life are women I've never met. One of them was the artist Beatrice Wood, who found her purpose as the creator of unique and radiant luster-ware pottery that she produced until the last months of her life—she died at the fierce age of 104 years—at her Ojai, California, studio. But it was her indomitable spirit—playful, intense, sensual, theatrical, irreverent, and, as she wished it for herself, peaceful—that I marveled at when I first came across some of her work. The photographer Joyce Tenneson learned this same message when she created *Wise Women,* a photodocument about women over sixty-five. "When I saw how dynamic these women were," said Tenneson at fifty-six, "I completely lost my fear of aging." As my friend Elizabeth would say, they are "women of lines"—the experiences that made them who they are inscribed on faces wise and radiant by their continuing wonder and the sheer passion for life.

And that's exactly the point. For until we ourselves become women with lines, we need plenty of role models to remind us how we might grow into ourselves. This is especially true for women alone, who during harder times need to read and see for themselves how other women not only endure but learn to live wisely and well. I have welcomed such exemplars of courage and even keep a running list of women who have personally inspired me. Among them, this small sampling: Gloria Steinem, who cofounded *Ms.* magazine, Women's Action Alliance, the National Women's Political Caucus, and the Ms. Foundation for Women; Eve Ensler, who started V-Day and whose life is dedicated to the worldwide campaign against violence toward women; Julia Butterfly Hill, who spent two years living in a thousand-year-old redwood to protest logging; Michelle Bachelet, who became the first female president of Chile; medicine woman Gladys Tantaquidgeon, who helped to revive and preserve the spiritual and cultural traditions of Native Americans; Esther Dyson, who helped tame cyberspace; and Oprah Winfrey, who tirelessly teaches women to care about themselves. This is not to say that we should "be like" any of these women; only that it gives us strength and courage to inhale the pure oxygen of adventurers and athletes and novelists and ministers and artists and crusaders when we need a pick-me-up. Sometimes an image or story or a few chosen words from one of the many Miss Dorans in this world is all the kindling we need to ignite; the day will come when we will be able to express our gratitude. The written words of one young woman to her mentor say it all: "To you, whose heart, soul, and imagination inspire me. Thank you for asking me to live my depth. You returned me to life."

COMMUNITY

The plan is to assemble at Gail's house, then head over to the nearby pond. A map pinned to the front door directs latecomers how to get there. It is an unusually hot day, so after greeting one another, the women—we'll be sixteen by the day's end—hurriedly shed their clothes and head straight for the water. Some early birds are already sunning themselves on the float. A few of us decide to swim to the island point and climb up on the bank to rest before going back. Gail scans the shoreline. "There's Tina," she says, pointing to a barely discernible figure who seems to be gingerly making her way into the water. Tina, a lawyer and single woman who works in Montpelier, Vermont, decided to mark the occasion of turning forty by bringing together her closest women friends—ranging in age from thirty-six to seventy-five—for a weekend celebration at the Inn at Shelburne Farms. The experience proved so rewarding that the women planned a daylong reunion in August, only this time each invited her own friend, too. That's how I come to be here—my friend Gail having been part of the original group. Gail decides to swim back and say hello to Tina. The rest of us follow leisurely behind.

On the float, Tina's nieces, Phoebe and Laura, age eleven and thirteen, take turns diving into the water. They're hoping to entice their mother, Ellie, to join them, but she refuses to budge from her nearby perch on a fallen tree trunk. After a while, Ellie's mother, Alice, the last to arrive, decides to head back to the house and begin assembling the potluck dinner. By the time we follow lazily along, the float is already covered in shadow. I fix wine coolers and gin and tonics and bring them out to the deck, where the conversation ranges freely from romance (Gloria is describing a man she's just met and "quite likes" after having been divorced and on her own for the past few years) to the new production at East Calais's summer theater (where Ellie, her mother, and her two daughters will soon be performing in a Gilbert and Sullivan operetta). Jan talks about her eighty-six-year-old mother, who had a stroke after bypass surgery, the doctors having neglected to inform her of the increased risk. "Mother is of an age when most women believed that doctors were gods and their word as binding as law," Jan says. Whether the stroke could have been avoided is hard to know, given her mother's age and deteriorating health; still, Jan would have liked to have been told the medical probabilities. Everyone present has her own story of medical negligence to tell. "We need a buddy system," Tina says. "Each of us should find a friend or family member who would agree to advocate on the other's behalf in case of any kind of medical emergency." Her plan is a spin-off of the winter emergency procedure initiated by the Vermont contingent of the group. For the last three winters, whenever the weather forecasts a dip below zero, the women phone each other at two A.M. as a reminder to stoke their woodstoves. "That way, we don't have to worry that we'll freeze to death in our sleep when it hits forty below," a spirited woman named Joia says. By the time the evening draws to a close, important information has been exchanged, old friendships have deepened, and new ones have been formed. High above the meadow, the moon is now pale copper. Silhouetted in its light, we cut across the road to our cars.

We need to find ways to acknowledge ourselves—by ourselves, but also with friends and with community, so that we may step out feeling replenished and enlivened. Many women are beginning to understand this basic need. Several years ago my friend Ivy called me from Iowa. Her daughter Toby, then aged twelve, had just started menstruating. Ivy had been searching for some ritual that might help Toby's passage across the threshold from girlhood to adolescence. Finding none, she decided to fashion a ritual of her own. With Toby's approval, she threw a celebratory party and invited her daughter's intimate female circle of family and friends. Each guest chose her own form of commemoration: poems were recited, anecdotes told, photographs compiled. Miriam, Toby's former babysitter and now her somewhat older, wiser friend, choreographed a dance. Throughout the event, Toby accepted her role without self-consciousness. When it was over, she folded this moment—her moment—into her memory like a flower pressed inside a book.

Most women do not meet in supportive clusters amid peaceful Vermont landscapes or in living rooms in Iowa; many do not have the education or the stamina to review medical conditions that might be unfavorable to them; nor do they have buddy systems or support networks that link them to one another. In fact, most women are not even aware of their basic human right to such help or to know and expect that it will be forthcoming. At the very bottom of the heap are the millions of women who helplessly live the ultimate horror story of the outcast woman alone.

The art of being a woman alone is founded on a contradiction: to exist alone successfully, we need the solid bracing of friends, mentors, and community. A woman who has been raped needs to know the hotline number to call as well as the location of the nearest rape crisis center in her area. A woman who learns she has breast cancer needs the support of other survivors. A woman who chooses to be artificially inseminated, or, alternatively, to adopt a child on her own, needs to know the shortcuts from women who have already cut trails. A woman thinking about having an abortion needs the guidance and support of knowledgeable and, above all, nonjudgmental women. A single mother or a divorced woman who hasn't learned to take care of her finances needs solid advice from those who have. A woman faced with caring for an elderly parent needs concrete information about the kind and range of health-care services that exist. So, too, does a woman who needs to enter an assisted-living community, or find a hospice. Every woman among us must learn how to find, and use, the best educational, psychological, and social resources that are available to her. Every woman among us must learn how to protect herself against violence. Every woman among us must learn how to take care of her health. Such information and resources are not luxuries: they are absolute necessities. The Resources section at the back of this book is offered as a beginning guide.

Some women can point to a single moment when they realized that their fates were inextricably linked to one another and in small or larger measure did something about it. Take Laura Nurse, for example. Once divorced and once widowed by the age of sixty, Nurse says, "It took me a couple of years after my second husband's death just to . . . wake up. You know, to feel myself when I pinched myself." Once she did, she started to think seriously about going to Africa.

After her mother died in 2000, Nurse decided it was time. She quit her job as a sales executive at NBC, took out some of her twenty years of savings, and, without having made specific plans, traveled to the black township of Guguletu in Capetown, South Africa. "There was some important kind of convergence about losing my mother and gaining this relationship with the motherland," she says. With limited time at her disposal, Nurse decided to bypass the local NGOs (nongovernmental organizations) "because they moved too slowly." Instead, she went to a shelter called Ikya LaBantu, which stands for hope and shelter, and told them, "I'll start a program, but I need you to promise me that somebody can give me a ride into the township and get me back every day." Her next stop was the local school-supply store, where she bought notebooks, pens, and paper; when she realized there were no textbooks to give to her students, she made her own. To this day, the literacy program Nurse started continues to operate with volunteers, and 70 percent of her thirty-five students are now gainfully employed. She also started a scholarship fund in her mother's name that now has four scholars, two of whom are studying to become doctors, the other two lawyers. "If you can dream it, you can do it," Nurse says.

Most of us are not going to be Laura Nurse, who imagines a world where all children receive a proper education, or Dr. Helen Caldicott, who imagines a world without weapons. Nor are we supposed to be. These women are blessed by being on fire all the time—by the true marriage of passion and vision. Pioneering spirits, they light the way for the rest of us to clarify our own vision and feel our own passion. And so the path is lit that we may each have enough light for our own journey.

The power to prosper as women alone resides within us. By virtue of belonging to half of the human race we are already part of one particular "family," many of whose members are in drastic need of help. In saying this, I am not suggesting that the other half is less important, or that men's needs are less significant than women's; rather, I want to emphasize that gender is not merely a biological fact but a social category in which the two sexes have generally existed in a subordinate/dominate relationship. *And still do.*

More to the point: the fact that women are disadvantaged in most societies—including our own—has enormous bearing on women alone. Women are already differentiated by many subcategories— including age, marital status, life-cycle stage, economic situation, class, ethnicity, and race. If, added to this, we are also women alone, then we are obliged to deal consciously with the many old, and new, influences that are daily being brought to bear on us. As participants in the larger community of women, we benefit from learning more about who we are. Women in different circumstances respond differently to being alone, on both a micro and a macro level. For example: Does a black woman have different emotional responses to being left by a partner than a white woman? What kinds of psychological and social supports are available to working-class women in contrast to those for middle-class women? Does a middle-class Latino woman feel more isolated than her working-class cousin? Do wealth and privilege effectively screen out a woman's awareness of self? What kinds of supports are available to women of all social and economic classes who are preparing to retire and afraid to be without community? How does our social conditioning prepare us for being women alone? How do women at different ages and stages of life form, and keep, friendships? Clearly, these are just of few of the many questions to address; many more will be forthcoming as the numbers of women alone in this country and throughout the world increase.

As we begin to test the waters for ourselves and step out of our old ways of thinking—indeed, out of our old lives—and into the new, we should keep in mind three basic elements of transformation that will best serve our interests: *knowing, naming, and speaking.* We want to know our deepest feelings and desires. We want to name them so that we can call them forth. And we want to be able to speak on our own behalf through an informed heart and with a developed sense of our legitimacy and authority to do so.

HERE IS MY own dream. It begins with a May Stevens painting called *Sea of Words* (1990–91), in which mysterious white-clad figures that are unmistakably female glide by in white skiffs, one behind the other, each one *on her own* across a great expanse of an iridescent blue sea. At first, the women look like gulls resting on the surface of the water. But when you look closely, you see that the sea is not composed of water but of countless words—words, in my imagining, that have been thought, spoken, and sometimes silenced, then voiced again, and again, and again—until they become part of the great sea that supports these women and allows them to continue their journey in serene yet alert attention. When I first saw this painting in the Boston Museum of Fine Arts years ago, I thought of the historian Gerda Lerner's injunction to women not to be ignorant of our own history—of what women before us, generation unto generation, have known and thought—lest we find ourselves struggling for insights already born and make the mistake of endlessly reinventing the wheel. Then I noticed that the women's oars dipped into the sea like arms so that their words could reach out in ever-expanding circles and be heard by all of us: we women who are alone and *all one*.

Notes

1. IF I AM A WOMAN ALONE, WHO AM I?

9   *Given the facts*   U.S. Census 2000, Summary Files 1 & 3. Note that of the nearly 13 million female-headed households (18 percent of households), almost 9 million included related children under the age of 18. Statistics for divorced women is from Brian Willats, *Breaking Up Is Easy to Do,* Michigan Family Forum, citing Statistical Abstract of the United States (1993): 385.

9   *de Beauvoir*   Simone de Beauvoir, *The Second Sex* (New York: Vintage, 1989 [1952]); see especially the Introduction, xix–xxxv.

11   *basic human need*   According to the U.S. Census, Current Population Survey, March 2002, women aged 65 and older were four times more likely to be widowed than their male counterparts (8.9 million widowed women versus 2.0 million men). Moreover, according to the U.S. Census 2000, Summary Files 1 & 3, 7,327,224 women over 65 live alone, versus only 2,395,633 men in the same group. The experience of living alone is one most women can expect to have; the same is not true for men, who are over three times less likely to live alone.

11   *Depressed men*   Terrence Real, *I Don't Want to Talk About It: Overcoming the Secret Legacy of Male Depression* (New York: Scribner, 1997). See also Jim Thornton's "So Tough It Hurts," *AARP,* May & June 2006, 26–28, 76–77. And for an interesting gender comparison, see Sarah Mahoney's "The Secret Lives of Single Women" in this same issue, 50, 52–56, 73–74.

15   *inevitably find ourselves alone*   Quantifying "women alone" through demographic data is challenging because of terminology confusions; for example, surveys classify women who live with a partner as "single"; also, the census data for women living alone doesn't reflect women who live with other people yet are without "partners." Two additional points deserve notice: first, given the shifting circumstances of women at any point in time, it would be impossible to estimate reliably the actual numbers of women who are "separated" or for other reasons fall into the category of women alone; second, women

who are marginalized (such as runaway adolescents, migrants, the homeless) are unlikely to be counted in any kind of survey and, certainly, will not be "legitimized" as women alone.

17   *James's*   Henry James, *The Portrait of a Lady* (New York: Penguin Books, 1963 [1881]), 161.

17   *Stoker's*   Bram Stoker, *Dracula* (New York: Bantam, 1981 [1897]), 62.

17   *Heilbrun*   Carolyn Heilbrun, *Writing a Woman's Life* (New York: Ballantine, 1989), 28.

17   *Caldwell*   Gail Caldwell, "A Solitary Life," *The San Diego Union-Tribune* (November 3, 1997), E-1, 4. See also Caldwell's Memoir, *A Strong West Wind* (New York: Random House, 2006).

18   *More than thirty million*   http://www.census.gov/Press-Release/www/2003/cbo3ffo3.html. The actual number is 30.7 million.

18   *Ten million of these*   U.S. Census, 2001.

2. WHAT IS ALONENESS?

24   *The great activist*   From "The Solitude of Self," Elizabeth Cady Stanton's last address to Congress, delivered to the Congressional Judiciary Committee in 1892. Stanton's essay first appeared in the *Woman's Journal,* Boston, January 23, 1892.

25   *"The Little Match Girl"*   For a complete version and illluminating interpretation of Hans Christian Andersen's fairy tale, see Clarissa Pinkola Estes, "Clear Water: Nourishing the Creative Life," chapter 10 in *Women Who Run with the Wolves: Myths and Stories of the Wild Woman Archetype* (New York: Ballantine, 1995 [1992]), 322–61.

26   *Meera Kim*   Ms. Kim's photograph by Joanne Kim appeared in "What They Were Thinking," *The New York Times Magazine* (July 18, 1999), 24.

28   *Anna Christensen*   Interview, New York City, November 12, 2003.

29   *old Buddhist scripture*   Anna is quoting from "Hsn Hsin Ming: On Believing Mind," by Seng-t'san, third Chinese patriarch of Zen, who died in 606 C.E.

31   *"It was marriage"*   Vivian Gornick, "On Living Alone," chapter 6, in *Approaching Eye Level* (Boston: Beacon, 1996), 137–49, 140.

31   *"the loneliest number"*   Lyrics to "One" by Harry Nilsson for the band Three Dog Night, on ABC-Dunhill/MCA Records, 1969; Gabriel Meckler, producer.

31   *When Brad Pitt*   Ginna Bellafante, "Brad, Jen and Hollywood's New Morality Tale," Sect. 4, *The New York Times Week in Review* (January 16, 2005), 12.

33 *aloneness and connection*   D. W. Winnicott, "The Capacity to be Alone," in *The Maturational Processes and the Facilitating Environment: Studies in the Theory of Emotional Development* (New York: International Universities Press, 1965), 29–36, 34.

33 *In his groundbreaking book*   Storr, *Solitude*. See also Ester Schaler Buchholz, *The Call of Solitude: Alonetime in a World of Attachment* (New York: Simon & Schuster, 1997). Both books are notable for a concentrated exploration of the aloneness we know as solitude for its healing, creative, and spiritual power; moreover, both authors are aware that connection, or "attachment," satisfies only part of our human needs. Storr concentrates on the creative aspect of solitude, Buchholz on our personal connection to solitude as a missing yet necessary dimension of living.

34 *the psychological community has not made*   See Frieda Fromm-Reichmann's unfinished essay, "On Loneliness," in *Psychoanalysis and Psychotherapy, Selected Papers of Frieda Fromm-Reichmann,* D. Bullard, ed. (Chicago: University of Chicago, 1959), 325–36. While Fromm-Reichmann's focus was the psychodynamics of loneliness, particularly the deep loneliness that leads to psychological isolation, she was aware of the psychological community's "avoidance" in dealing with aloneness in all its variations as an explicit category of human experience. Having said this, I want to acknowledge a distinguished contribution to the subject of loneliness in *Contemporary Psychoanalysis,* Vol. 26, No.2, April 1990, journal of the William Alanson White Institute, which devoted considerable space to analytic reflections on Fromm-Reichmann's last work. In particular, Myer D. Mendelson's thoughtful essay, "Reflections on Loneliness," 330–55, suggests that the fear of loneliness in Western societies is a culturally-conditioned phenomenon, and speculates that the shame and fear of rejection associated with loneliness inhibits people from openly declaring their loneliness. He concludes: "Accordingly, loneliness in and of itself may not necessarily be a condition to be 'cured'. . . . And where one calls upon creative resources to make the best of a stressful situation, loneliness may be turned to good account." Ildiko Mohacsy stresses this same point in "Solitude in a Changing Society: A Discussion of Fromm-Reichmann's 'Loneliness,'" stating that "the best route . . . is to help people live happily alone," 360–64. Finally, in "A Note on Fromm-Reichmann's 'Loneliness,'" George Satran suggests that analytic supervisors can teach their students, wherever possible, "to ask patients to be specific about the details, context, and texture of their loneliness," 367–69.

36 *Romero*   Christianne Zehl Romero, Ph.D., Interview, August 18, 2005.

36 *Jan Roy*   Interview, August 10, 2005.
37 *Schachtel*   Zeborah Schachtel, Ph.D., Interview, December 15, 2004.

3. SHAME-IN-HIDING: A WOMAN'S CULTURAL HERITAGE

41 *the spinster*   For etymology, see, among other sources, Adrian Room, ed., *Cassell's Dictionary of Word Histories,* (London: Cassell, 2002).

42 *we identified our longings*   For some examples, see E. M. Forster's *A Room with a View,* Tennessee Williams's *Glass Menagerie,* Henry James's *Daisy Miller,* Edith Wharton's *The Old Maid* and *The House of Mirth,* and any of Jane Austen's novels.

42 *American artist Thomas Eakins*   John Wilmerding, ed., *Thomas Eakins (1844–1916): The Heart of American Life* (London: National Portrait Gallery, 1993), 160. Addie is Mary Adeline Williams.

43 *114 million adult women*   In the strictest sense, about 15.5 million women live alone at any given time, and about half of all women age 15 and above are not married. If we count the total number of separated, divorced, widowed, or never-married women who are over 34, breaking down marital status by age, the statistics also include 33 percent of females aged 35 to 59 and 53.6 percent of females aged 60 and older. Note also that the population of women alone nearly doubled from 7.3 million in 1970 to 15.3 million in 1998. U.S. Census 2000, PHC-T-27, Table 3.

45 *"My father tried to kill"*   Annie Ernaux, *Shame,* T. Leslie, trans. (New York: Seven Stories Press, 1998 [1997]), 14.

46 *Stephanie Gonzalez*   Interview, Santa Fe, New Mexico, February 22, 2002.

47 *one out of every six*   "Prevalence, Incidence and Consequences of Violence Against Women Survey," National Institute of Justice and Centers for Disease Control and Prevention, 1998, via RAINN.org.

48 *past thirty-five*   Two decades ago, *Newsweek*'s cover story, "The Marriage Crunch," formidably announced that "a 40-year-old single woman was more likely to get killed by a terrorist attack than to find a husband." In the June 5, 2000, issue, *Newsweek* retracted its earlier findings. See Daniel McGinn, "Marriage by the Numbers," 40–46, and Stephanie Kootz, "Three 'Rules' That Don't Apply," 49. Both authors say that the inaccuracy of old assumptions and predictions results from the changing nature of marriage, the fact that the average age at which women now marry is twenty-six, and that a forty-year-old single

woman has a 17 to 23 percent probability of eventually marrying, not the 2.6 percent originally forecast. On the other side, there are the still-looming facts that 50 percent of marriages end in divorce, and that 45.1 percent of survey respondents say their marriage is "less than 'very happy'" (see Mark Bain's compiled statistics, 44–45).

49   *women's antiaging movement*   see Maureen Dowd's eye-opening *Are Men Necessary?*, especially chapter 7, "Whence the Wince?" (211–56, 240), which describes how women's cosmetic obsession has ballooned profits for the antiaging market from 1 billion a year in 1990 to $15 billion in 2005.

49   *believed herself defective*   Regarding forlorn contenders, see Bill Maher's response to *The Bachelor:* http://www.safesearching.com/billmaher/print/a_details_0103.htm

51   *Woolf*   Virginia Woolf, *A Room of One's Own* (New York: Harcourt Brace, 1957 [1929]), 118.

52   *Freud asked*   Freud told Marie Bonaparte that after researching "the feminine soul" for thirty years, he still was baffled by women; hence, his question, *Was will das Weib?*—"What does woman want?" This famous remark, as Freud's biographer Peter Gay points out, "is an age-old cliché in modern guise," man's defense against woman as unfathomable. But it is also Freud's confession of his limited understanding of woman. See Peter Gay, "Flickering Lights on Dark Continents," chapter 10, in *Freud: A Life for Our Time* (New York: W. W. Norton, 1988), 470–523, 501–02.

52   *"rules"*   Ellen Fein and Sherrie Schneider, *The Rules: Time-Tested Secrets for Capturing the Heart of Mr. Right* (New York: Warner Books, 1995).

52   *Greenwald's*   Rachel Greenwald, *Find a Husband After 35 Using What I Learned at Harvard Business School* (New York: Ballantine, 2003).

55   *research has documented the link*   In a survey of girls nine and ten years old, 40 percent have tried to lose weight, according to an ongoing study funded by the National Heart, Lung and Blood Institute (*USA Today,* 1996). A 1996 study found that the amount of time an adolescent watches soaps, movies, and music videos is associated with their degree of body dissatisfaction and desire to be thin (Tiggmann & Pickering, 1996). One author reports that at age thirteen, 55 percent of American girls are "unhappy with their bodies." This number grows to 78 percent by the time girls reach seventeen (Brumberg, 1997). These and other relevant studies are at: http://www.mediafamily.org.

56   *exposé of the advertising world*   Jean Kilbourne, *Can't Buy My Love: How Advertising Changes the Way We Think and Feel* (New York: Simon & Schuster, 1999), 81.

58   *we take risks anyway*   Marla Ruzicka's story was reported by Robert F. Worth, *New York Times,* April 18, 2005, A4.

59   *her baby had died*   For a powerful story about stillbirth, see Daniel Raeburn, "Vessels," *The New Yorker* (May 1, 2006), 48–53.

4. THE AWAKENING: CHILDHOOD

65   *"I remember at a very young age"*   Alexandra Bloom, Ph.D.: Interview, July 20, 1998.

65   *Jung*   For a concise definition of individuation, see C. G. Jung, *Memories, Dreams, Reflections,* A. Joffe, ed., R. and C. Winston, trans. (New York: Vintage, 1965), 383–84.

66   *active self-awareness*   For our earliest experiences of a forming sense of self in infancy, see Daniel N. Stern, *The Interpersonal World of the Infant: A View from Psychoanalysis and Developmental Psychology* (New York: Basic Books, 1985) and Annie Bergman's *Ours, Yours, Mine: Mutuality and the Emergence of the Separate Self* (Norvale, New Jersey: Jason Aronson, 1999).

68   *A "Thing-Finder"*   Astrid Lingren, *Pippi Longstocking* (New York: Puffin Books, 1997 [1950]), 11.

69   *"What are we going to do now?"*   Lingren, *Pippi Longstocking,* 26–27.

70   *Gilligan*   Carol Gilligan, *In a Different Voice: Psychological Theory and Women's Development* (Cambridge, Massachusetts: Harvard University Press, 1982). See also essays by Judith V. Jordan, Alexandra G. Kaplan, Jean Baker Miller, et al., in *Women's Growth in Connection: Writings from the Stone Center* (New York: The Guilford Press, 1991).

71   *we develop a false self*   See especially D. W. Winnicott, "Ego Distortion in Terms of True and False Self" (1960), in *The Maturational Processes and the Facilitating Environment: Studies in the Theory of Emotional Development* (New York: International Universities Press, 1965), 140–52; see also his "The Concept of the False Self," in *Home Is Where We Start From: Essays by a Psychoanalyst* (New York: W. W. Norton, 1986), 65–70.

71   *the "liveliness" of children*   Winnicott, "The Effect of Loss on the Young," in *Thinking About Children,* R. Shepherd, J. Johns, and H. T. Taylor, eds. (Reading, Massachusetts: Addison-Wesley, 1996 [1968]), 46–47.

72   *Atwood's*   Margaret Atwood, *Cat's Eye* (New York: Anchor, 1998 [1989]), 124.

75   *the shadow of her mother*   For a probing study of the lingering unconscious effects of early grieving experiences, see Christopher

Bollas, *The Shadow of the Object: Psychoanalysis of the Unthought Known* (New York, Columbia University Press, 1987).

76   *When we are mourning*   See also Joan Didion, *The Year of Magical Thinking* (New York: Knopf, 2005).

76   *the Greek word* melancholia   Robert Burton, *The Anatomy of Melancholy,* Vol. IV, J. B. Bamborough with M. Dodsworth, eds. (New York: Oxford University Press, 1998); see especially, "Love-Melancholy," 40–256.

77   *Freud*   Sigmund Freud, "Mourning and Melancholia," in *Collected Papers,* Vol. 4, Ernest Jones, ed. (New York: Basic Books, 1959), 152–70, 161.

81   *Herman*   Judith Lewis Herman, *Mother Daughter Trauma and Recovery: The Aftermath of Violence—From Domestic Abuse to Political Terror* (New York: Basic Books, 1992) 1.

86   *Simmons*   Rachel Simmons, *Odd Girl Out: The Hidden Culture of Aggression in Girls* (New York: Harvest, 2003). See also Deborah Cox, Susan S. Stabb, and Karen H. Brucker, "The Formation of Socialized Anger in Women," chapter 3 in *Women's Anger: Clinical and Developmental Perspectives* (Philadelphia, Pa.: Brunner/Mazel, 1999), 61–84.

87   *lazy eye*   The medical term is Amblyopia, a condition in young children of reduced image quality in one eye, the other eye able to focus better.

92   *Winterson*   Jeanette Winterson, *The World and Other Places* (New York: Vintage, 1999). See also Larissa Macfarqhar's "Horse Country" in "Letter from Virginia," *The New Yorker* (August 21/28, 2000) 70–81.

92   *Stark*   In 1928, at age thirty-five, the intrepid traveler and writer Freya Stark journeyed as a woman alone into the Syrian Druze and, later, through Turkey, southern Arabia, Greece, and Italy. See Freya Stark, *Baghdad Sketches* (Evanston, Illinois: Marlboro Press/Northwestern, 1998 [1938]), x.

93   *When Mary Lennox*   Frances Hodgson Burnett, *The Secret Garden,* T. Tudor, illust. (New York: J. B. Lippincott, 1962 [1911]), 80–81.

5. THE HALL OF MIRRORS: ADOLESCENCE AND YOUNG ADULTHOOD

99   *Pipher*   Mary Pipher, "Saplings in the Storm," chapter 1 in *Reviving Ophelia: Saving the Life of Adolescent Girls* (New York: Ballantine, 1995), 17–28.

105   *good-enough mothering*   Since there is no such thing as perfect mothering, it can still be a "good enough" adaption to the infant's ges-

tures and needs. See especially Winnicott, chapter 12, in *Maturational Processes* (see Note to page 71).

105 *Apter*   Terri Apter, *Altered Loves: Mothers and Daughters During Adolescence* (New York: Ballantine, 1990).

111 *In her memoir*   Mary Gordon, *The Shadow Man: A Daughter's Search for Her Father* (New York: Vintage, 1996), 2002.

112 *Pruett*   Kyle Pruett, *Fatherneed: Why Father Care Is as Essential as Mother Care for Your Child* (New York: Broadway Books, 2001), 19. While Pruett addresses the needs of both genders, Daphne Merkin's point in "Daddy's Forgotten Girl," *The New York Times Magazine* (June 18, 2006), 17–19 that the significance of the bond between sons and fathers has been stressed far more than that between daughters and fathers, is still true. One only has to look on Amazon.com to see that there are more than twice as many books about "mothers and daughters" than "fathers and daughters," and while a number of psychological books that discuss the relationship between fathers and daughters supply excellent and much needed corrective material—see especially Jessica Benjamin's *Like Subjects, Love Objects: Essays on Recognition and Sexual Difference* (New Haven, Connecticut: Yale University Press, 1995)—the rank order of the following phrases on Google tells all: "Fathers and Sons", "Mothers and Daughters", "Mothers and Sons", and, lastly, "Fathers and Daughters". Is this perhaps the least considered relationship of the four? My own reponse is an unequivocal "yes"; certainly "Fathers and Sons" continues to outpace all the other configurations.

113 *Freud's ideas on female development*   With the advent of the feminist movement in the late sixties and early seventies, women began speaking out against Freud's model of the defective and limited female. The French voice included Luce Irigaray, Sarah Kofman, and Helene Cixous; and in the United States, Margaret Mead, Karen Horney, and Nancy Chodorow were among the many who voiced a new and positive self valuation for women.

123 *"Adolescence is a beauty pageant"*   Rosalind Wiseman, *Queen Bees & Wannabes: Helping Your Daughter Survive Cliques, Gossip, Boyfriends & Other Realities of Adolescence* (New York: Three Rivers Press, 2002), 77.

124 *Girls fourteen to eighteen years of age*   National Center for Health Statistics (CDC), 2002.

124 *Many adolescent girls*   Eating disorders have doubled since the 1960s, increasingly in younger age groups, as young as seven; 40–60 percent of high school girls diet; and 13 percent of high school girls purge. From: http://www.eatingdisorderscoalition.org/reports/statistics.html.

124 *"unthought known"*   Bollas, *The Shadow of the Object*; see especially "The Unthought Known: Early Considerations," chapter 15, 277–83 (see Note to page 75).

125 *The Red Shoes*   See both the story and a revealing interpretation in Estes, "Self-Preservation: Identifying Leg Traps, Cages, and Poisoned Bait," chapter 8 in *Wolves*, 230–75.

126 *Self-destructure behavior*   The 2003 film *Thirteen*, written and directed by Catherine Hardwick in documentary style and starring Holly Hunter, Evan Rachel Wood, and Nikki Reed, reveals the startling range of secret behaviors that signal a teenager's profound distress.

127 *Freud*   Sigmund Freud, *Civilization and Its Discontents*, James Strachey, ed. and trans. (New York: W. W. Norton, 1962), 25.

128 *O'Faolain's*   Nuala O'Faolain, *Are You Somebody: The Accidental Memoir of a Dublin Woman* (New York: Henry Holt, 1988), 93, 95.

129 *Wurtzel*   Elizabeth Wurtzel, *Bitch: In Praise of Difficult Women* (New York: Doubleday, 1998), 391.

6. BEFRIENDING ALONENESS

144 *"duplicating machine"*   The first time I heard Adyashanti say this was at a two-day intensive at Omega Institute, New York, September 30–October 2, 2005.

145 *Housden*   Maria Housden, *Hannah's Gift: Lessons from a Life Fully Lived* (New York: Bantam, 2002), the story of the death of her young daughter and the "gift" she left behind. She is founder of the nonprofit organization, Grief in Action (see "Resources").

145 *Kübler-Ross*   Elizabeth Kübler-Ross, *On Death and Dying* (New York: MacMillan, 1969).

148 *"Life changes fast"*   Didion, *The Year of Magical Thinking*, 3. Text in italics.

148 *The film* Blue   The two other films in Kieslowski's triology *Three Colours* (*Trois Couleurs*) are *White* (1994) and *Red* (1994).

155 *She tells Torvald*   Henrik Ibsen, *A Doll's House*, C. Barslund, trans., Frank McGuinness (London: Faber and Faber, 1996), 101.

156 *British actress Janet McTeer*   Interview, July 25, 1997. I have seen at least six Noras, including Claire Bloom and Jane Fonda, and McTeer's performance at the Belasco Theater in New York City surpassed all of them.

157 *Pinned above my desk*   The cartoon was published in the September 6, 1999, issue of *The New Yorker*. BEK is the pseudonym for the cartoonist Bruce Eric Kaplan.

157 *Carson*   Anne Carson, *The Beauty of the Husband: A Fictional Essay in 29 Tangos* (New York: Knopf, 2001), 5.

159 *Orenstein's*   Peggy Orenstein, "Mourning My Miscarriage," *The New York Times Magazine* (April 21, 2002), 38, 40–41.

159 *Kinnell*   Galway Kinnell, "Saint Francis and the Sow," from *Mortal Acts, Mortal Words* (Boston: Houghton Mifflin, 1980). Quoted in Roger Housden, *Ten Poems to Open Your Heart* (New York: Harmony, 2002), 35–44, 35–36.

7. STEPPING OUT

162 *In her illuminating work*   Sharon Salzberg, *Faith: Trusting Your Own Deepest Experience* (New York: Riverhead, 2002), 1.

163 *As she expressed it*   Salzberg, *Faith,* 11.

166 *Goodchild*   Chloe Goodchild, *The Naked Voice* (London: Rider, 1993), 4.

168 *Chodron*   Pema Chodron, *Start Where You Are: A Guide to Compassionate Living* (Boston: Shambhala, 2001), x, 34.

170 *Fraser*   Kennedy Fraser, *Ornament and Silence: Essays on Women's Lives* (New York: Knopf, 1997), xiv–xv.

172 *Milner*   Marion Milner, under the pseudonym Joanna Field, *A Life of One's Own* (New York: Tarcher/Putnam, 1981 [1936]), 11.

172 *some "gap"*   Milner, *A Life of One's Own,* 13.

172 *"the whole of my body"*   Milner, *A Life of One's Own,* 24. Text in italics.

174 *"Creative living"*   D. W. Winnicott, *Playing & Reality.* See especially chapter 4, "Playing: Creative Activity and the Search for the Self," 53–64, and chapter 5, "Creativity and its Origins," 65–85.

175 *Huizinga*   Johan Huizinga, *Homo Ludens: A Study of the Play Element in Culture* (Boston, Massachusetts: Beacon Press, 1955 [1950]), 1.

175 *"let's consult* The I Ching"   R. Wilhelm, trans., *The I Ching or Book of Changes,* 3rd ed., Bollingen Series XIX (Princeton: Princeton University Press, 1967 [1950]), 240.

176 *Simpson*   Joe Simpson, *Touching the Void: One Man's Miraculous Survival* (New York, HarperPerennial, 2004 [1998]). See also the 2003 film adaptation of Simpson's book directed by Kevin Macdonald.

176 *Ackerman*   Diane Ackerman, Preface to *Deep Play,* P. Sis, illus. (New York: Vintage, 1999), ix–xiii.

177 *Sendak's*   Maurice Sendak, *Where the Wild Things Are* (San Francisco: HarperCollins, 1984 [1963]).

178   *"no idea can be safely shut out"*   Milner, *A Life of One's Own,* 153 (see Note to page 172).

178   *"Do I contradict myself?"*   Cited in *Creators on Creating: Awakening and Cultivating the Imaginative Mind,* F. Barron, A. Montuori, and A. Barron, eds. (New York: Tarcher/Putnam, 1997), 88.

178   *Miles Davis put it this way*   Cited in Barron, Montuori, and Barron, eds., 56.

178   *turning forty*   Maria Housden, Interview, August 24, 2002.

180   *"the thing that matters"*   Milner, *A Life of One's Own,* 43–44 (see Notes to pages 172, 178). Text in italics.

185   *Lessing's*   Doris Lessing, *The Golden Notebook* (New York: Perennial Classics, 1999 [1962]), 10.

185   *Woolf*   Woolf, *A Room of One's Own,* 113, 117 (see Note to page 51).

194   *victim of "gaslighting"*   The reference is to George Cukor's 1944 thriller *Gaslight,* in which the husband (Charles Boyer), systematically attempts to drive his wife (Ingrid Bergman) insane.

195   *Photojournalist Paula Allen*   Interview, December 11, 1998.

199   *"I was at the piano"*   Kitty Carlisle Hart, Interview, July 9, 2002.

8. REAPING THE HARVEST: SOLITUDE, THE SACRED, AND THE REDISCOVERY OF THE SELF

201   *Sarton*   May Sarton, *Journal of a Solitude* (New York: W. W. Norton, 1973) 11.

202   *"quiet of the heart"*   Quoted in Elizabeth Frank, *Louise Bogan: A Portrait* (New York: Columbia University Press, 1986), 150.

202   *"Only when one is connected"*   Anne Morrow Lindbergh, *Gift from the Sea* (New York: Pantheon Books, 2005 [1955, 1975]), 38.

206   *Spending time alone in nature*   Diane Haug, Interview, August, 29, 1997.

206   *Caldwell*   "A Solitary Life," E4 (see Note to page 17).

207   *Freya Stark*   Stark, *Baghdad Sketches,* x (see Note to page 92).

207   *"The ambience here"*   Sarton, *Journal of a Solitude,* 12.

207   *I am sitting in the Bombay apartment*   Ramesh Balsekar has written many books, including *Your Head in the Tiger's Mouth, A Net of Jewels,* and *Consciousness Speaks.*

210   *Dillard*   Annie Dillard, *Pilgrim at Tinker's Creek* (New York: Bantam, 1974), 9.

211   *Katherine Kurs*   Interview, March 14, 2003.

211   *Norris*   Kathleen Norris, *The Cloister Walk* (New York: Riverhead, 1996), 276–77.

212 *Ozelsel*   Michaela Ozelsel, Interview, December 1998. See also Ozelsel's *Forty Days: The Diary of a Traditional Solitary Sufi Retreat,* Andy Gaus, trans. (Brattleboro, Vermont: Threshold Books, 1996), 69–70.

213 *"On the planet"*   Dillard, *Pilgrim at Tinker's Creek,* 99.

213 *In the last of seven years*   Haug Interview.

214 *"I have had the experience"*   Tara Brach, Ph.D., Interview, September 2, 2001. See also Brach's *Radical Acceptance: Embracing Your Life with the Heart of a Buddha* (New York: Bantam, 2003).

215 *Wheeler*   Sara Wheeler's "Drawing Inspiration from Antarctica's 'Heavenly Music,'" excerpted from her book *Terra Incognita: Travels in Antarctica* (New York: Modern Library, 1999), excerpted in *The New York Times* (May 12, 1999), F4.

215 *"Like the moth drawn"*   Shakina Reinhertz, *Women Called to the Path of Rumi: The Way of the Whirling Dervish* (Prescott, Arizona: Hohm Press, 2001), xvi; other quoted material from the Interview with author, April 3, 2003.

216 *they encourage us* not *to take things personally*   See William James, *Varieties of Religious Experience: A Study in Human Nature* (New York: Modern Library, 1929 [1902]); see also Christina Feldman, "Stillness and Insight," *Insight* (Fall/Winter 2001), 34–37, 35, excerpted from a program offered by Feldman, Barre Center for Buddhist Studies, September 1999.

216 *Salzberg*   Salzburg, *Faith,* 151 (see Note to page 162).

217 *Lippe*   Toinette Lippe, *Nothing Left Over: A Plain and Simple Life* (New York: Tarcher/Putnam, 2002), 131.

217 *On an ordinary morning*   Anna Christensen, Interview, November 12, 2003. The story is based on a dharma talk Anna gave on May 1, 2001, "A Walk Down Lexington Avenue," based on a personal experience that took place in 1997.

218 *"Little by little, wean yourself"*   Jelaluddin Rumi, *Mathnawi, III.*

9. ALONENESS AND RELATIONSHIP

225 *De Rougement*   Denis De Rougement, *Love in the Western World,* M. Belgion, trans. (New York: Schocken Books, 1983 [1956]), 310.

231 *Rilke*   Rainer Maria Rilke, "Rilke's Letters on Love," in *Rilke On Love and Other Difficulties,* J. J. L. Mood, trans. (New York: W. W. Norton, 1975), 27–28.

233 *Regarding sex*   Paula Kamen, *Her Way: Young Women Remake the Sexual Revolution* (New York: New York University Press, 2000).

233   *Sheehy's*   Gail Sheehy, *Sex and the Seasoned Woman: Pursuing the Passionate Life* (New York: Random House, 2006).

233   *killjoy assessment*   Daphne Merkin, "What's So Hot About Fifty?" *The New York Times Magazine,* (February 12, 2006), 17–18.

233   *"Why don't you come on up"*   For this and other great one-liners, Google "Mae West Quotes."

233   *assert our sexual desires*   Jane Juska, *A Round Heeled Woman: My Late-Life Adventures in Sex and Romance* (New York: Villard, 2004), 12. Text in italics.

235   *friendship, at its best*   Ellen Goodman and Patricia O'Brien, *I Know Just What You Mean: The Power of Friendship in Women's Lives* (New York: Fireside, 2000).

235   *"Women's friendship"*   Lithe Sebesta, Conversation, April 19, 2005.

235   *Tannen*   Deborah Tannen, *You Just Don't Understand: Women and Men in Conversation* (New York: Quill, 2001 [1990]) 18.

236   *Graham*   Barbara Graham, Conversation, April 8, 2001.

236   *Psychotherapist Stephanie Hanks*   Conversation, April 6, 2001.

236   *Martin*   Steve Martin, *Shopgirl* (New York: Share Productions, 2000), 63. Martin also wrote the screenplay for the same-named film version directed by Anand Tucker, costarring Steve Martin and Claire Danes, 2005.

238   *"I have lost friends"*   From Virginia Woolf's *The Waves,* cited in B. Graham, "The End of the (Friendship) Affair," *O* (August 2001), 134–35, 176.

241   *the story of her seduction*   Personal communication, May 7, 2006. Barbara Graham first wrote about her experience in the play *Camp Paradox,* produced off-Broadway at the WPA Theater in 1992. She is also writing a memoir.

241   *Beatrice Wood*   See Francis M. Naumann, ed., *Beatrice Wood: A Centennial Tribute* (New York: American Craft Museum, 1997). Published on the occasion of the exhibition, March 3–June 8, 1997.

241   *Tenneson*   Joyce Tenneson, *Wise Women: A Celebration of Their Insights, Courage, and Beauty* (New York: Bullfinch Press, 2005). See also Kitty Carlisle Hart's photograph in *Wise Women,* 90.

245   *Take Laura Nurse*   Interview, December 5, 2002.

248   *It begins with a May Steven's painting*   See catalog, *May Stevens: Images of Women Near and Far: 1983–1997,* Barabara S. Shapiro, curator of the exhibition, May 1–Aug. 8, 1999 (Boston, Massachusetts: Museum of Fine Arts, 1999).

248   *Lerner's injunction to women*   Gerda Lerner, *The Creation of Feminist Consciousness: From the Middle Ages to Eighteen-Seventy,* Vol. 2 (New York: Oxford University Press, 1993). See, for example, 14, 281.

Select Bibliography and Recommended Reading

Angier, Natalie. *Women: An Intimate Geography*. Boston, Massachusetts: Houghton Mifflin, 1999.

Apter, Terri. *Altered Loves: Mothers and Daughters During Adolescence*. New York: Ballantine, 1990.

Bakker, Rosemary. *Elder Design: Designing and Furnishing a Home for Later Years*. New York: Penguin, 1997.

de Beauvoir, Simone. *The Second Sex*. Translated by H. M. Parshley. Middlesex, U.K.: Penguin, 1986.

Becker, Ernest. *The Denial of Death*. New York: The Free Press, 1973.

Bergman, Anni W. *Ours, Yours, Mine: Mutuality and the Emergence of the Self*. Northvale, New Jersey: Jason Aronson, 1999.

Borysenko, Joan. *A Woman's Book of Life: The Biology, Psychology, and Spirituality of the Feminine Life Cycle*. New York: Riverhead, 1996.

Chodron, Pema. *When Things Fall Apart: Heart Advice for Difficult Times*. Boston, Massachusetts: Shambhala, 1997.

———. *Start Where You Are: A Guide to Compassionate Living*. Boston, Massachusetts: Shambala, 1994.

Didion, Joan. *The Year of Magical Thinking*. New York: Knopf, 2005.

Dowd, Maureen: *Are Men Necessary?: When Sexes Collide*. New York: G. P. Putnam, 2005.

Edelman, Hope. *Motherless Daughters: The Legacy of Loss*. New York: Delta, 1994.

Ehrenrich, Barbara. *Nickel and Dimed: On (Not) Getting By in America*. New York: Henry Holt, 2001.

——— and Arlie Russell Hochschild, eds. *Global Woman: Nannies, Maids, and Sex Workers in the New Economy*. New York: Metropolitan Books, 2002.

——— and Deidre English. *For Her Own Good: 150 Years of Experts' Advice to Women*. Garden City, N. Y.: Anchor, 1979.

Ensler, Eve. *Insecure at Last: Losing It in Our Security Obsessed World*. New York: Random House, 2006.

———. *The Good Body*. New York: Random House, 2005.

———. *The Vagina Monologues*. New York: Villard, 1998.

Estes, Clarissa Pinkola. *Women Who Run with the Wolves: Myths and Stories of the Wild Woman Archetype.* 1992. New York: Ballantine, 1995.

Etcoff, Nancy. *Survival of the Prettiest: The Science of Beauty.* New York: Anchor Books, 1999.

Faludi, Susan. *Backlash: The Undeclared War Against American Women.* New York: Anchor, 1992.

Gloeckner, Phoebe. *The Diary of a Teenage Girl: An Account in Words and Pictures.* Berkeley, California: Frog, Ltd., 2002.

Gordon, Linda. *Woman's Body, Woman's Right: Birth Control in America.* New York: Penguin, 1990.

Grumbach, Doris. *Fifty Days of Solitude.* Boston, Massachusetts: Beacon Press, 1994.

Hanauer, Cathi., ed. *The Bitch in the House: 26 Women Tell the Truth About Sex, Solitude, Work, Motherhood, and Marriage.* New York: Counterpoint, 2003.

Heilbrun, Carolyn G. *Writing a Woman's Life.* New York: Ballantine, 1989.

———. *The Last Gift of Time: Life Beyond Sixty.* New York: Ballantine, 1997.

Herman, Judith. *Trauma and Recovery: The Aftermath of Violence—From Domestic Abuse to Political Terror.* New York: Basic Books, 1997.

Israel, Betsy. *Bachelor Girl: The Secret History of Single Women in the Twentieth Century.* New York: HarperCollins, 2002.

Juska, Jane. *A Round-Heeled Woman: My Late-Life Adventures in Sex and Romance.* New York: Villard, 2004.

Kilbourne, Jean. *Can't Buy My Love: How Advertising Changes the Way We Think and Feel.* New York: Simon & Schuster, 1999.

Knapp, Caroline. *Appetites: Why Women Want.* New York: Counterpoint, 2003.

Lerner, Gerda. *The Creation of Feminist Consciousness: From the Middle Ages to Eighteen-Seventy,* Vol. 2. New York: Oxford University Press, 1993.

Levine, Stephen. *Who Dies?: An Investigation of Consciousness Living and Consciousness Dying.* New York: Anchor, 1982.

Lindbergh, Anne Morrow. *Gift from the Sea.* New York: Pantheon, 2005.

Love, Susan M., with Karen Lindsey. *Dr. Susan Love's Breast Book.* 3rd revised edition. Cambridge, Massachusetts.: Perseus, 2000.

Northrup, Christiane. *Women's Bodies, Women's Wisdom: Creating Physical and Emotional Health and Healing.* New York: Bantam, 1994.

———. *The Wisdom of Menopause: Creating Physical and Emotional Health and Healing During the Change.* New York: Bantam, 2001.

Orenstein, Peggy. *Schoolgirls: Young Women, Self-Esteem, and the Confidence Gap.* New York: Anchor, 1994.

Pipher, Mary. *Reviving Ophelia: Saving the Selves of Adolescent Girls.* New York: Ballantine, 1995.

――――. *Another Country: Navigating the Emotional Terrain of Our Elders.* New York: Riverhead, 1999.

Richesin, Andrea N., ed. *The May Queen: Women on Life, Love, Work, and Pulling It All Together in Your 30s.* New York: Jeremy P. Tarcher/Penguin, 2006.

Rich, Adrienne. *Of Woman Born: Motherhood as Experience and Institution.* New York: Bantam, 1977.

Rufus, Anneli S. *Party of One: The Loner's Manifesto.* Baltimore: Atomic Books, 2003.

Sarton, May. *Journal of a Solitude.* New York: W. W. Norton, 1973.

Simmons, Rachel. *Odd Girl Out: The Hidden Culture of Aggression in Girls.* New York: Harvest, 2002.

Slugocki, Lillian Ann, and Erin Cressida Wilson. *The Erotica Project.* San Francisco: Cleis Press, 2000.

Spiegel, Maura, and Lithe Sebesta. *The Breast Book: Attitude, Perception, Envy & Etiquette.* New York: Workman, 2002.

Stern, Daniel N. *The Interpersonal World of the Infant: A View from Psychoanalytical and Developmental Psychology.* New York: Basic Books, 1985.

Storr, Anthony. *Solitude: A Return to the Self.* New York: Ballantine, 1988.

Tannen, Deborah. *You Just Don't Understand: Women and Men in Conversation.* New York: Quill, 2001.

Winnicott, D. W. *Playing & Reality.* London: Tavistock, 1982.

Wiseman, Rosalind. *Queen Bees and Wannabes: Helping Your Daughter Survive Cliques, Gossip, Boyfriends & Other Realities.* New York: Three Rivers Press, 2002.

Wolf, Naomi. *Misconceptions: Truth, Lies, and the Unexpected on the Journey to Motherhood.* 2001. New York: Anchor, 2003.

――――. *Promiscuities: The Secret Struggle for Womanhood.* New York: Random House, 1997.

――――. *The Beauty Myth: How Images of Beauty Are Used Against Women.* New York: Anchor, 1991.

Resources

Domestic Violence *(see also Sexual Violence/Abuse/Incest)*

The following publication on **Intimate Partner Violence** from the Centers for Disease control examines the causes and consequences of violence between intimates.

http://www.cdc.gov/ncipc/factsheets/ipvfacts.htm

Through the **National Domestic Violence Hotline,** help is available to callers 24 hours a day, 365 days a year. Hotline advocates are available for victims and anyone calling on their behalf to provide crisis intervention, safety planning, information, and referrals to agencies in all 50 states, Puerto Rico, and the U.S. Virgin Islands. Assistance is available in English and Spanish with access to more than 140 languages through interpreter services.

800-799-SAFE (7233)
800-787-3224 (TTY)

Education

The **American Association of University Women (AAUW)** promotes equity for all women and girls, lifelong education, and positive societal change. Since 1881 AAUW has been the nation's leading voice promoting education and equity for women and girls.

American Association of University Women
1111 Sixteenth St. N.W.
Washington, DC 20036
800-326-AAUW (2289)
info@aauw.org
aauw.org

Grants and Fellowships for Women: The Michigan State University Libraries host a collection of web links to funding sources for women considering higher education.

http://www.lib.msu.edu/harris23/grants/3women.htm

Women in Higher Education publishes a monthly newsletter that covers various topics affecting women on campus.

> Women in Higher Education
> 5376 Farmco Drive
> Madison, WI 53704
> 608-251-3232
> 608-284-0601 (fax)
> career@wihe.com
> wihe.com

Gender Identity and Sexuality Issues

The Gay & Lesbian Alliance Against Defamation (GLAAD) is dedicated to promoting and ensuring fair, accurate, and inclusive representation of people and events in the media as a means of eliminating homophobia and discrimination based on gender identity and sexual orientation.

> GLAAD
> 5455 Wilshire Blvd, #1500   248 West 35th Street, 8th Floor
> Los Angeles, CA 90036   New York, NY 10001
> 323-933-2240   212-629-3322
> 323-933-2241 (fax)   212-629-3225 (fax)
> glaad.org

The Gay, Lesbian & Straight Education Network strives to assure that each member of every school community is valued and respected regardless of sexual orientation or gender identity/expression.

> The Gay, Lesbian & Straight Education Network
> 90 Broad Street, 2nd Floor
> New York, New York 10004
> 212-727-0135
> 212-727-0254 (fax)
> glsen.org

Created in partnership with a Canadian advocacy group for transgendered and intersexed people, the **Trans Care Project** offers extensive information and resources for people exploring issues related to gender.

vch.ca/transhealth/resources/tcp.html

GIRLS' SELF-ESTEEM

Girls Incorporated is a national nonprofit youth organization dedicated to inspiring all girls to be strong, smart, and bold. With roots dating to 1864, Girls Inc has provided vital educational programs to millions of American girls, particularly those in high-risk, underserved areas.

GIRLS INCORPORATED
120 Wall Street
New York, NY 10005-3902
1-800-374-4475
girlsinc.org/ic/

The mission of the **Girls Leadership Institute** is to fight the crisis of confidence and dissociation that often occurs in adolescent girls. Its curriculum uses educational theater and is grounded in the research on girls pioneered by psychologist Lyn Mikel Brown, Carol Gilligan, and their colleagues.

girlsleadershipinstitute.org/home2.htm

Founded as a catalyst for positive change within schools and communities nationwide, **The Ophelia Project** is committed to helping youth form healthy peer relationships while creating safe social climates for all.

THE OPHELIA PROJECT
718 Nevada Drive
Erie, Pennsylvania 16505
888-256-KIDS (5437)
ophelia@opheliaproject.org
opheliaproject.org

GRIEVING

Grief in Action is a nonprofit organization dedicated to creating contexts in which grief is recognized as a powerful, transformational force—a force that can inspire and motivate those who suffer as a result of the death of a loved one, loss, or trauma, to live more honest, compassionate, and productive lives.

MARIA HOUSDEN
110 Hance Road
Fair Haven, New Jersey 07704
maria@griefinaction.com
www.griefinaction.com

HEALTH AND WELLNESS: *General*

DrNorthrup.com offers information, community, and resources tied to the work of women's health guru Dr. Christine Northrup.

http://www.drnorthrup.com/index.php

The National Women's Health Information Center (NWHIC) is a clearinghouse of reliable health information for women put together by the U.S. Department of Health and Human Services. By accessing the website or calling the hotline number, women can gain access to information on special topics like pregnancy, breast-feeding, body image, HIV/AIDS, girls' health, heart health, menopause and hormone therapy, mental health, quitting smoking, and violence against women.

1-800-994-9662 (English or Spanish) or TDD 1-888-220-5446 for the hearing impaired. NWHIC's phone lines are open Monday through Friday, 9 A.M. to 6 P.M. EST (excluding federal holidays).
4women.gov

Planned Parenthood affiliate health centers provide culturally competent, high quality, affordable health care to millions of diverse women, men, and teens every year. Planned Parenthood welcomes everyone, regardless of race, age, disability, sexual orientation, or income.

plannedparenthood.org

HEALTH AND WELLNESS: *Meditation/Relaxation*

The World Wide Online Meditation Center was created to provide clear, straightforward meditation instruction to people anywhere on the planet and includes sections on basic meditation, healing meditation, and other relaxation techniques.

meditationcenter.com

HEALTH AND WELLNESS: *Mental Health Issues*

The National Eating Disorders Association (NEDA) is the largest not-for-profit organization in the United States working to prevent eating disorders and provide treatment referrals to those suffering from anorexia, bulimia, and binge eating disorder and those concerned with body image and weight issues.

NATIONAL EATING DISORDERS ASSOCIATION
603 Stewart St., Suite 803
Seattle, WA 98101
Business Office: 206-382-3587
Toll-free Information and Referral Helpline: 800-931-2237
info@NationalEatingDisorders.org
NationalEatingDisorders.org

The National Hopeline Network helps people through such emergencies as attempted suicide, drug overdose, and psychotic episodes.

800-784-2433

See this website for an overview of depression from the National Institutes of Mental Health.

http://www.nimh.nih.gov/publicat/depression.cfm

See this website for an overview of postpartum depression from the U.S. Department of Health and Human Services.

http://www.4woman.gov/faq/postpartum.htm

Information and articles on eating and body image disorders from the National Eating Disorders Association can be found here.

http://www.edap.org/p.asp?WebPage_ID=294

Overeaters Anonymous offers a program of recovery from compulsive overeating using the Twelve Steps and Twelve Traditions of OA. Worldwide meetings and other tools provide a fellowship of experience, strength, and hope where members respect one another's anonymity. OA charges no dues or fees; it is self-supporting through member contributions. To find a meeting near you, visit:

>	oa.org

The Renfrew Center Foundation is a tax-exempt, nonprofit organization advancing the education, prevention, research, and treatment of eating disorders.

>	THE RENFREW CENTER FOUNDATION
>	475 Spring Lane
>	Philadelphia, PA 19128
>	877-367-3383
>	215-482-2695 (fax)
>	foundation@renfrew.org
>	Renfrew.org

HEALTH AND WELLNESS: *Specific Concerns and Populations*

The mission of **Gilda's Club** is to provide meeting places where men, women, and children living with cancer and their families and friends can join with others to build emotional and social support as a supplement to medical care. Free of charge and nonprofit, Gilda's Club offers support and networking groups, lectures, workshops, and social events in a nonresidential, homelike setting.

>	GILDA'S CLUB WORLDWIDE
>	322 Eighth Avenue, Suite 1402
>	New York, NY 10001
>	888-GILDA-4-U
>	info@gildasclub.org
>	gildasclub.org

The National Coalition for Lesbian, Gay, Bisexual and Transgender Health is committed to improving the health and well-being of lesbian, gay, bisexual, and transgender individuals and communities through public education, coalition building and advocacy that focuses on research, policy, education, and training.

> THE NATIONAL COALITION FOR LGBT HEALTH
> 1407 S St. N.W.
> Washington, DC 20009
> 202-797-3516
> 202-797-4430 (fax)
> coalition@lgbthealth.net
> lgbthealth.net

SusanLoveMD.org contains resources for women with breast cancer including community, information, advice from survivors, and more.

> susanlovemd.org

Women's Cancer Network was developed by the Gynecological Cancer Foundation and CancerSource in order to provide women information specific to women's cancers, as well as a risk assessment tool, links to clinical trials, and other resources.

> wcn.org

HOSPICE AND END OF LIFE ISSUES

Compassion & Choices is a nonprofit organization working to improve care and expand choice at the end of life. As a national organization with over 60 chapters and 30,000 members, Compassion & Choices help patients and their loved ones face the end of life with calm facts and choices of action during a difficult time. They also aggressively pursue legal reform to promote pain care and legalize physician aid in dying.

> COMPASSION & CHOICES
> PO Box 101810
> Denver, CO 80250-1810
> 800-247-7421
> 303-639-1224 (fax)
> compassionandchoices.org

HospiceNet offers a clearinghouse of information, directories, and articles for patients and families facing life-threatening illness.

> http://www.hospicenet.org/index.html

LEGAL

The **ACLU's** Women's Rights Project was founded in 1972 by Ruth Bader Ginsburg. Through litigation, community outreach, advocacy and public education, WRP empowers poor women, women of color, and immigrant women who have been victimized by gender bias and face pervasive barriers to equality. To find a local ACLU office, or for more information, visit:

aclu.org

The Legal Services Corporation (better known as the Legal Aid Society) is a private, nonprofit corporation established by Congress to seek to ensure equal access to justice under the law for all Americans by providing civil legal assistance to those who otherwise would be unable to afford it. To find a local Legal Aid office, visit the following website:

rin.lsc.gov

MONEY MATTERS: *Investment*

Path to Investing is a website dedicated to investment advice with a special section on "Financial Self-Defense for Women," which cover issues of particular concern to women, including divorce, home buying, and planning for long-term convalescent care.

pathtoinvesting.org

Women and Company (affiliated with Citigroup) was created to address the needs of women who continue to face financial challenges and concerns unique unto themselves. Fee-paying members have access to workshops, advice, investment products and other financial information.

citibank.com/womenandco/homepage/index.htm

The Women's Institute for Financial Education is the oldest nonprofit organization dedicated to providing financial education to women in their quest for financial independence.

WOMEN'S INSTITUTE FOR FINANCIAL EDUCATION
PO Box 910014
San Diego, CA 92191
760-736-1660
WIFE.org

MONEY MATTERS: *Small Business*

The Business Women's Network was founded ten years ago by Edie Fraser to fulfill her desire to help women and minorities achieve success in the work world of today. Now owned and operated by iVillage, BWN continues to serve as a networking and educational resource for working women.

> BUSINESS WOMEN'S NETWORK
> 1990 M St. N.W., Suite 700
> Washington, DC 20036
> 202-466-8209
> 800-48-WOMEN
> 202-833-1808 (fax)
> bwni.com

Online Women's Business Center, part of the United States Small Business Administration, is an online resource designed to assist women start and run successful businesses, regardless of social or financial situation, race, ethnicity, or business background.

> OFFICE OF WOMEN'S BUSINESS OWNERSHIP
> Small Business Administration
> 409 Third St. S.W., Sixth Floor
> Washington, DC 20416
> 202-205-6673
> owbo@sba.gov
> onlinewbc.gov

Philanthropy News Digest is an online publication of the Foundation Center and provides a collection of links to grants aimed at women, including those that support microenterprise.

> fdncenter.org/pnd/rfp/cat_women.jhtml

OLDER WOMEN

The Elder Cohousing Network promotes an innovated approach to long-term care by helping elders re-create a new version of the "old-fashioned neighborhood"—a community where neighbors know one another and help take care of one another. Cohousing is about having a positive influence upon the wider society, helping us reduce our ecological footprint and live more consciously on the earth by encouraging building and land use that preserves more of the earth's resources.

> THE ELDER COHOUSING NETWORK
> 1460 Quince Ave. #102
> Boulder, CO 80304
> 303-413-8067
> Info@ElderCohousing.org
> Eldercohousing.org

The Elder Wisdom Circle is an online resource in which members, all over sixty, offer advice and wisdom gleaned from their lifetimes. Writing from the EWC appears as a column in several small newspapers.

> elderwisdomcircle.org

As the only national grassroots membership organization to focus solely on issues unique to women as they age, the **Older Women's League (OWL)** strives to improve the status and quality of life for midlife and older women. OWL is a nonprofit, nonpartisan organization that accomplishes its work through research, education, and advocacy activities conducted through a chapter network. Now in its twenty-third year, OWL provides a strong and effective voice for the more than fifty-eight million women age forty and over in America.

> OLDER WOMEN'S LEAGUE
> 3300 N. Fairfax Drive, Suite 218
> Arlington, VA 22201
> 703-812-7990
> 800-825-3695
> 703-812-0687 (fax)
> owlinfo@owl-national.org
> owl-national.org

The Red Hat Society promotes the idea that life begins at fifty. Founded by Sue Ellen Cooper, satellite Red Hat Societies have sprung up all over the country, encouraging woman over fifty to have fun, support each other, and celebrate the wisdom that age brings.

> THE RED HAT SOCIETY, INC.
> 431 S. Acacia Ave.
> Fullerton, CA 92831
> 714-738-0001
> redhatsociety.org

PLEASURE

CAKE, a female-run, women's sexuality enterprise, is designed to cultivate a community of women who believe in the importance of sexuality in women's daily lives. CAKE, through events, website, membership program, and newsletter, provides a safe and fun environment where women can express their sexuality.

cakenyc.com

Mama Gena's School of Womanly Arts trains men and women to use the power of pleasure to have their way with the world. It enhances and expands the voice of women by fanning the flames of their desires, which opens the doors of fun and pleasure for everyone.

212-787-2411
mamagenas.com

Toys in Babeland and **Good Vibrations** are two stores that promote female pleasure through a broad range of women-centric sex toys, books, videos, and more.

babeland.com
goodvibrations.com

REPRODUCTION/ADOPTION/FERTILITY/PARENTING

The **American Fertility Association (AFA)** was founded in 1999 by Executive Director Pamela Madsen and works to transform the lives of couples faced with infertility, raise awareness, and fight for social and legislative change around infertility issues. From Ms. Madsen's collective experience with a group of committed health care providers, patient advocates, and consumers who had been working together on infertility issues since 1994, she recognized the need to serve people before, during, and after infertility.

AMERICAN FERTILITY ASSOCIATION
666 5th Avenue, Suite 278
New York, NY 10103-0004
888-917-3777
theafa.org

BabyCenter.com, the leading destination on the Internet for new and expectant parents, together with its companion site ParentCenter.com, a Web resource for parents of children ages two to eight, is dedicated to helping women find the information and support they need during pregnancy and in caring for a baby, toddler, or child.

www.babycenter.com

MomsRising has a goal of championing core motherhood and family issues in political, social, and economic spheres. MomsRising is working to build a massive grassroots online resource to move motherhood and family issues to the forefront of the country's awareness and to provide grassroots support for leaders, as well as organizations, addressing key motherhood issues. The intent is to reach millions of women who have not previously been active, to educate people about the problems facing mothers and families, and to provide avenues for commonsense solutions to those problems.

momsrising.org

The **National Adoption Center** expands adoption opportunities for children throughout the United States, particularly for children with special needs and those from minority cultures.

NATIONAL ADOPTION CENTER
1500 Walnut Street, Suite 701
Philadelphia, PA 19102
800-TO-ADOPT
adopt.org

SEXUAL VIOLENCE/ABUSE/INCEST

The Rape, Abuse & Incest National Network (RAINN) is the nation's largest anti–sexual assault organization. RAINN operates the National Sexual Assault Hotline at 1-800-656-HOPE and carries out programs to prevent sexual assault, help victims, and ensure that rapists are brought to justice. Its website provides statistics, counseling resources, prevention tips, news, and more.

RAPE, ABUSE AND INCEST NATIONAL NETWORK
2000 L St. N.W., Suite 406
Washington, DC 20036
202-544-1034

800-656-4673, extension 3
202-544-3556 (fax)
info@rainn.org
rainn.org

SINGLES ADVOCACY

The Alternatives to Marriage Project (AtMP) advocates for equality and fairness for unmarried people, including people who are single, choose not to marry, cannot marry, or live together before marriage. They provide support and information for this fast-growing constituency, fight discrimination on the basis of marital status, and educate the public and policymakers about relevant social and economic issues.

AtMP
PO Box 320151
Brooklyn, NY 11232
unmarried.org

Declaring herself "deeply single," Sasha Cagen founded **QuirkyAlone** as an independent-minded movement for a diverse community of individuals uncomfortable with the "tyranny of coupledom." While embracing fun, friendship, and even romanticism, QuirkyAlone has spawned a website, book, and a national movement with events on "QuirkyAlone Day" (February 14th).

QUIRKYALONE
PO Box 40128
San Francisco, CA 94140
info@quirkyalone.net
quirkyalone.net

Single Mothers by Choice (SMC) was founded in 1981 by Jane Mattes, C.S.W., a psychotherapist and single mother by choice. The group's primary purpose is to provide support and information to single women who are considering, or who have chosen, single motherhood.

SMC
PO Box 1642
New York, NY 10028
212-988-0993

smc-office@pipeline.com.
mattes.home.pipeline.com/index.html

SUBSTANCE ABUSE

Al-Anon (which includes Alateen for younger members) offers support and fellowship to families and friends of alcoholics through dedicated meetings. For meeting information in Canada, the United States, and Puerto Rico, call 1-888-4AL-ANON (1-888-425-2666) Monday through Friday, 8 A.M. to 6 P.M. ET or visit:

al-anon.alateen.org

Alcoholics Anonymous is a fellowship of men and women who share their experience, strength, and hope with one another that they may solve their common problem and help others to recover from alcoholism. To find a meeting in the United States or Canada, look for "Alcoholics Anonymous" in any telephone directory or visit:

alcoholics-anonymous.org

Narcotics Anonymous adapts the Alcoholics Anonymous principles for individuals addicted to drugs. Members share their successes and challenges in overcoming active addiction and living drug-free productive lives through the application of the principles of NA.

NA WORLD SERVICE OFFICE
PO Box 9999
Van Nuys, California 91409
United States
818-773-9999
818-700-0700 (fax)
na.org

TRAVEL

Journey Woman is an online resource offering tips, advice, and travel narratives to women travelers of adventurous spirit.

http://www.journeywoman.com/

The Women's Travel Club was designed for women by women—it organizes group tours the world over for women only.

THE WOMEN'S TRAVEL CLUB
36 West 20th Street, Suite 301
New York NY 10011-4212
800-480-4448
360-935-5080 (fax)
womenstravelclub.com

Women Traveling Together is another company that organizes group tours for women.

WOMEN TRAVELING TOGETHER
1642 Fairhill Drive
Edgewater, MD 21037
info@women-traveling.com
410-956-5250
women-traveling.com

WOMEN'S POLITICAL ISSUES AND ADVOCACY

The Stop Violence Against Women Campaign is **Amnesty International**'s international campaign to spare women and girls around the world from being threatened, beaten, raped, mutilated, and killed with impunity.

AMNESTY INTERNATIONAL USA
5 Penn Plaza
New York, NY 10001
(212) 807-8400
(212) 627-1451 (fax)
aimember@aiusa.org
amnestyusa.org

EMILY's List, the nation's largest grassroots political network, is dedicated to electing pro-choice Democratic women to federal, state, and local office. As part of their mission, they recruit and fund viable women candidates, help candidates build and run effective campaign organizations, train the next generation of activists, and mobilize women voters to help elect progressive candidates across the nation.

EMILY's LIST
1120 Connecticut Avenue N.W., Suite 1100
Washington, DC 20036
202-326-1400
202-326-1415 (fax)
information@emilyslist.org
emilyslist.org

The Feminist Majority Foundation (FMF), which was founded in 1987, is a cutting-edge organization dedicated to women's equality, reproductive health, and non-violence. In all spheres, FMF utilizes research and action to empower women economically, socially, and politically. The organization believes that feminists—both women and men, girls and boys—are the majority, but this majority must be empowered.

THE FEMINIST MAJORITY FOUNDATION

1600 Wilson Boulevard,
Suite 801
Arlington, VA 22209
703-522-2214
703-522-2219 (fax)
Feminist.org

433 S. Beverly Drive
Beverly Hills, CA 90212
310-556-2500
310-556-2509 (fax)

INTERSECT is dedicated to social mobilization across countries worldwide to end the co-epidemics of HIV and violence against women and girls.

INTERSECT
77 West 15th Street, #6L
New York, New York 10011
212-989-9388
212-989-9394 (fax)
sfintersect@aol.com
intersect-worldwide.org

The **League of Women Voters,** a nonpartisan political organization, has fought since 1920 to improve our systems of government and impact public policies through citizen education and advocacy. The League's enduring vitality and resonance comes from its unique decentralized structure.

The League is a grassroots organization, working at the national, state, and local levels.

> LEAGUE OF WOMEN VOTERS
> 1730 M St. N.W., Suite 1000,
> Washington, DC 20036-4508
> 202-429-1965
> 202-429-0854 (fax)
> lwv.org

The National Council of Women's Organizations is a nonpartisan, non-profit umbrella organization of over two hundred groups that collectively represent more than ten million women across the United States. The only national coalition of its kind, NCWO has over twenty years' experience uniting American women's groups.

> NATIONAL COUNCIL OF WOMEN'S ORGANIZATIONS
> 1050 17th St. N.W., Suite 250
> Washington, DC 20036
> 202-293-4505
> 202-293-4507 (fax)
> womensorganizations.org

The National Organization for Women (NOW) is the largest organization of feminist activists in the United States. Since its founding in 1966, NOW's goal has been to take action to bring about equality for all women. NOW works to eliminate discrimination and harassment in the workplace, schools, the justice system, and all other sectors of society; secure abortion, birth control, and reproductive rights for all women; end all forms of violence against women; eradicate racism, sexism, and homophobia; and promote equality and justice in our society. To find a local chapter or for more information, visit:

> now.org

The National Partnership for Women & Families is a nonprofit, nonpartisan organization that uses public education and advocacy to promote fairness in the workplace, quality health care, and policies that help women and men meet the dual demands of work and family.

National Partnership for Women & Families
1875 Connecticut Avenue N.W., Suite 650
Washington, DC 20009
202-986-2600
202-986-2539 (fax)
info@nationalpartnership.org
nationalpartnership.org

Created in December 2001, the **Sex Workers Project** is the first program in New York City and in the country to focus on the provision of legal services, legal training, documentation, and policy advocacy for sex workers. Using a harm reduction and human rights model, the SWP protects the rights and safety of sex workers who, by choice, circumstance, or coercion, remain in the industry.

Sex Workers Project
Urban Justice Center
666 Broadway, 10th Floor
New York, NY 10012
646-602-5690
212-533-0533 (fax)
sexworkersproject.org

V-Day is a global movement, created by award-winning performer and playwright Eve Ensler (*The Vagina Monologues*) to stop violence against women and girls. V-Day is a catalyst that promotes creative events to increase awareness, raise money, and revitalize the spirit of existing anti-violence organizations. V-Day generates broader attention for the fight to stop violence against women and girls, including rape, battery, incest, female genital mutilation, and sexual slavery.

V-Day Administrative Offices
127 University Avenue
Berkeley, CA 94710
vday.org

Comprised of the Center for Research on Women and the Stone Center for Developmental Services and Studies, the **Wellesley Centers for Women (WCW)** has been promoting positive change for women and men, girls and boys for over thirty years. WCW brings together an interdisciplinary community of scholars engaged in research, training, analysis, and action through groundbreaking work dedicated to looking at the world through the eyes of women with the goal of shaping a better world for all.

WELLESLEY CENTERS FOR WOMEN
Wellesley College
106 Central Street
Wellesley, MA 02481 USA
781-283-2500
781-283-2504 (fax)
wcw@wellesley.edu
wcwonline.org

Founded in 1993, **Women for Women International** helps women in war-torn regions rebuild their lives by providing financial and emotional support, job skills training, rights awareness, leadership education, and access to business skills, capital, and markets. Through the program, women become confident, independent, and productive as they embrace the importance of their roles in rebuilding their families, their communities, and, ultimately, their nations.

WOMEN FOR WOMEN INTERNATIONAL
1850 M St. N.W., Suite 1090
Washington, DC 20036
202-737-7705
202-737-7709 (fax)
general@womenforwomen.org
womenforwomen.org.

Acknowledgments

This book was brought into life on the wings of many angels, named and unnamed, all of whom nourished its growth in incalculable ways. Being angels, I hope you will know who you are and how your wisdom, compassion, encouragement, and patient support made it all possible. My boundless and heartfelt gratitude especially to Mark Matousek, who listened to my idea for this book, instantly gave me the green light, and has unfailingly supported me with love and devotion; to Elizabeth Retivov, who spent six weeks with me in Santa Fe as ideas first became words and who remains a source of endless wisdom and encouragement in my life; to the wise and loving Barbara Graham, who has always kept compassionate vigil with me in my work and in my life; to Sidney Mackenzie, one of the most nurturing and insightful people I know; to Susan Dalsimer, whose editorial wisdom was a profound source of inspiration; to Sarah Jane Freymann, whose clarity of mind and purpose instilled new life into my writing; and to Erin Cressida Wilson, angel of light par excellence.

Thanks beyond words to my esteemed agent Anne Edelstein, whose energy, enthusiasm, and rock-solid support on my behalf have been a source of manna throughout; to the peerless Lithe Sebesta, who guided me through the first draft and has stayed close by ever since; to the masterful Ginny Faber, whose keen intelligence, sensitivity, and staying power produced the miracle of turning a sprawling manuscript into a book; to the indefatigable Amanda McCormick, who was always available to find the answer to yet one more research question; to Sally Fisher, Milly Milster, and Linda Fisher, who made troves of resources available to me; to Randee Marullo, who copyedited the manuscript with a vivid eye and sharp mind; to my publisher, Shaye Areheart, for valuing the vision of this book, and to her assistant, Joshua Poole, who stood ever-ready to answer my every question.

Thanks, too, to my friends and colleagues, old and new—especially the courageous women who gave their time to tell me their stories and offer me close-up views of their lives; to my loyal friends, Celia Candlin, Anna Christensen, and Annette Breindel, whose generosity of spirit is a teaching unto itself; to Gail Osherenko, Jan Roy, Christianne Zehl Romero, Lois Eby, and all my Vermont friends, whose lives express how much they cherish the power of both solitude and community; and to my patients, great teachers all, and, in the deepest sense, my collaborators.

Above all, I am grateful more than words can express for the special angels in my own family and the bond that unites us—my mother, Pauline, whose love and devotion are truly a force of nature; to the two joys of my life, my loving and beloved sons, Dimitri and Noah, who never lose faith in me; to my precious daughter-in-law, Karolin, who brought forth the great gift of a first grandchild, Juliet; to my brother Richard, stalwart believer and my dear friend; to my adored cousins Stephanie and Peter Hanks; and to Stephanie's mother, my own guardian angel, Alexandra Hoffman.

READING GROUP GUIDE

ABOUT THIS GUIDE

In *On My Own*, women who are alone, want to be alone, or are figuring out how to be alone will find themselves in excellent company—and anything but "alone." In her book, psychotherapist and author Florence Falk addresses a remarkable social shift underway: Single women over eighteen and without a spouse now represent a stunning 49 percent of the female population. Yet most of these women, from young graduates starting out in the workplace to single moms, divorcees, and widows, have internalized society's notion that a woman alone is defective—inherently flawed in some way. Beset by shame and fear, they do not know how to cope with being alone.

This consideration of "the art of being a woman alone" is written for *all* women, inasmuch as all women, by default, choice, or necessity, inevitably experience our own life crossings that set us apart. *On My Own* invites women to reimagine aloneness—to see it as a gift rather than a burden—so that we can be fully realized as women alone *and* in relationships. The "art" lies in learning how to harness solitude and use its shaping and transformative power to attune ourselves to our own needs and desires and begin to find our own path toward an authentic selfhood—in a word, to *thrive* rather than merely survive.

The questions in this guide are intended as a framework for your group's discussion of *On My Own*.

ABOUT THE AUTHOR

Florence Falk, Ph.D., is a writer, teacher, and psychotherapist in private practice for more than twenty years. She has given lectures and workshops throughout the United States.

FOR DISCUSSION

1. The book opens with this short quotation from Anne Morrow Lindbergh's *Gift from the Sea*: "Woman must come of age by herself. This is the essence of 'coming of age'—to learn how to stand alone." How does this quote express the book's intended purpose? Was this the author's personal experience? How does it correspond to your own? Would you agree that aloneness is an interior state as well as an external condition?

2. The author suggests that the book's subject matter concerns *all* women, inasmuch as all women inevitably find themselves alone, not once but many times during our lives. Does this strike you as true? If so, can you point to any moment in your own life where, by default, choice, or necessity you found yourself alone? Did you feel prepared for the experience? If so, how? If not, what held you back?

3. Do you think the book's subject matter is as important for married women as singles? Why or why not?

4. Chapter 1 begins with Lisa's story and this question: "If I am a woman alone, who am I?" How does it resonate for you? How do you feel about Lisa's distress after her breakup with Sam? Do you think the experience was a turning point in her life? What did it teach her?

5. "We often mistake aloneness and loneliness for each other, but they are not the same." How do they differ? Discuss the author's point

that the issue for women is not that we will never feel lonely—considering that some degree of loneliness exists in all our lives—but how aloneness makes us feel about *ourselves*.

6. Do you agree that we need to "befriend" aloneness? If so, what difference do you think accepting aloneness would make in your life?

7. "For each of us in different ways, aloneness is the portal we enter to find our way into solitude and to the harvesting of the self." What does this statement mean to you? Do you agree that stable relationships with others—partners, parents, children, or friends—are based on the solid foundation of a secure self? How does harnessing solitude help us to establish this goal?

8. "Women in our culture breathe in shame like oxygen and don't even know it." Consider whether this statement applies to you. If so, in what ways? Do you agree that despite having more social opportunities and independence than ever before, we still feel guilty nurturing ourselves? How might you begin to change this?

9. How do cultural messages women receive aggravate our sense of shame, fear, and inadequacy? Do you think these messages play into our fears about being women alone? How do our negative feelings keep us from forging a strong sense of self? Do you think the media has had a debilitating effect on women's self-esteem? If so, how can we stay more alert to negative messages in future?

10. Discuss some of the differences between the cultural messages women and men receive. How does the spinster vs. bachelor dichotomy help clarify some of the differences?

11. Discuss a moment in your childhood or adolescence when "you first knew you're you" and no one else. Consider how your childhood and/or adolescent experiences made you aware that you had to protect your "private self." Do you remember feeling inside or outside a

"magic circle"? What was that like for you? How might being a woman alone bring up some of the same kind of feelings?

12. Consider the secret garden as metaphor for a place of solitude in which to begin growing our private self. Do you remember your own secret garden? As an adult, do you feel you've lost touch with the solitude it provided? Discuss ways to retrieve it for yourself.

13. What does the author mean by the "art" of being a woman alone? Can you think of ways in which harnessing solitude might help you to find your own path to selfhood? Why does the author use the terms "active" or "creative" solitude? How would practicing active solitude help you?

14. The process of transitioning into aloneness begins with acceptance. Discuss some of the obstacles a woman faces that can interfere with that process. What does it mean to "start where you are"? How would faith and patience help you "revision" your story? What would "stepping out" mean for you?

15. The last chapter explores the relationship between aloneness and relationship. It suggests that rather than seek "rescue" by another person, we learn to accept aloneness. How can harnessing solitude to hear our own "voice" enhance our relationships with friends, partners, family, and the community at large—or, as the author says, from being alone to all one?

16. Describe some of the benefits that await a woman—with or without a partner—who has learned how to be on her own. Do you think the stories in the book help clarify the value of being on one's own? If so, which ones were helpful to you? How might you help other women alone achieve some of the same benefits?

Index